D0849090

LATIN AMERICA: THE HOPEFUL OPTION

LATIN AMERICA: THE HOPEFUL OPTION

EDUARDO FREI

Translated by John Drury

ORBIS BOOKS

Maryknoll, New York 10545

Library of Congress Cataloging in Publication Data

Frei Montalva, Eduardo, Pres. Chile, 1911–
    Latin America, the hopeful option.

    Translation of América Latina, opción y esperanza.
    1. Latin America—Politics and government—1948–
2. World politics—1945–   3. Democracy.   I. Title.
F1414.2.F713   320.9'8'003   78-1358
ISBN 0-88344-277-9

Originally published in 1977 as *América Latina: Opción y esperanza* by
Editorial Pomaire, S.A., Avda. Infanta Carlota, 114, Barcelona, 29,
Spain

This translation copyright © 1978 by Orbis Books, Maryknoll, New
York 10545

Printed in the United States of America

The Catholic Foreign Mission Society of America (Maryknoll) recruits
and trains people for overseas missionary service. Through Orbis
Books Maryknoll aims to foster the international dialogue that is
essential to mission. The books published, however, reflect the opinions of their authors and are not meant to represent the official position of the Society.

CONTENTS

PART II

LATIN AMERICA AT CROSSROADS

PART III

SHORING UP THE FOUNDATIONS
OF DEMOCRACY

Preface

For a whole lifetime I have been fighting for the ideas I advocate here. I have done so in books and speeches, in public-opinion campaigns and in elective offices conferred on me by the people. Never have I doubted their validity. Now that they are under attack, I felt it was the right moment to reaffirm my faith in them. That is why I have written this book.

The book consists of three main sections. They might seem rather different but they are intimately interconnected. In Part I, I analyze what might be called the crisis of democracy. As I see it, that crisis can be traced back to a real crisis in western civilization itself, due, among other reasons, to profound changes brought about by scientific-technological achievements.

The democracies have grown weak because they are neglecting or forgetting the values that are essential to them. They have also been weakened by the rancorous attacks of extremists on the Left and the Right, both of whom seek to destroy democratic governments. The rightist extremists oppose democracy because its full implementation will eliminate their privileges; the leftist extremists want to use democracy as a stepping-stone to the takeover of power and then suppress it.

But the present crisis does not afflict the democracies alone, as some would claim. It is also evident in the communist world and is practically a global reality. Every day we find a growing number of witnesses confirming that fact.

All of humanity, not just one country or one continent, is facing a historical upheaval unparalleled in extent and depth. In the midst of such a situation there are many people who think that freedom is a utopia today; that what is needed now are governments exercising complete authority over the people and free of all checks and balances.

In such a situation does democracy offer us a way out? If it does, what are its essential values and what new institutions are needed to give it concrete embodiment?

In Part II I examine the repercussions of all this in Latin America, where the crisis takes on its own distinctive characteristics. To understand the situation, we cannot rest content with a consideration of the present. We must also consider the principal features deriving from the past. We must look at its sociological structure, its evolving history, and the transformations that have taken place in more recent times. If the crisis of democracy is little more than a latent danger on other continents, here in Latin America it is already a fact affecting a population of more than two hundred million people, that is to say, two-thirds of its total population.

In Part III I stress the need to shore up democracy where it now exists and to recover it where it has been lost. This entails defining its essential bases and proposing a concrete historical project for Latin America.

It is my conviction that this undertaking calls for a philosophy which will serve as its underlying inspiration and which will give it real content. Such a philosophy cannot be local or provincial; it must embody and represent universal values.

No one can undertake these questions without possessing some conception of the human being, society, and the state. All the great movements that have had a real impact on human destiny were grounded on ideas that defined them and on ethical norms that gave them their true dimensions. The task of politics, in turn, is to translate them into a historical project that will serve a specific society and take due account of its own distinctive reality.

On September 24, 1970, at the end of my term as president of Chile, I received a letter from Jacques Maritain. At one point in that letter he wrote:

It is on the level of truth and testimony that Christians are summoned to act. It is on that level that they can fulfill their duty in the temporal order and wage their social and political battle. In other words, they must work in terms of an authentic vocation, and for this task good will and lofty inspiration will not suffice. It calls for a faith that is completely whole and integral. It also calls for a solidly outfitted reason capable of comprehending the real world and directing action in the light of that integral faith. . . . These are the truths that must be proclaimed today. Christians simply must take cognizance of them, not just in Chile but throughout the world.

That letter was a reflection of others I have received in the course of a long-standing friendship. The letters have given me the opportunity and the privilege of associating with one of those human beings in whom the transparency of the spirit is physically visible. We are now living through a time of testing for the whole world, including Latin America and Chile. It is my belief that the writings of that philosopher, Jacques Maritain, not only anticipated the present situation but have great significance today.

Changes continued to take place after his death. They are more rapid and profound than any experienced by a previous generation. New factors, hardly foreseeable yesterday, are now altering the forms of human existence. All the latent implications of certain ideas and inventions have now come to the surface, and we can now confirm the practical consequences of statements that seemed innocuous only a short time ago.

In his last letters to me the old master benevolently urged me to carry on my analysis of the new facts and events in the light of the principles of humanism that he has spelled out in visionary terms. Thus, taking up some of his essential ideas, I have looked at the new experiences through which I have been allowed to live. I have tried to spell out what might be the bases and characteristics of a modern, effective, living democracy grounded on humanism.

I am convinced that this is the only rational course open to our peoples if they want to maintain or recover their freedom, realize justice, and overcome poverty and violence. There is no other possibility of living in peace and freedom.

September 1977

PART I

HUMANISM AND DEMOCRACY

1

Uneasiness Over the Future

New Models of Existence

One could say that never before in history has such an overwhelming amount of information gone hand in hand with such serious difficulty in trying to shed light on what is really happening.

People today are besieged with a flood of novelties and news, but in itself this wealth of information does not increase our knowledge or our understanding. The mass communications media provide us with a mosaic of strange or tragic events that is usually fleeting and disconcerting.

Another source of information is the vast output of essays and scientific studies designed to describe the changes in human living conditions. They are reflected in our everyday language, which has incorporated a vocabulary that was practically unknown yesterday but which is now irreplaceable. The new terminology is not the result of artifice. It follows from the need to characterize countless facts that previously had not been known, or at least not labelled.

Humanity now confronts new situations that have overthrown its earlier models of human existence and

3

have nothing to do with the past. They do not even have much to do with the recent past, when people had not even glimpsed the character and dimensions of the instruments now available to us. People would find it difficult, if not impossible, to do without those instruments and models today; for they have become part of our lifestyle, or else they have given rise to undertakings that could not even been imagined without them.

Moreover, the very nature of these changes confers a planetary dimension on many problems. They involve the life of the human species itself, and so they cannot be considered in isolation.

Whatever present-day conditions might be, however, we can say that the same age-old questions keep occurring—more anguishing than ever. Toward what end is this tide taking us? Are we in control of it? Or are we simply being dragged along by it toward some unknown destiny?

One of the most characteristic signs of our time, then, is uneasiness over the future and over the implications of certain inventions and their manifold by-products.

This has given rise to many different entities, some of which are now known around the world, which try to scrutinize the future by projecting the effects of present phenomena and extrapolating their developmental curves. They want to plot the course of certain data and events confronting humanity as a whole: e.g., population growth, population control, and population distribution; the indiscriminate use of renewable and non-renewable natural resources; water reserves; the availability of foodstuffs; the contamination of the environment; and the transference of new technologies. Living on an earth that we now see to be limited, we must know if we can pollute our air and water, if we can destroy living organisms and the earth's crust.

Obviously it was difficult or even impossible in the past to realize this desire to scrutinize the future. Only the new tools of computer science and their antecedents on a global level have made this possible, and they were not available to humanity before. It is they that enable people to make projections with some foundation and probability, to examine certain phenomena and forecast their later impact on the living conditions of human societies. For the first time we are really facing up to the fact that we live on an earth that does not seem to hold back any mysteries and that has contours that are growing more reduced every day.

One can hardly deny the usefulness of such studies, which seek to inform and warn people about the future consequences of a course that now seems to be out of control. On the one hand they provide us with a diagnostic tool and point up the short-term effects of our actions, thereby placing them in perspective. On the other hand they enable us to glimpse ways of managing and correcting them in the face of a dizzying and accelerating rate of growth that is all too often neglected.

That is the contribution of analysts, programmers of "simulation models," and, to some extent, those who are called futurologists. They collect and classify the different variables, feeding them into the computer to get mathematical answers. Plunging into the thicket, they select, classify, arrange, and stress various basic tendencies that have a determining influence.

Right now that particular concern is an important one because in recent decades we have covered distances that once took centuries. Consider the problem of population growth, for example. In less than a century the world's population has grown more than it did in the previous half-million or million years. It should not surprise us when we are told that the very process of globalization obliges us to take control of our future. The adverse effects of industrial society and its power combine with the complexity of our present problems to render our world more fragile and vulnerable.[1]

Like the human beings of today, human beings of past ages were worried about the destiny of their souls beyond the unknown frontiers of death. But they were less worried about the future of the world around them. It had been much the same for their ancestors and it probably would remain much the same for their descendants. They trod solid and familiar ground. Today things are very different. The world is not the same world one's parents knew, nor is it the same world we knew yesterday. Furthermore, we know that it is not going to be the same world tomorrow. We know that right at this very moment, in places we do not know and in laboratories we cannot even envision, changes are taking place that may alter our lives. People may be finding new ways to poison the atmosphere or to save life from some ill that had been incurable up to now. They may be inventing some new weapon that can be fired thousands of miles away and end up killing us, in a war that is not our own.

People also know that their efforts as individuals and as nations do not ensure them of success. They can be profoundly affected by changing conditions in one of the great centers of power. Changes in the composition or use of a given product, expansions and contractions in economic activity, and alternations in the pattern of consumption may profoundly affect them. Such happenings offer practical verification of the fact that we are living in a world that grows more interdependent every day. The network of interdependence grows ever thicker, and this is evident in every area of living and every area of knowledge.

That is why people now show an unwonted interest in catching a glimpse of the future. At the very least we want to make projections some distance ahead, so that we will be able to estimate the consequences of our actions today.

The Relativity of Certain Concepts

At the present time people are also experiencing much uncertainty in various spheres of knowledge. New concepts appear and intellectual fads take over, only to disappear quickly or fall prey to controversy. This happens in the physical sciences, and we also find it happening frequently in the social and political sciences.

It was only two or three decades ago that people believed they had found an almost mathematical formula for measuring the "progress" of a society. That formula considered the annual growth rate, the gross national product, and the per-capita income. It was based on the fiction that the distribution of this income would be not only fair but perhaps even equal.

Today there are many arguments and reservations about these notions. Development no longer is equated simply with an increase in the production of goods and services; nor is it viewed as an end in itself. In the eyes of many there is great potential danger in the way such development is channeled. The figures and statistics themselves now prove convincingly that such "growth" is being realized at a terrible price. The vast majority of the human race is the victim of terrible exploitation and inequality because a small minority is unrestrainedly using and abusing goods that are the common patrimony of all humankind.

This cannot help but raise questions in people's minds. Where is this growth leading? Why is the exponential and permanent growth of goods and services limited to certain regions of the world when most of the world is still mired in extreme poverty?

Suppose, for example, that we have an annual growth rate of 5 percent in some countries, as some estimates predict. By the end of the next century their economy will have grown by an enormous compounded multiple. The ever-increasing gap between them and backward countries will create worldwide incompatibilities that we can scarcely imagine or appreciate today. This leads us to conclude that growth for growth's sake cannot go on indefinitely.

Nor has it proven to be absolutely true and certain that the social sciences have reached the point where we can know the laws governing economics precisely or that crises are things of the past. We cannot even accept some simplistic classification of nations into developed and underdeveloped ones. A fairly strong power is not a superpower. The "rich" countries of the OPEC cartel cannot be equated with the "middle-class" countries of Latin America on the one hand, or with the impoverished countries of the Fourth World, where millions of people live in dire straits.

Furthermore, people today can readily see that today's world is fraught with unpredictable elements. On the one hand there seems to be an irreversible and growing trend toward viewing facts and events in terms of the future of the species and the world as a whole. On the other hand there is a growing trend not only toward exacerbated nationalism, but also toward cultural regionalism and linguistic separatism; these latter factors tend to undermine the classic national units. On a planet whose destiny is becoming more and more one, we find small communities rising and flourishing. They embody and affirm the distinctive and individual features of human beings who love their own way of life and their own past, often flying in the face of all reason and convenience.

Who can say what the future might bring? Within the framework of a world government it might be possible to have the most varied kinds of human community. These communities might be composed of human ties that are closer to the roots of life, of habits and sentiments that will allow each individual and each group to enjoy its own distinctive physiognomy. More than one person might feel that humanity could fulfill itself better in such a framework than in the present world of nation-states.

The customary analyses, projections, and solutions seem to be akin to drugs. Some drugs are beneficial. Others seem to be superb and indispensable when they are first discovered. Then, as time goes on, they prove to be pernicious or to have side-effects that are worse than the affliction they cure.

Those who first began to study the future and to compose "models" were content to limit themselves to a certain number of variables. They soon discovered, however, that the variables were more complex and more numerous than they had ever imagined. Their mutual influence and interaction made it difficult to reduce them to mathematical curves that could convincingly reflect the variety of factors at work in any human happening.

What has happened here is similar to what has happened in the realm of science. Mathematical concepts were developed and humanity moved forward in our knowledge of the physical makeup of matter and the atom. At each step we thought that we had arrived at the ultimate, basic element. But time and again we discovered another basic element, plunging deeper and deeper into a process that seems to have no end. Now we have arrived at the notion of the infinite, the impalpable: pure energy.

Human Factors

Not surprisingly, then, some of those exploring the future of humankind are turning their attention more and more to moral, human and socio-political factors. These, even more than economic and mathematical factors, are at the root of the problems under investigation.

A study put out by the University of Sussex explicitly warns about deceptive oversimplifications in this area.[2] Alluding to the famous MIT report for the Club of Rome *(The Limits to Growth)*, it suggests that the problems of the future and their implications are not purely technical or technological. The seeming neutrality of a computational model is illusory, since every model in a given social system necessarily contains presuppositions about the way the system works. It is also influenced by the attitudes and values of the individuals or groups engaged in programming the model. Thus the validity of all computer calculations depends entirely on the quality of the antecedent factors that underlie them—in this case, on the mental models behind them.

In other words, the operation of the models is influenced by the philosophical and socio-political presuppositions that are implicit in choosing and evaluating the variables. Furthermore, the programming process cannot concentrate solely on the economic and mathematical aspects and omit changes in subjective values, since the latter should be the most important and dynamic factors in the system as a whole. There must be proper balance between the social and political factors of development on the one hand and the mathematical and economic factors of growth on the other.

This point has been increasingly stressed in subsequent publications. It was brought out strongly in the second report for the Club of Rome by Mihajlo Mesarovic and Eduard Pestel.[3] It pointed out that all quantification, measurement, and model-formation provide us with only an impoverished picture of reality. There is much uncertainty in the fragmentary features chosen. There is ignorance about some aspects of the system one proposes to understand. There is a basic unpredictability about certain events. And there is a subjective element in every value judgment and every political act that can effect our view of causes and consequences.

Insofar as Latin America is concerned, the authors of the report put out by the Fundación Bariloche start out by saying that any long-term prognosis about the evolution of humanity is grounded on a worldview. That worldview, in turn, is based on a system of values and a concrete ideology. Contrary to what some people maintain, we are not proffering an "objective" view of reality when we assume that the structure of the present-day world and its supporting value-system can be projected without change into the future. Such an assumption means that we have already taken an ideological stand. It is therefore false to assume, as is often done, that there is a difference between long-range projective models and long-range normative models. The report goes on to say:

The model presented here is explicitly normative. It is not concerned with predicting what will happen if humankind's present tendencies continue. Instead it is concerned to point out a way to arrive at the ultimate goal of a world liberated from poverty and backwardness. It does not seek to be "objective" in the neutral valuational sense in which that term is often used. It embodies the conception of the world that its authors share and to which they are deeply committed.[4]

It is interesting to see how these studies have grown and developed. As they have perfected their technique, they have gone beyond mathematical-economic models to confront a more invisible realm, namely, the spiritual, cultural, moral, and political world that is the distinguishing mark of human activity.

The influence and variability of the latter factors show up notoriously in the fact that it is easier to construct a world model than it is to construct a continental model. And it is even more true when one gets down to outlining a national project. On the macro-world level it is easy enough to trace out some central lines with respect to central problems. The situation is quite different when one gets down to the level of micro-projections, so to speak. For then one begins to deal with the complex web of real life and the consequences of specific measures directly affecting the individual person in society.

Besides being a serious investigative effort, these projections reflect the anxiety of people today. Insofar as we have not been turned into an anonymous mass and stripped of our own consciousness, we stop to think now and then. We try to understand where our course is leading us and what its end will be. It is not that such reasoning inevitably leads to fatalism. It is that it just does not seem reasonable to keep pursuing a course of uncontrolled progress without trying to take control of it and foresee its potential effects. Indeed more than a few people nowadays are coming to recognize that a policy of *laissez innover* (unrestricted innovation) in the area of technological change may be no more desirable than a policy of *laissez faire* in the area of social and economic policy.[5]

So we can say that any projection of the future or of a given model corresponds to some parameter of thought, and that the latter frames the former in some way or another.

Roger Garaudy has formulated some statements about the ideas of past, present, and future that are apposite here. "Man," he says, "is defined only by his future, by his possibilities. Even history itself can only be approached from the standpoint of tomorrow. . . . It is not a deterministic passage from cause to effect but a specifically human, finalized transition from the possible to the real."

Humankind, then, is a looking ahead, a moving ahead with the intention of transforming the world. We are "not the prediction of the future but the invention of the future. The positivist futurologist (such as Herman Kahn) is the opposite of a prophet. Extrapolating from the present and the past, he promotes a preventive war against the future. His aim is to colonize the future for the benefit of the present. But hope cannot be deduced or derived from any concrete experience. There is necessarily an ongoing and perduring conflict between concrete experience and hope. For experience relates to the past and the present whereas hope is the militant anticipation of the future."

Although we leave aside any discussion that might arise about his essential ideas, we do find in Garaudy a wise warning against the temptation of imagining the future as a mere projection of the present. To do that would be to forget the unpredictable: "Just as Cuvier boasted of reconstructing a prehistoric animal on the basis of fragmentary remains, we would then be trying to construct a kind of archeology of the future."[6]

The case is quite different when we are trying to study, analyze, and offer programmatic models of a reality close at hand. With all the limitations we have pointed out above, the use of new systems to this end helps us to measure and weigh the different possibilities that are available to a national community and the alternative choices it has in planning its further development.

To sum up once more, these studies and projections will make use of mathematical formulations and the indispensable computer. They help us to visualize, better than we ever could before, the complexity of the problems facing us. They provide us with objective bits of data that are extremely useful. Nevertheless our answers will always be conditioned by the nature of the projects and the vision of the human being and society that we hold or seek. At the very least every model contains an implicit doctrine that cannot possibly be measured mathematically.

Programmers and Philosophers

From the above it is clear that today, more than ever before, we need the presence of people who stop to think, that is, philosophers, in the original sense of the word. We need people who love wisdom, who are willing to look beyond the pressure of turbulent events and the accumulating mound of data provided by technical means, who try to probe deeper and find the why and wherefore. In short, we need people who offer us a "conception of the world," who can and should inspire those who fabricate "simulation models."

The basic, age-old questions about the origin and destiny of humankind perdure today. The questions we formulate and the answers we arrive at will depend on the ideas we hold. The technician, the futurologist, and the analyst provide us with indispensable material. This is evident from real-life facts, since the nature of many arguments and debates would be inexplicable if their investigations, studies, and practices were ignored. But it is up to the philosopher to go deeper and further.

The fact is that the problem does not end with the work of the investigators: As I have indicated, we must determine what we think about the destiny of humanity. Is indefinite and unlimited growth in production permissible? Does that objective lead to a happier, more humane society? Or does purely material satisfaction and unlimited consumption lead ultimately to satiety, rebelliousness, licentiousness, and the loss or negation of essential values? Does it ultimately corrupt and degrade everything?

In other words, the problem is to find out what criteria are the underlying inspiration for those who are inventing, creating, and consuming; what sort of civilization they are trying to build; what vision of the world is guiding them. Their present actions may derive from some conception of their own happiness and some view of the nature of their own force, power, and "progress." Is it perhaps the antithesis of a system of ideas, of a philosophy, that interprets the human being in terms that go beyond the mere satisfaction of personal ambitions? Do we need a different philosophy, one that can generate different aspirations and objectives and offer a sound response to the questions that underlie any vision of the future?

As I noted, every philosophy implies some conception of human destiny and generates a vision of humanity. That is evident from the time of Plato and Aristotle to the time of Hegel and Marx. The curious thing today is that there is much talk about the end of ideologies, when in fact their influence is quite strong. Grand cosmogonic visions guide the major social, cultural, and political movements of our time, as well as those who fabricate the new "models."

2

The Feigned Death of Ideologies

The Presence of Marxism

Consider the presence of Marxism in today's world, for example. As an interpretation of human history and society, the range and depth of its impact is quite considerable. This fact clearly belies the assertion of those who proclaim the death of ideologies.

In reality more than 1.2 billion people live in countries that recognize Marxism as their official doctrine. Its influence has also spread to almost every area of the world, especially through the mass communications media, the intelligentsia, and university centers. Sometimes it works directly through organized groups in the fields of politics and labor. They claim to be inspired by that philosophy, regarding it as the best way to explain and give direction to the whole social process. Indeed we might say that for the first time in history an ideological system born in the West has conquered China and other sections of Asia and Africa. The range of its influence seems to outstrip that attained by any of the older religions.

To some extent Marxism has also made inroads into the Christian churches. Clearly influenced by it, some

15

segments of the churches are trying to make Marxism and Christianity compatible. They are organizing such groups as "Christians for Socialism" and elaborating "liberation theologies." These trends, which began in Latin America and have spread to other continents, adopt some Marxist theses and apply them in their own exegesis.

Marxism appears in a variety of forms. It may take the form of a pure philosophy. It may appear as Maoism, a trend that seems to have had a rapid rise and a no less rapid decline. Or it may take the orthodox Russian form of Marxist-Leninism. In any case it does not simply affect those who are members of Communist or Socialist parties. Many people who do not belong to such parties still declare that they are adherents to the doctrine itself.

This ideology, which covers a wide spectrum of the human population, is the most challenging and powerful motive-force behind the socio-political changes that are shaking today's world. This is not the place to provide a detailed analysis of its basic principles, which I have done in earlier publications. But there can be no doubt that it is a major motivating force in world history. It has highlighted and accelerated certain elements in the process of human evolution. Whatever judgment it may ultimately merit, there can be no doubt that it contains large doses of truth. It would be hard to explain how something totally erroneous could have achieved such widespread and profound influence. And no one can fail to recognize the contributions of Marxism. It has provided analytical tools for both the social and the economic planes. It has stressed the value of human labor as the basic foundation of society. It has criticized inequality between different social classes and stressed the dialectical interaction between classes in the transformation of society. It has highlighted the problems of human alienation, particularly in modern industrial society. It has also underlined the substructural influence of material conditions vis-à-vis ideological super-structures.

Marxism was born near the start of the modern industrial era, as capitalism was preparing to expand in every direction. It scrutinized the world of its time, denouncing its inhumanity and injustice (which we can scarcely imagine today). Today, however, Marxism has been fundamentally superseded and is out of date, e.g., in its theory of labor-value, its doctrine of ends and means, its atheism, and its concept of man and freedom.

Nevertheless, because it has all the features of a religious phenomenon, Marxism awakens faith and hope in its adherents. For this reason it has been able to withstand the various critiques of its theoretical constructs as well as the unfortunate results of its practical application. However, what once seemed like a monolithic phenomenon is now splintering under the obvious weight of national, military, and imperial designs. The experiences of China, Poland, Czechoslovakia, Hungary, and the Baltic states prove this beyond a doubt, and more such cases could be cited.

Moreover, it has not been proved clearly and indisputably that all racial and regional antagonisms will disappear almost automatically within a socialist formula of government. No amount of secrecy and repression has been able to conceal the underlying conflicts between different peoples, cultures, and nationalities. There is no guarantee that socialist societies will always find a peaceful solution to the problems that exist between them, as is evident from the border disputes and political in-fighting between Russia and China.

It has become obvious that human liberation in a classless society is nothing but a myth. It did not happen under Stalin. It has not happened under the totalitarian rule of one party and its elite *apparatchiki*. This has been brought out clearly and forcefully by Russia's top writers, scientists, historians, and artists. With great personal risk to themselves, they have brought to light the true characteristics of a totalitarian society: the way it deals with human beings, the true status of human rights, and the concrete functioning of the government.

Neither have any of Marxism's fundamental predictions turned out to be true. There has been no ultimate crisis of capitalism, no progressive impoverishment of the laboring classes, no revolution in the most industrialized countries.

Yet, for all this, the Marxist current does continue to make advances both in the East and the West, in the northern and the southern hemispheres. Its evident flaws and contradictions have not diminished its expansive force and influence.

Liberalism is not an adequate response to this threat. It did make its own historical contribution, and its principal features have already been incorporated into the democratic, parliamentary regimes to be found in North America and the West. Today, more fully than ever before, we can appreciate the importance of affirming human freedom, the desire for justice and equality, respect for the rights of the individual, and freedom of expression. We can see how important it is that fresh blood be injected into government and national leadership through periodic elections based on universal suffrage and the secret ballot.

These principles must be maintained, defended, and elaborated more fully because they form an integral part of human heritage and progress. Nevertheless, some have proposed to sacrifice those principles in order to realize their own new versions of utopia. In every instance this has meant a serious loss, and some nations have taken tragic steps backward as a result. These principles must be affirmed, deepened, and extended, but that can be done only with an up-to-date vision of the world and a broader, more adequate conception of the historical cycle through which we are living.

The positive contributions of the liberal doctrine must

be incorporated into a new perspective that will enable us to defend human freedom amid the conditions of post-industrial society and the demands now being voiced by the poor peoples of the earth who are attempting to achieve their economic "take-off points." The pragmatic empiricism of the United States and the successful functioning of its democratic government and economy may suit the peculiar context of that continental nation. It may accord well with its traditions and way of life. But it may not work as well in other countries that do not possess the same characteristics and resources.

The capitalist mode of production is not a philosophy; nor is it a response to the great human questions. It may have proved its effectiveness in certain economic aspects and in certain countries, but in itself it does not constitute what I would call a "civilization project," that is, a projected plan for the elaboration of a civilization.

An Ideological Vacuum

What we find, then, is an ideological vacuum that is profoundly affecting the foundations of the "free" world. In the face of aggressive totalitarian philosophies, this ideological vacuum is the root cause of the crisis that now threatens democratic regimes. It is quite apparent in the nations of Europe, some of which seem to be highly vulnerable already.

H. Trevor Roper has pointed out that Europeans feel they are living through a period of decline rather than progress. There is good reason for such a feeling when the shadow of superpowers looms over the divided countries of Europe, when a new despotism based on mass technologies threatens to destroy freedoms that Europe boasted of discovering.

The crisis is not just economic or political. It has to do with basic values, with the basic structure of consensus that allows the system to function normally. More than one person has already pointed out that the greatest challenge to the democratic societies now comes from the intellectuals and various groups led by them.[1] They have criticized the corruption, the materialism, and the inefficiency of democratic governments that have succumbed to the domination of "monopoly capitalism." A counterculture has developed among the intellectuals, and it is now spreading to professors, students, and the middle classes. It proposes a set of countervalues that are designed to undermine all leadership, to defy authority, to unmask and delegitimize all institutions. This challenge to democratic government is serious in an age when there is widespread education on the high school and college level, when the middle class is expanding, and when the manual laborer is being replaced by the professional and the office worker. It is at least as serious as the threat once posed by aristocratic elites, fascist movements, and organs of the Communist party.

Significant here is the fact that it is members of the thinking elite and the middle classes, not the proletariat, that are now undermining the bases of democratic government and its functioning. This fact can be observed in every area of activity. Consider the field of education, for example. Professors no longer believe that they have a "sacred mission," and students no longer accept what they are taught without questioning. Dogmatic structures are disintegrating in both the secular and the religious sphere; and no one really knows how to operate when new forms have not arisen to replace the old ones.

This process, which generally affects all democratic nations, cannot be attributed to any one single cause. Human societies and their problems are now much more complicated than they were in the past, even in the recent past. Increased education and culture, the technological revolution, and new systems of communication and interrelation have changed people's living conditions and created a situation that goes beyond the old institutional framework. The old institutions are not adequate for the new realities. They go on functioning, but they are more suited to the society of the nineteenth century than to that of the upcoming twenty-first century.

The existing forms of authority and social control are not effective in the face of heightened human aspirations. Or else they are not accepted as legitimate by those who are unaware of their foundations. This produces a lack of basic discipline so that people cannot really face up to problems. It appears in all sorts of forms. As is the case with inflationary pressures, for example, they cannot be solved solely on the basis of economic theorems. They call for socio-political perspectives and visions that will take in the social body as a whole.

All these phenomena are the result of a world confronting a major historical change. It cannot face up to that change without some basic consensus. Certain values must be shared by all segments of society.

In underdeveloped countries these problems take on a different cast and are far more serious. There we find a lack of integration, inefficiency, serious economic and social deficiencies, inadequate institutions, and aspirations that go unsatisfied because of fragile economies. It is much more difficult, therefore, for the society as a whole to accept certain common values. In such countries the ruptures are more serious and questions are soon phrased in the most radical terms. Practical formulas are not enough to solve them.

Limited Responses

Technology, know-how, and economic development are a necessary part of the response, but they will not suffice to answer the deeper human unrest provoked by this current process.

Aid and cooperation from the more powerful nations

are also necessary and commendable, but that cannot constitute the full response to the underdeveloped nations. One complaint occurs frequently in this connection. Those nations that are sending the most aid often complain that they do not receive adequate thanks for what they are doing while other nations, which are not sending any aid, seem to be looked upon with admiration and affection.

It is the age-old story of Martha and Mary. One invests worry and effort into common domestic necessities; the other pays attention to a life-inspiring word or message. In our present case it should be pointed out that the aid is rather limited and the message often far from true.[2] Nevertheless, broad segments of humanity now feel a great need for some sort of interpretation that at least offers them a coherent framework for establishing discipline, social control, and the hope needed to continue the struggle.

It has been possible to see the lack of an adequate response in the vagaries of the policy of "detente." In the United States and the other nations of the West many have been inclined to believe, or at least have acted as if they believed, that if an understanding were reached with the U.S.S.R. and the communist world, this would oblige the latter to make important ideological concessions.

Experience suggests that this is not the case, and so there has been much ambivalence surrounding the notion of detente. If it were simply a matter of easing tensions, of using dialogue to avoid armed conflict or to set limitations on certain kinds of armament or to broaden contacts between people, then certainly no one could raise objections to it. But it is a serious mistake to think that detente has signified a suspension of ideological warfare. No amount of arms-limitation agreements is going to stop people from thinking their own ideas and trying to share them with others, particularly when a militant faith constitutes an essential part of their raison d'être as a world power.

The fact is that the communist countries, and particularly the U.S.S.R., have never renounced the idea of aggressively spreading their doctrine. Their leaders have expressly dedicated themselves to that task. With the increase of economic, commercial, and tourist contacts in recent years, they have stressed the need for vigilance and urgent effort on the ideological front. In March 1974 a conference of ideological activists took place in Warsaw. They arrived at this conclusion: "Neither now nor in the future can peaceful coexistence be equated with a termination of the class struggle or the removal of antagonisms and contradictions between socialism and capitalism. . . . The conditions fostering peaceful coexistence greatly enhance the significance and importance of the ideological struggle." Thus the policy of peaceful coexistence has engendered an ideological offensive and an intensification of domestic controls.

Some years ago Arnold Toynbee pointed out that material tools are not the only kind in this sort of contest:

All tools are not of the material kind; there are spiritual tools as well, and these are the most potent that Man has made. A creed, for instance, can be a tool; and, in the new round in the competition between Russia and the West that began in 1917, the Russians this time threw into their scale of the balances a creed that weighed as heavily against their Western competitors' material tools as, in the Roman story of the ransoming of Rome from the Gauls, the sword thrown in by Brennus weighed against the Roman gold.[3]

Arms agreements, therefore, will never still the ideological struggle; nor will they cause either party to renounce its own particular vision of the future. When it is a matter of easing tensions, there are two levels involved. One has to do with the material level of reducing armaments; the other has to do with the ideological struggle. If people rest content with the first level but have little to say on the second level, then the latter struggle, which is much more important and decisive, will be lost beforehand. They will have no course left but to resort to force, and their own force will already have been undermined from within.

Such seems to be the lesson of history. In no epoch of human history has the course of events been left in the control of those who limited themselves to self-defense and relied on force alone. Force itself is simply the by-product of a chance position. It may allow people to be victorious for a fleeting moment, but it does not guarantee them the future.

In one of his books Henry Kissinger showed us how the conservative forces of an earlier day tried to withstand the revolutionary forces of their time.[4] The illustrative example was Metternich. Convinced of the basic weakness of the empire he represented, he used all his ingenuity to form a Holy Alliance that would halt the march of the liberal, republican revolution. This shrewdly constructed edifice could hold up for a time, but its eventual downfall could well be expected. It postponed the march of events for a time, but eventually the structure crumbled. History cannot be confined in spider webs, however artfully they may be constructed. The Austrian minister tried to preserve a particular system in the face of a changing world, knowing full well that its day was past and that he was only stalling for time.

Examples and comparisons are often dangerous when pushed too far. But allowing for differences in time and circumstance, we could say that something similar is happening today. One part of the world, smug and self-satisfied, is trying to defend itself against the onslaught of new ideas and emerging nations; but it has not gotten beyond mere self-defense.

The situation may not stand out so clearly when one looks directly at the relations existing between the superpowers, or between them and other highly developed nations. It becomes quite obvious, however, when we consider other regions of the world such as

Africa or Latin America. There the effects of the notion
and policy of detente have been more readily observa-
ble.

On this southern continent, for example, people are
certainly anxious to see a nuclear conflict avoided. Like
all human beings, they want to avoid the terrible suffering such a war would entail. But the problem does not
end there. The nations on this continent are not interested in maintaining the present state of affairs.
They are vitally interested in social change. Indeed profound and rapid change is called for if we want to maintain certain values of the present that are essential for
the existence and preservation of freedom. Marxism,
however, offers a different formula and a way to implement it. It seeks to capture the will of those who are
desperately looking for some method that will give
meaning to their actions. It is quite possible that Marxism, without firing a shot, may come to dominate most if
not all of our continent.

At this point we might well ask what the democracies
have to offer in the way of a philosophy, in the way of
ideas, values, and an interpretation of the future. What
sort of tools or weapons do they have to offer for this
serious battle? The fact is that the peoples of Latin
America and elsewhere have not been aware of any
clear answer to these questions. They have known of no
effective, feasible answer that offered hope to the vast
majority of the people. The only response of conservative groups, particularly of conservative extremists, is
to use force and repression. An important part of their
political view can be summed up in the theory of "national security." To confront the threat of insurrection
they have not hesitated to destroy democracy. Their
economic recipe has meant huge advantages for small
minorities and general impoverishment for most of the
populace.

So what we have had is not detente but a series of
localized conflicts and formulas designed to maintain

"order." With due allowance for differences in time and methods, it is the same procedure that was used by the members of the Holy Alliance in the last century.

This is not a matter of mere conjecture. The vision and the type of response just described has been amply treated in writing and embodied in concrete actions. At this point we might do well to quote the words of Robert McNamara when he was the U.S. secretary of defense. He posed the problem authoritatively and in very clear terms:

We now recognize formally the low probability of conventional attack on any American State from outside the hemisphere [i.e., end of the Cold War—detente]. As a result we see no requirement for Latin American countries to support large conventional military forces, particularly those requiring expensive and sophisticated equipment. Outlays for such forces are an unwarranted diversion of resources from the more urgent and important tasks of economic and social development.

The absence of a major external threat to this hemisphere also has helped us to focus the energies of the Rio Treaty nations toward the widely shared problem of armed insurgency. Indeed, another major change in our policy reflects the need to deal with the threat of externally inspired insurgencies. This threat has been a major challenge to some of our Latin-American allies, and we have tried to help them by providing training, advisers and assistance in the equipment and techniques of counterinsurgency.

But counterinsurgency alone is an inadequate response to this problem. Removal of the causes of human suffering and deprivation is essential if stable political institutions are to flourish free of the threat of violent revolution.[5]

That political response never materialized, despite the wisdom of the advice. We can now point to what is actually going on, some ten years after those words were written. Military expenditure is greater in Latin America than it has ever been, absorbing funds and resources essential to economic and social development.

Human suffering and poverty probably go deeper and range further today, not only objectively but subjectively; for today people in Latin America are more explicitly conscious of their comparative situation. On the domestic front energy has been concentrated on the counterinsurgency struggle. Foreign contacts have centered around advice, training, and supplies connected with counterinsurgency warfare and political policing.

Terrorism and armed struggle have in fact furnished an excellent pretext for the establishment of anti-insurrectional regimes. As a result Latin America is now going through one of the most regressive epochs in its history. It has taken a long step backward with respect to freedom and human rights. Not only ignoring the possibility of some rational and stable political solution, it has actually put further obstacles in its way. The only response to the existing problem has been the use of force. This has been backed up by a pseudoideology that has promised "security," but has not responded to any of the needs and demands now pulsating in the anguished consciousness of Latin Americans.

This has been the prevailing situation in Latin America in recent decades, but it is obvious that the international situation has been undergoing constant alteration.

The threat of communism has not diminished in importance, but on the ideological plane it has lost its impetus. Various phenomena are indicative of this fact. Communism has been weakened by the breakup of monolithic unity in its international conduct and by the rise of varied heretical movements. Moreover, it is no longer possible to hide the fact that the communist system in Russia has not been successful in certain areas. While the U.S.S.R. has made rapid progress in such areas as space exploration, military technology, and industry, it has not been successful in agriculture and livestock-raising. Nor has it been successful in applying technology to other areas of production. But perhaps the most obvious flaw in the system is its ongoing rigidity, the lack of personal freedom, and its bureaucratic centralism. This has stifled or retarded the process of political, cultural, and even scientific creativity. Once upon a time the communist system aroused much enthusiasm in certain sectors of public opinion in the western democracies. This is giving way to greater objectivity, to more critical analyses, and to a process of demythologization. Its ideas and its practical applications are coming under closer scrutiny. Fuller information and the testimony of a growing number of dissidents have forced the Communist parties of Europe to pay closer attention.

These factors and others have also brought about a change in attitude in democratic countries. The threat of communism no longer seems so fearsome. Marxist-Leninism no longer seems to be an inevitable fate. This has done much to reduce blind, irrational reactions of an anticommunist bent. Speaking at the University of Notre Dame, President Carter summed up the new attitude: "Being confident of our own future, we are now free of the inordinate fear of Communism which once led us to embrace any dictator who joined us in our fear. For many years we were willing to adopt some of the imperfect principles and tactics of our adversaries, sometimes abandoning our values for theirs. We were fighting fire with fire, never stopping to think that it is better to fight fire with water."

The implementation of a policy seeking to defend human rights has also transformed the nature of the ideological debate and its national and international repercussions. Military and economic strategy in the struggle are no longer the sole focus of that debate. Today there is much talk about relations between people, the values that should guide such relations, and the terms in which coexistence should be conceived.

All this offers new horizons for humanism and a revitalized conception of democracy. More and more importance is being attributed to the forms in which human beings can express their freedom and to their desire to participate in the life of individual nations and the international community.

The Crisis in Nondemocratic Regimes

These failings in democratic countries should not lead people to conclude that dictatorships and totalitarian regimes are not facing similar or even greater problems simply because they give the appearance of having solved all problems. One need only look at recent events in history to settle that question.

Every now and then the myth that dictatorships are more efficient comes to life once again. Once upon a time the mythology of Nazi and Fascist invincibility glorified the achievements of those regimes. Today we know much more about the true inner reality of those regimes and their workings. Aside from their total lack of respect for human rights, they were riddled with weakness, corruption, disorganization, and deceit; but all that was covered over by official propaganda and the silence imposed on dissent. Now we know the tragic consequences that they brought upon their nations and peoples.

The case is much the same with Greece and Portugal under earlier regimes. I could go on citing many such examples, and our own Latin America has provided many.

For many years there was also the claim that democratic governments were ineffective and that the communist countries would overtake them on the economic front. Today that thesis is scarcely defensible. No communist country has matched the socio-economic growth rates of the European democracies, Canada, Japan, Australia, and of course the United States. Much of the apparent per capita growth in the communist world has been due to the growth of goods and services related to expanded war and military production. When the proper corrections have been made, it turns out that their growth has been relatively meager, especially if we consider that there has been a steady decline in the national product of those countries in recent years.

Inflation has not been absent under collectivist systems either. As Valery Giscard d'Estaing points out, there is an imbalance between supply and demand so that the prices fixed by the authorities are not always a reliable indicator. There is much poverty, and one can judge from the long lines waiting to buy food and supplies. At times the imbalance has resulted in social explosion. "It is no accident that the monetary units of the collectivist economies are not convertible and lack value in the international sphere."[6]

These situations have been kept under wraps or suppressed for the most part, but at times they break out into the open. Worker protests led to the deposition of Gomulka in Poland in 1970 and to the resignation of Gierek in 1976.

Sakharov had this to say about life in the U.S.S.R.:

Our society is ill with apathy, hypocrisy, egotism, and underhanded cruelty. The vast majority of the elite class—the administrative apparatus of both the party and the government as well as the favored intelligentsia—cling obstinately to their secret or not so secret privileges. They show profound indifference to the violations of human rights, the demands of progress, and the security of man's future.

Garaudy has insisted that the struggle of the laboring class against the bourgeoisie did not end in victory for the workers. In the U.S.S.R. it has ended in a monopoly of power being held by the technocracy: "The fact that the state appropriates the surplus . . . on the national level does not automatically mean that the people have control over the use of that surplus, that political life is democratized, or that the workers are any less alienated."[7]

Indeed Sakharov went so far as to say that absolute monopoly by the state inevitably engenders servitude and excessive conformity, thereby destroying culture and ideologies. This basic thesis is confirmed by the witness of an ever growing number of dissidents.

We must not forget Maoism either. A few years ago it became a sacrosanct dogma and in various parts of the world Soviet communism found itself displaced and hounded by China's ideological offensive. In Latin America, for example, some years ago the Maoist current struck many young people as the new and exciting thing. The Muscovites were old-hat reactionaries, and everyone was expected to adopt the new ideological fashion.

The picture reported by visitors to China was that of a new paradise. A new, original kind of society and economy had come into being in China. Even more importantly, a new human species grounded on solidarity and brotherhood had appeared and was apparently capable of transforming the natural environment around it. In the new society there was no conflict and no ambition to wield power. Mao Tse-tung was practically a god. With his death and the end of his reign those illusions have gone up in smoke. We now can see the deep divisions that existed within the party and the armed forces. Some have fallen from favor and others have risen to power in the wake of ferocious intramural attacks. As Willy Brandt points out:

We now know that in communist countries the elimination of private economic power has *not* as a general rule led to the liberation of the workers. It has led primarily to a tremendous concentration of power in the hands of an uncontrolled bureaucracy and to the formation of a new kind of dictatorship.[8]

We have thus reached the point where no one can gloss over the intrinsic defects of these systems, not to mention the lack of freedom. Twenty or more years ago this objective examination could not be carried out. The regimes in question seemed not only monolithic but invulnerable to any real information-gathering. Criticism was considered a form of heresy, and one could scarcely predict that the Communist parties of the western world would rebel in any way. Today such rebellion is a common fact. The Communist parties of the West are expressing their own reservations and objections, while simultaneously asserting their own independence on the ideological level.

Yet, for all that, one cannot say that an ideological vacuum exists in the communist world. Its vision of a new model of society can withstand any disillusionment suffered by its adherents, so the faith remains immutable. Even for those who have abandoned the ranks of the Communist party, such as Garaudy in France, Marxism remains the most solid and scientifically unobjectionable system of ideas. Criticism may point up the "perversions of socialism" to be found in its historical model, but it cannot undermine its validity as a philosophy.

Some dissidents have gone further. They have challenged the truth and form of these totalitarian societies, pointing up the dangers to human freedom that they embody. As a result many of these dissidents have been expelled from their country or have sought refuge in the West. Unfortunately the West has little more to offer than refuge. Today they cannot really ask the West to give them the inspiration that will help them to rediscover their soul. In the West we do not find any rush of examples or creative ideas that might give rise to a new civilization.

The dissidents are voicing criticism of collectivist society, but they can also see the sores festering in many democracies. They know that the societies marked by high consumption have lost their inner unity, that for all their well-being they are nursing deep dissatisfactions, egotism, hypocrisy, and moral corruption.

Money has become the driving force as never before.

The yearning for profit and economic power knows no limits. And a thousand and one sophistries are corrupting the ethical standard that should govern people's conduct. Many expressions of youthful revolt are rooted in this fact, though they too may move toward irrational excesses.

It is certainly true that other grave defects can be seen in totalitarian countries. However, that does not mean that people in the socialist world or in the under-developed world feel that the existing forms of democracy are the solution they are seeking. From the western world they want only to learn about its technologies and take advantage of them, to acquire its capital so as to be able to match its levels of production and consumption.

Lacking any real message in this overall context, the democracies seem to be weak. Lacking faith in themselves, they do not seem to project any message or image that opens prospects for the future or bolsters the will for survival. As if that were not disillusioning enough, surprising views are beginning to be heard more frequently in intellectual and government circles within the great democracies. Speaking cautiously but explicitly, some are suggesting that freedom and democracy may not be feasible among certain peoples who have not attained certain economic and cultural levels. Perhaps it is excusable, and even reasonable, that freedom should be repressed among such peoples, at least for the time being. Such is the view that is now bandied about.

From there it is an easy step for many people to conclude that democratic values are not essential, that it is more advisable for such peoples or nations to adopt some "authoritarian" form of government. And if it does come down to a choice between various kinds of authoritarian government, it is quite possible that the people or nation in question might want to opt for some sort of socialist dictatorship. For at the least the latter can offer a dialectical framework and structure that is much better thought out than other nationalist dictatorships that are simply repressive.

Humanism and Democracy

The power of Marxism lies in the fact that it proposes a system of ideas, a theory of history, an interpretation of the human being, and a vision of a future society. For a Marxist-Leninist like Mao, "dialectical materialism is a proletarian conception of the world and, at the same time, a method created by the proletariat to become acquainted with the world around them and to carry out revolutionary action. It is the union of a universal point of view and a methodology."

We might add here that it may be such, not only for the proletariat, but also for certain sectors of the middle class and for intellectual groups. Indeed there may be greater understanding involved with the latter two groups. In any case it is on that foundation that Marxism elaborates its strategy and its tactics.

On the other hand, for many the power of democracy lies in the fact that for all its weaknesses it remains the one and only rational route for human progress. But the fact is that it is not enough to point out that route as the only rational one. Indeed that will do little good if many of its proponents have vitiated it from within, if they simply hold on to a world that has lost all meaning for them and that is often used only to conceal their own scepticism.

Democracy must be more than a political formula. It must flow from a certain conception of the human being and society, from the wellsprings of law and right, from the raison d'être of the institutions that give it formal structure.

We cannot pretend to organize the state and its juridical framework without some specific conception of the human being. As Giorgio La Pira has pointed out, the fact that the state is inspired by one set of principles rather that another is not a matter of indifference. Being an organ of the collectivity and enjoying a certain supremacy, the state functions to serve justice and culture as well as to legislate and guide economic activity. Thus it creates the general atmosphere in which the human person must live and find fulfillment.

Contemporary political currents depend first and foremost on the sustaining worldviews or *Weltanschauungen* for which they have opted beforehand. In the last analysis, therefore, they are based on metaphysical concepts.

And yet there is much mistrust of such concepts, because some people use them as an excuse for not facing up to reality. In that respect Marx's critique of democracy and its ideology was incisive but also distorted. In the last analysis we can say that he created his own *Weltanschauung*.

My thesis is that it is in humanism, as a philosophy and a conception of society, that we find both the theoretical foundation of democracy and its practical projection. The terms "humanism" and "democracy," however, may mean a great deal or practically nothing at all. They have been used and abused to apply to the most flagrantly contradictory positions, and sometimes they have been combined with adjectives that strip them of their true nature. Adding to this confusion is the fact that even the worst enemies of human freedom and human rights now dare to call themselves "humanists," "Christians," and "democrats," when their every deed belies such appellations.

So there is a real need to define the meaning of these terms and spell everything out precisely. Of all the philosophers of this century, Maritain may well be the one who carried out that objective with the greatest care and precision. While he recognized different forms of humanism, his own thinking was rooted in Christian thought. That in itself is important, quite aside from other considerations, because more than a billion human beings claim to profess Christian belief—though of course it does not mean that all agree on the nature of integral humanism or adhere to its social consequences. Toynbee has rightly pointed out that at different points in history Islam and communism broke to the surface as programs designed to reform the abuses in the contemporary practice of Christianity: "It was a Western criticism of the West's failure to live up to her own Christian principles in the economic and social life of this professedly Christian society."[9]

Such reactions are bound to happen when a large segment of the human race abandons the practice of its guiding principles. It inevitably loses its spiritual initiative and cannot maintain its forms and structures. Now hollow, these forms and structures can no longer defend themselves against the incursion of outside ideologies or heresies born within their own boundaries.

Revitalizing Christian and humanistic principles is therefore a matter of life and death. They must gain new vigor and project themselves into the tasks of history. This effort must be undertaken not only with respect to individual nations but also for the sake of the world community. Though different religions can be found in it, they all are humanist ones. And since profound changes and new orientations are called for, we must go beyond the social and economic boundaries to concern ourselves with the very existence or renovation of the civilization created by Christianity, its precursors, and other great prophets of theological doctrine before and since.

If Christianity and the other religions are not faithful to their mission on the temporal and historical front, they will leave a vacuum that will destroy contemporary civilization.

Maritain proposes to avoid this vacuum with a Christian version of humanism and its socio-political significance. But though he is rigorous in its exposition, he nowhere excludes others.

The very clarity of Christian humanist teaching enables it to be open in dialogue and to seek agreement with other forms of humanism coming from different religious sources. There can be a consensus on the values that will enable us to elaborate a civilization project in which freedom, justice, brotherhood, and human solidarity have real meaning.

It is only under these conditions that democracy will be able to achieve authentic expression. At the center will stand human beings as members of a community that enriches them without absorbing them. It will be a society focused, not on profit or power, but on the full development of the human person.

This humanist conception can revitalize the moral foundations on which democracy rests. Having shored up its own consistency, it will be able to withstand assaults from within and without. It will thus offer real hope to those peoples and nations who are seeking justice and development without having to sacrifice their own freedom.

3

A Civilization in Crisis

A Call for Heroic Effort

In 1939 Maritain published a small book entitled *Le crépuscule de la civilization.* In it he confronted a question that had already been asked by other thinkers such as Spengler and Berdyaev: How desperate is the plight of western civilization? Is it on its way out?

Maritain spurned both the "professional optimists" and the "pessimism of the fatalists." Salvation or ruin depended on whether or not people would undertake the difficult but not impossible task of tapping their spiritual energies and working for human freedom. The situation would become critical if those who appreciated the price and value of freedom were not willing to undertake that task. What was needed was "heroic" effort in the cause of "integral humanism." In our day, said Maritain, integral humanism is the "only thing that can remedy the ills of the world."[1]

Implemented in the contemporary world, this humanism would have two basic traits according to Maritain. First, the effort would not be restricted to ensuring the rights and development of ivory-tower thinkers or small elites. It must touch all human beings, making real their rights to the necessities of existence and the life of the spirit. In our day we are definitely confronted with "the problem of the masses." That is the first thing that humanism must take into account.

The totalitarian solution attempts to take advantage of the natural misery of human beings. It attempts to turn them into carefully guided instruments bred on illusions and lies. People will be turned into slaves who think they are happy. Massification erases everything individual and personal in people, closing the door on the creative freedom.

The second feature of this new humanism is that it would "take on the task of profound transformation in the temporal order. Our mercantile civilization and our economy rooted in the fecundity of money would be replaced, not by a collectivist economy, but by a 'personalist' civilization and economy reflecting the temporal splendor of the gospel truths."[2]

Almost forty years after that small book was written, it is easy enough to see that we have not fulfilled the conditions Maritain laid down for any effort that might truly salvage or replace our civilization. Insofar as the first point is concerned, it is becoming ever clearer that there is a real danger that the masses might be turned into carefully guided instruments and truly enslaved people in the collectivist economies and the totalitarian states. Even Lenin himself began to fear the growing power of bureaucracy before he died. Insofar as the second point is concerned, we have seen a further intensification of "our mercantile civilization and our economy rooted in the fecundity of money." It is now taking on new forms and modalities in the so-called "consumer societies," where there is a dizzying growth spiral in production and the demand for goods. It does not simply take in the necessities of life. It also includes highly sophisticated luxuries, which are provided to satisfy the urge for profit, to multiply money, and to effect a concentration of power.

The high-consumption society could be justified insofar as it liberates people from material bondage. Rationally organized and operated, it would undoubtedly provide us with instruments that make our existence easier. Instead, however, it has been turned into a huge machine for exciting appetites, the satisfaction of which leads to inconceivable waste. The resources of this planet are being used to the very limit, if not beyond it, for the benefit of a small portion of the world's population. The basic capital of humanity as a whole is being squandered to this end; and vast sectors of humanity and the physical globe, even within the developed countries themselves, are subjected to great misery and destruction.

The market economy and the high-consumption society have brought about the exploitation of underdeveloped countries. Sometimes it equals that of the earlier colonial period, exhausting the resources and reserves that those countries need for life and survival.

For its part the collectivist system has accentuated the process of massification. Here again the objective is to attain higher living standards at the cost of enormous sacrifices. In this case the price is the loss of personal freedom, complete lack of participation in societal processes and decisions, and the absence of freedom of expression and all the other rights that make human life gracious and dignified. And all this has happened without any proof that it has produced greater efficiency in the operation of the economy.

Curiously enough both societies display similar characteristics in many instances. Both are moving toward standardized massification. Both are aiming to develop high-consumption societies more or less rapidly. As superpowers, both resemble each other insofar as the military-industrial-technological complex holds great power. But we should remember that this is even more true in totalitarian states, where the technobureaucracy does not allow for any real decentralization of power.

Thus things have moved in precisely the opposite direction from the one that Maritain pointed out as the precondition for saving our present civilization. The twilight that he saw falling in 1939 is turning into night. In 1939 the symptoms were lit up by the glare of war and Nazi aggression. Today the backdrop may not seem so dramatic, but the disintegration is far more extensive and profound.

Certainly it is not the first time that a civilization has reached its twilight. The question now is whether the effort of which Maritain spoke in 1939 is still possible. I am convinced that it is, so long as our effort is energetic and heroic.

Inalienable Rights

This twilight is not the result of chance. It is due to a substantial and ongoing alteration of the bases on which western civilization was built. It is also due to a conception of what human beings are, one that limits them to the temporal realm and excludes any values transcending their own nature. All humanism is threatened by the desire of some to define it in such a way that "all orientation toward the supra-human and all transcendence is ruled out."[3]

If there is no ruling principle prior and superior to us, then order and rights in the real world must flow from a pact in which the law of the majority prevails. Thus the majority become the exclusive origin of right and law; nothing can oppose it. The individual becomes a fleeting particle in the mass. It is the mass whose existence and physical gravitation perdures, finding expression in the state that represents it.

Lacking any higher personal destiny, human beings come to depend on such things as race, class, technology, or the idea embodied in the state. Sooner or later they come to depend on the very idols that they themselves erected.

No one can fail to realize that the majority is the

expression of the people's will. But their margin of decision cannot be absolute; there must be limits to it. For example, there are the inalienable rights of the human person, which cannot be disregarded by any state or majority. Norms laid down by a majority are the best system for societal living, so long as they are not so unique and absolute that they deny human rights.

Human beings have a right to enjoy life and freedom, to form a family, to organize and express themselves. These rights do not arise from some compact. They can find recognition and expression in such a compact, but no "Social Contract" can eliminate them, because they are part of human nature. Human beings have an origin and a destiny that does not depend on any majority. There is no other way to guarantee respect for individual persons. If one adopts a different vision of the human being, there is great danger that human rights will disappear soon afterwards.

It is true that social classes do exist, and that there is conflict between them. But that conflict must not replace human persons or absorb them and their integrity. If it does, then human beings will cease to be the essential objective and will be turned into mere instruments. Their rights will be sacrificed in a war without quarter where there is no room for freedom, justice, and peace.

If absolute reason is the one and only norm, then charity, hope, kindness, and understanding will disappear. Pride and base appetites will prevail. Indeed Solzhenitsyn claims it is already happening: "Our twentieth century has turned out to be more cruel than those preceding it. . . . The same old caveman feelings—greed, envy, violence, and mutual hate, which along the way assumed respectable pseudonyms like class struggle, racial struggle, mass struggle, labor-union struggle— are tearing our world to pieces."[4]

We have seen the rise of a counterhumanism or an antihumanism. As Maritain pointed out forty years ago, there are those who want to have done with false optimism and illusory moralities: "Enough of the idealism that is killing us. Let us return to the spiritual fecundity of the absurd, the abyss, and the ethics of desperation! Poor Nietzsche! "[5]

But it is not really the voice of Nietzsche, says Maritain. It is the voice of a mob whose meanness, mediocrity, and futility stand as apocalyptic signs. It sows the gospel of hatred of reason, propounding the cult of war, or the cult of race, or the cult of blood.

As the decade of the thirties ended, this new theory was embodied in the new superman who danced his way through concentration camps, in the ghettos where thousands of Jews were condemned to a slow death, in the bombed cities of Europe and the Far East. "Nietzsche did not see that there are only two choices open to human beings—the road to Calvary or the road to mayhem and murder."[6]

The myths to which Maritain referred forty years ago still survive today. Disguised under new appellations, they continue to nourish the current forms of antihumanism.

Antihumanism

Many people nurtured the hope and belief that the terrible experience of the last world war would be a sufficient lesson for humanity. Since then, however, it has become clear that none of the causes that unleashed antihumanism have been removed or called into question. Egotism, hatred, and the thirst for power have continued on their way. Today we are once again confronted with decisions of major importance. Only now it is the fate of all humanity, not just that of a single nation, that hangs in the balance.

Worse still, the possibilities for destruction are much more obvious, because we now possess awesome nuclear and biological weapons. Every day the gap between developed nations and the starving millions of the world grows wider. The greatest powers in the world find themselves in a mad arms race, deriving rich side-benefits from the sale of those arms to other nations. Paying billions of dollars, rubles, or francs, small nations ruin themselves to acquire these weapons.

Democracy cannot exist without some minimum consensus. There must be shared acceptance of certain basic ethical values if people are to live together in society. Yet such consensus is now disintegrating. Growing groups are espousing violence as a system; their actions are prompted by the thirst for hatred and destruction. Segments of our young people are rebelling against the established order, and in some cases their protest goes so far as self-destruction.

We are also witnessing another spectacle to which Maritain alluded forty years ago. Our focus on ourselves continues to grow and move toward extremes. Rationalist hopes are becoming not only a philosophical religion but a religion lived and practiced every day:

Thus we confront Marxism. The belief that man's salvation lies in himself has come full circle: Man's destiny is wholly and exclusively temporal. Of course salvation takes place without God, since man cannot exist or operate unless God does not exist. Indeed man's salvation operates against God, that is, against everything in man and the human milieu that is the image of God. . . .

And yet this position claims that it is humanist. But it is radically atheistic, and hence destroys the reality of the humanism that it professes in theory. Consider the way the materialistic revolutionary dialectics has been implemented and lived over the past twenty years [now sixty years] in the country it conquered. It has used every possible means to eradicate moral consciousness in order to serve its own ends. It has persecuted thousands and thousands of suspects, interning them in concentration camps or condemning them to death. The evidence should be enough to convince us on that score.[7]

Maritain wrote those words in 1939, when we did not know the full dimensions of the situation that now stares us in the face. He felt that only heroic effort could contain the "demons" unleashed in the name of race, class, or exacerbated nationalism. Yet today we find that they have only intensified in one form or another.

Not long ago Georges Pompidou, the former president of France, wrote a book that constitutes an authentic political testament. Though he himself is dead, his words deserve to be remembered in our present context:

This parallel growth . . . of anarchy in behavior and of unlimited government power . . . entails an immense danger. We can fall prey to this danger in one of two opposing ways. First, if anarchy prevails, then the foundations for progress will rapidly crumble and we will move toward leftist or rightist totalitarianism. Or, on the other hand, we may move directly towards the totalitarian solution. The danger is not an illusory one. . . .

We have reached such an extreme that we clearly must put an end to speculation and re-create the social order. Someone will cut the Gordian knot. The question is how it will be done. Will it be done by imposing a democratic form of discipline that guarantees liberties? Or will some strong man . . . cut it with the sword of Alexander? Fascism is not an unlikely prospect. Indeed I believe that it is closer at hand than communist totalitarianism. . . .

When all beliefs have crumbled, when people have inculcated the rejection of all social order and authority without proposing anything in their place, then nothing will serve to keep a disoriented humanity together. It will inevitably fall prey to the domination of even more blind and brutal forces. . . .

God is dead. That cry has sounded in history over and over again. Each time humanity has found the way back to faith again, almost always it has been through suffering and killing. From the strictly social and human viewpoint of which I am writing here, faith has enormous value. It is not that it drugs them, as some say, or that it makes their submission easier. Faith is valuable in preventing man from falling prey to the extreme temptations of pride. The conviction that there is a power over human beings serves as a sort of safeguard for both human beings and their leaders. This is all the more useful today, when the instruments at man's disposal are more terrifying than ever before.[8]

Clearly enough the crisis we face today is nothing but the logical result of the ideas and forces that have been operating since World War II. Today they go deeper than ever before. Of course that should not really surprise us. Anything else would have been a miracle. The prevailing political and religious organization of humanity has been strained and then overrun by the forces at work: i.e., the unwonted growth of the economies of the industrialized nations; the possibility of acquiring new kinds of power, thanks to technological inventions; and the simultaneous weakening of moral ties and forces in those same countries.

A new type of materialism is suffocating the virtues that would enable us to perfect ourselves. The curious thing is the response that we see to the execrable "materialism of Marxism." It is an even more vulgar form of materialism, completely devoid of respect for higher human destiny.

New Ingredients

So we find new, unfamiliar ingredients as well in today's historical process. The dimming of civilization and the threatening growth of extremes combine with the fact that we now find ourselves facing new and sometimes wholly unfamiliar situations. We are forced to reconsider the terms in which we had previously organized our life and our societal existence. Without falling prey to any false kind of structuralism, we can assert that we must re-examine our ideas; that we must move forward with alacrity and effectiveness to project the institutions that will make a new social order possible.

In a relatively short time we have moved from a world

organized around national industrial societies and colonial empires to a world that is one interconnected planet. The resulting imbalances pose problems that were heretofore unknown. We need only note the fact that today there are at least 150 sovereign nations; but they are so interdependent that none of them could exist wholly on its own. Moreover, the transfer of knowledge-data and technology is just as important to them as the transfer of capital funds. Sometimes, however, those nations are not really capable of selecting, adapting, and utilizing these things correctly, so they are readily penetrated by huge multinational businesses. And one clear indicator of the new world situation is the fact that some of these multinational companies are more powerful than some nation-states.

Never has it been so true that knowledge is the source of power. Yet despite the general advance of information and mass instruction, there is a steadily growing concentration of the sources of knowledge and an even more rapid growth in the gap between nations. While some nations are painfully moving into the Iron Age, some of the superpowers are exploring the universe beyond us and living in the Computer Age.

This complex of facts is more powerful than any political revolution because it is changing the very foundations on which the societal systems used to function. Institutions and procedures that seemed valid only yesterday are being rendered obsolete. Many of the upheavals we witness today are rooted in that fact.

So we confront a need for changes on the one hand, and the consequences of ideologies that would dehumanize us on the other. Together they give us the measure of the critical juncture at which humanity as a whole, not just one nation or one continent, has arrived.

4

Freedom and Responsibility

Neither Complacent Ease nor Anarchy

All the great turning points of history have been marked by disorientation. Today it is greater than ever before, and so is the temptation to disown freedom. When we feel helpless in the face of threatening forces that we cannot control, our first reaction is to look for a protector. The risks of freedom wear us down. When it is "every man for himself," freedom is the first thing we are inclined to throw overboard. We think that is the price we must pay for saving our skin. Too late we discover that we have lost our dignity and perhaps even our soul.

We know that history is a constant vacillation between progress and retrogression. When people have sought only to secure the present, they have always gone backward; when they have shouldered the risks in the cause of freedom and justice, they have always moved forward in a real and progressive sense.

In any case freedom is not complacent ease or the easy way out on the one hand, nor anarchy on the other. It is the most serious commitment to responsible action that humankind knows. When people want to enjoy its benefits but are incapable of taking on its demands, they break the inner spring that sustains it. That is why dictatorships often prove to be the fatal result of a prior collapse of moral supports.

When Alexander Solzhenitsyn was chosen Man of the Year in 1975, he was interviewed by the journal *Le Point*. This is part of what he had to say about freedom in the West and in the world at large:

You people in the West have forgotten the meaning of freedom. When Europe achieved freedom in the eighteenth century, it was a sacred notion flowing directly from the older religious world that it both denied and continued. Freedom cannot be dissociated from its goal, which is specifically the exaltation of the human being. Its function was to make it possible for those values to emerge, and hence it was affirmed on the basis of virtue and heroism. This is what you have forgotten. Time has changed the notion of freedom. You have kept the word but formulated a different notion. Now it is a petty freedom, a caricature of the real thing. It is a freedom devoid of obligations and responsibilities, a freedom that comes down to the enjoyment of certain goods. No one is prepared to die for it. For us in my country freedom is the tiny flame that illumines our night. For you it is a diminished reality, a sometimes disillusioning reality of tinsel and hollow riches. . . .

Now you have entered the era of calculation. You are no longer capable of any sacrifices for the phantasm of the older freedom. All you can do is compromise. . . .

No political combine, no military combine can save you. Inner willingness and resolution is more important than politics. . . .

You people say that today's world is a hard world. But you don't really think so. At bottom you really think that freedom is something you can latch on to once and for all, and so you indulge in the luxury of scorning it. . . .

Forty years after Maritain, Solzhenitsyn seems to be saying the same thing: The precious gift of freedom is in imminent danger.

The Rational Organization of Freedom

The response of integral humanism is grounded in a particular conception of the human being. It maintains that human destiny transcends our own nature. Hence no one can deny us the possibility of achieving it in and through democracy. For democracy is the only system we know that really guarantees the exercise of freedom. It is the only one that defends the rights of persons so that they can attain self-fulfillment. It is the only one that protects people from arbitrary rule.

Viewed in this light, Maritain's definition of democracy becomes quite comprehensible. He defines it as "a rational organization of freedoms that are grounded in law." Then he goes on to say:

With democracy, humanity has set out on the only authentic road: i.e., the moral rationalization of political life. It is the road that leads to the fullest earthly realization of which people are capable in this world. . . .

Democracy can be crude, torpid, defective. Perhaps it merits the severe judgments passed on its capabilities. . . . But it is the only true path for the progressive forces and capacities of human history to take.[1]

Today we can readily tabulate the price we must pay for our accumulated mistakes. The most serious mistakes have been our moral failings, for they do most to undermine the confidence of people in those who represent them. They do most to undermine the credibility of rulers, parliaments, political parties, judges, and leaders in the mass communications media.

Time and again in different democratic countries we see moderation being thrown to the wind and liberties being abused. This cannot help but discredit them. People take advantage of certain freedoms to engage in the most exaggerated deviations.

Such is the case, for example, with the so-called process of "liberation." No one can object to the basic idea that through this process human beings would try to overcome the alienations that openly or subtly oppress them. In itself liberation implies respect for the values that give authentic scope to the human person and au-

thentic independence to nations. Social and economic
liberation certainly is feasible, if it is grounded on an
existing ethical, spiritual, and cultural foundation. But
such a foundation can be put together only if there is
solidarity between human beings and nations, mutual
understanding to overcome antagonism, a real spirit of
service and, most important of all, a real tenacious
struggle to make sure that justice reigns completely.

For the Christian, liberation means renouncing both
the haughty pride that leads us to oppress our neighbor
as well as the dominant position that leads us into imperial ambitions. It calls for more than simple tolerance.
We must be willing to place the common good above
private egotism. That idea, by the way, underlies the
wisdom of all the religions and philosophies of East and
West. It provides an ecumenical starting point for bring-
ing together all people of good will.

Yet it is quite clear that some view the process of
"liberation" in an entirely different light. They see it as
giving free rein to every appetite, spurning all responsibility, and rejecting all social control and authority.
They would annihilate all moral norms, undermine the
most honored institutions. Even such basic institutions
as the family would have to go. So the road is open to
every sort of excess: e.g., the "liberation" of the sexes,
pornography, immodesty, drug-use, and the kidnapping
or murder of one's enemies as well as innocent third
parties.

Liberation, the noblest of undertakings, calls for a
long and difficult process of overcoming. It calls for
inner strength and faith in people.

We cannot take the easy way out, the way of those who
want to "live their own lives." That leads to the worst
forms of individual and social alienation, and almost
always to enslaving regimes.

We must appreciate the responsibility that weighs
down upon those who would defend the cause of freedom
and the democratic faith. If we do not, we will only offer

aid and comfort to the enemy. So we must be faithful to
our mission of clearing the path of democracy, for it is
the path of the progressive forces in human history.

Machiavellian Sophistry

Of course there are more than a few people who feel
that democracy itself is too weak, that it cannot withstand the pressures and assaults of our agitated world.
They think we must have recourse to other means in
order to ensure discipline and promote development.
Some other way must be found to control the appetites
of the masses and to dominate the power centers and
feudalistic urges that threaten to undermine existing
societies.

This view is far more tempting, of course, in countries
that see themselves falling further and further behind
the highly developed nations, who are in a position to
grow more rapidly by virtue of the very mechanics of the
system.

Those who act on the basis of moral principles and
norms seem to be fools. Over against them stands the
power of force and violence alone. And "violence can
only take refuge in lying, even as lying cannot only look
to violence for support. Those who choose violence as
their means must inevitably choose lying as their
norm."[2]

Not without reason Maritain rejects this alternative
forcefully: "Let us not be deceived . . . by the Machiavellian sophistry. They say that justice and respect for
moral values spell weakness and doom, and that
strength is strong only if raised to the supreme standard
of political existence. That is a lie."[3]

This lie has found its principal support in the most
"conservative" sectors. In the distant past they supported the union of throne and altar. Then they joined
with the most reactionary wing of the bourgeoisie to
impede the thrust toward democracy. Now they do not

hesitate to swear off the liberal principles that they once upheld and to reject even the outer forms of democracy. All that is left standing, clear and naked to the sun, is their own desire to cling to their advantages and privileges.

To achieve what they wanted, they did not hesitate to use Christianity; and on the surface it did seem to be in league with them. As Maritain points out, it is one of the great scandals of history. The working classes sought their salvation by rejecting Christianity while conservative Christian sectors sought their salvation by rejecting the temporal demands of justice and love.

As Maritain pointed out long ago, democracy will win the peace, as it won the war, only if there is a reconciliation between the principles of Christianity and the principles of democracy.

That reconciliation, seemingly difficult and remote, is the task that faces those who claim to profess humanism. The two cannot be kept separate, because the pernicious effects of such separation are all too clear.

At the same time we have been able to see the dubious possibilities of the technological tools for "progress." They can be used for progress or for oppression. In particular, they can be used in the latter sense when people ignore the moral norms that could channel them in the right direction and point them in the service of human beings.

Today the state has tools such as it has never known before. Never has humankind been so directly threatened with the possibility of enslavements. Worse still, it is a new kind of enslavement that threatens us. We are asked to become happy, contented slaves, hearing and thinking what we are supposed to, completely lacking all privacy, and victimized by a system of terror of which we may be scarcely aware.

Consider the present-day use of computers, for example. They are a mark of our new age, and they are indispensable to human progress. But they may just as well serve as a highly efficient means of political and police control. It is now possible to record all the data on people's public and private lives, and to process that information so that they stand naked to the gaze of an inquisitorial government. The more perfect the techniques of oppression and mutual espionage on a worldwide level, the more difficult it will be to avoid abuse of those Machiavellian robots.

As Garaudy puts it: "In four or five seconds you can learn all the facts about a labor leader or politician in Tanzania . . . or about an available seat on a plane between Sidney and Melbourne, Australia. The computer now permits us to create a police state far beyond the dreams of a Hitler, a Stalin, or a Mussolini."[4] This is no page from science fiction. Information of this sort is already recorded on the national level and is fully operational.

The computer can be an ideal means for providing useful information to individuals and governments. It can tell them what the objective facts are and what options are at their disposal. It can also serve to improve the functioning of a direct democracy, enabling the individual citizen to participate more frequently and directly in the basic decision-making process. That possibility is close to reality right now. By the same token, it can also be put to perverse uses by the state, serving as a police instrument to control the public and private lives of the citizenry.

These are the possibilities and alternatives, some of them already operational. They make it all the more urgent that democracy be implemented here and now, so that human freedom and dignity may perdure in the midst of technological progress. Greater information-gathering and technological advances are not enough to construct or maintain a free society.

The alternative is clear enough. Those who exercise power may use the new means at their disposal to keep themselves in power and thus undermine the life of their nation. If they do, then the tendency toward totalitarian regimes is more of a threat than ever before in history. The only thing that can offset it is an alert and vigilant spirit on both the private and public level. Only that can counterbalance and control those who administer the affairs of state.

Aurelio Peccei, the founder of the Club of Rome, has pointed out the need to keep things within proper limits and to maintain control over the new tools. He says:

We generally neglect these limits because they are imponderable, and concern the noosphere, the field of the intellect, of reason, of understanding oneself and the world, and finally of the spirit. Man has committed himself so deeply to constructing ever larger and more complex artificial systems that it has become difficult for him to control them, thereby losing a sense of his destiny and at the same time that of his communion with Nature and with the transcendent.[5]

From this disturbing growth of technological tools it should be clear that we need to synthesize the Christian message with the democratic way of life and its implicit moral values. That synthesis will not be effected by good intentions alone. Today it will take will, effort, witness, and opposition to extremist oppressors. In particular it will take reflection and imagination to create the concrete forms of a democracy that is more real and subject to improvement every day.

That of course will call for what might be called a process of theoretical enrichment. We must constantly try to imagine and define new formulas and institutions that will allow us to implement an open and free way of life. Just as there are people in the scientific world who devote themselves to research, so there must be people who will explore new political, economic, and social formulas. They must find formulas that will enable us to adapt the substantive values of democracy to the new realities arising every day. We need rational instruments of analysis, further clarification of ideas, progress in the expression of democratic humanism. We cannot allow that humanism to be trodden underfoot while we simply go about automatically repeating formulas whose content means nothing to many of us.

5

*The New Axis
of History*

A New Project

Other facts run their course beneath the ones just mentioned. One cannot help but be a source of puzzlement. In many places people's rights and the law are violated time and again; yet those who commit the violations claim to be the defenders of rights, and those who seek to destroy democracy claim to be operating under its aegis. In truth never has the reign of falsehood been so widespread, and never before has it had such powerful tools at its disposal.

Still the course of truth has its own potentialities. Democracy does have its errors and its limitations, as I noted earlier. But every day it is becoming clearer that it also entails a sense of respect, community, solidarity, friendship, renunciation, and prudence that allows for mutual understanding and coexistence. And without such things there can be no justice, no freedom, no solidarity, and hence no possibility of peace in societal living.

The worldwide recognition of this fact, which cannot be suppressed, is appearing in the most varied and unsuspected forms. It must tie in with an irresistible tendency in history itself. It results from the continuing

growth of human moral consciousness. Despite all its
avatars, this consciousness is moving toward greater
knowledge and clearer judgments.

Many different historical factors are helping people
toward this new awareness of the proper road to take in
order to find human freedom and dignity. People today
are now in a position to judge the real consequences of
errors that presented themselves with all the force and
truth of myths only a few years ago. By now every
ideological system has shown where it and its consequences lead, and many idols have toppled from their
pedestals.

There has been a broad extension of knowledge and
information beyond physical and political frontiers.
Education has been spread far and wide. Postindustrial
society has posed a demand for millions of specialists.
All human beings have a clearer sense of their own
importance and that of their fellow workers. On us all
depends the functioning of a complex network that is
the very framework of modern society.

While millions of qualified people are needed to ensure
that everything functions correctly, a very few people
can create chaos. A handful of human beings can leave a
city without light or power. They can paralyze airport
traffic or even the nerve center of our huge urban conglomerates. So while these new technological possibilities do entail great danger, they also are engendering
an awareness that the intelligence and knowledge of
each individual person is important, that people cannot be treated as children who have not yet come of
age. People want to be respected and to participate,
for they are convinced of their own worth and importance.

So we are at a historical juncture that is fraught with
risks but also fraught with hopes. It is within this context that we must try to think out a new "civilization
project," developing ever more perfectible forms of
democracy.

At this point it might be well to cite Toynbee's view of

the rise of civilizations and their meaning, for I think it applies to these comments on a new project:

In human terms, I should say that each of these civilizations is, while in action, a distinctive attempt at a single great common human enterprise, or, when it is seen in retrospect, after the action is over, it is a distinctive instance of a single great common human experience. This enterprise or experience is an effort to perform an act of creation. In each of these civilizations, mankind, I think, is trying to rise above mere humanity —above primitive humanity, that is—towards some higher kind of spiritual life.[1]

I think there is no doubt that the progressive energies of history take that route. In the end they must take the route of reason and consensus, not of force and violence; of freedom and respect for human rights, not of enslaving submission; of an order based on justice and participation, not an order imposed on people from without. Only in that way will human beings be able to create a human society moving "towards some higher kind of spiritual life."

By its very nature this new project can be effective only if it derives from the will of peoples and nations on a broad base. It can be fleshed out only in a society where human kinship is real, where people recognize in practice that all human beings are fundamentally equal and possess personal inalienable rights. Only in that way can we form natural communities of a basic sort, whose independence and full expression will be guaranteed by the fact that they are respected as such. These communities would take in the family, the neighborhood, regional units, political units, and the many others that can take shape through the activity of human beings in a free society.

Toward a New Society

This march toward a new society does have an axis —not excluding but compelling. It involves taking cognizance of the fact that historical evolution basically involves the recognition of people's dignity as producer-workers. Hence I would say that the historical ascent of the proletariat would assume the principal role in the upcoming phase of social evolution.

Humanism acknowledges the reality of social classes and their conflict; but it does not believe in any class conception that would destroy or annul the human person as such. Hence it does not believe that the conflict can be resolved in a struggle designed to demolish or physically destroy one class or another. In the eyes of the humanist it can be resolved only through a process that is progressive, ascendent, and integrative.

The class-oriented notion, transformed into the central motivating force of history in recent times, has not led to human liberation. Whatever form it has taken, it has always led to the most rigid forms of alienation and of institutionalized violence.

The life of humanity has moved in an ascending direction over the long term, and that movement seems irreversible. Social classes have had a determining role in that ascent. The bourgeoisie, for example, brought an end to feudalism and wrought the great changes that were reflected in the eighteenth and nineteenth centuries. Through liberalism it conquered Europe and spread to America. Its contribution has been invaluable, but now it has lost its creative impetus.

The new guiding impulse now comes chiefly from the world of labor, from the humble existence of the anonymous common people. It is they who are ascending to take first place on the historical stage, and this movement seems obvious and irresistible.

The problem is that this ascent may be taken over by the wrong people. Instead of looking for a higher synthesis and a new historical situation, some want to use the historical process to annihilate other classes and to establish a new system that is bound to end up in totalitarian states. That would subject the world to a gloomy process of regression in which the accumulated progress would be lost for a long time.

So obvious is the regression that the dictatorship of the proletariat has now been declared indefensible by certain of its former supporters. They have adopted a new position that could scarcely have been predicted only a few years ago. Eurocommunism is a fact that can scarcely be overlooked in our present analysis.

Some think that the new stance of the Italian, French, and Spanish Communist parties is merely a stratagem to penetrate societies that are too highly developed to accept the dogmas of Soviet communism. Others regard it as honest and valid, particularly in the case of Italy where there is an intellectual tradition going back to Gramsci. Be that as it may, we can hardly overlook the fact that those parties have publicly rejected a unified international command. They have asserted their independence from Soviet control, recognized the values of "formal" democracy, accepted pluralism, and rejected a thesis as fundamental as the dictatorship of the proletariat.

The Italian Communist party has expressed its view of a socialist society in this new perspective: "The state and its democratic organization are grounded on principles of a secular rather than an ideological nature. This entails a plurality of political parties, the possibility of various majorities holding alternate control of the government, autonomy for unions and syndicates, religious freedom, freedom of expression, and freedom for education, the arts, and the sciences."

The proclamation of these truths is a fact, even though it may not alter their underlying inspiration in Marxist philosophy. Whatever the underlying intentions may be, it marks a new stage in the history of international Communism and confirms what humanist philosophers and thinkers have been saying all along: i.e., that the dictatorship of the proletariat leads, not to the liberation of the people, but to a new form of subjection. Concrete experience of what has occurred in orthodox Marxist societies has forced people to admit that, and hence to reject at least for now, theses that were once basic tools of the Marxist struggle.

When humanists and democrats expressed the same positions, they were regarded as "reactionaries." They were behind the times for not accepting what many Communists in Western Europe now claim to reject, and what many people in Eastern Europe would also repudiate if they could express their real opinion.

Taking due note of the signs of history and the determining presence of the labor world, humanist philosophy does not believe that the process should evolve into dehumanizing dictatorships, even if they be only a transitional stage. By virtue of their real characteristics today, the newly emerging societies need a higher and better synthesis that will make full use of the resources already acquired by modern societies. Seen in this context, the fight to crush other sectors or classes now seems antihistorical. It leads to serious regression, or it costs too high a price in time and human suffering.

The whole scheme of the dictatorship of the proletariat has to be dropped. It is part of an analysis that now goes back more than a century, and that is therefore far from complete in the light of present-day trends. It fails to take into account the changes that have taken place in the mechanisms and structures of contemporary society. Consider, for example, the democratic nations of northern Europe, which have achieved a high degree of social development. And some of that has filtered down to lesser developed countries, even to underdeveloped ones.

Some people still claim that the only course is to have one class impose its dictatorial rule on all if we are to move toward utopia. In so saying, they overlook the degree and extent of power held by the middle classes, by technical sectors, and even by skilled segments of the proletariat. Seeing themselves threatened, these segments become the basis for a resistance movement. This is used to advantage by the very people who seek to stop the process of rational, legitimate change. The appearance of terrorist extremists intensifies feelings of fear, insecurity, and anarchy—which societies tend to reject almost by instinct. And so the middle sectors end up serving the interests of the most reactionary and backward segments at the other extreme.

A real, solid synthesis can be effected only with the help of a humanist conception. It will come about through the reconciliation and union of people of every condition. Their will for social renewal will enable them to attain real human freedom and personality. Maritain tells us the sort of freedom and personality involved: "It is not that of a class which absorbs human beings and crushes them. It is that of human beings who share and communicate their own dignity in order to establish a society in common with others. Not all differentiation and hierarchy will have disappeared in that new society, . . . but the present class divisions will be gone."

This approach will bring together people of different classes, races, and nations who are one in thought, love, and will, who are inspired by a passion for the common task to be carried out. The community to be developed will not be based on biology (e.g., on race) or on sociology (e.g., on class). "It will be truly human. The idea of class, of the proletariat, is thereby transcended."[2]

Here we find the real creative forces for a new civilization. Love of the people is a central element, and Maritain has spoken eloquently about it. Many people fear, despise, and even hate the common people. For Maritain, on the other hand, they are human beings united by common human tasks and by a shared awareness of the work that all must do to find their place in the sun. They are also united by "long experience of sufferings and of joys, . . . by a common capital of wisdom gathered in the course of heavy labors, by human sentiments, human traditions, and human instincts that nurture each one. . . . However limited it may be, the people do engage in a real effort of reason and freedom. They are the tide of human activities, of human intelligence and effort, which courses through the soil of civilized life."[3]

In his vision we can readily see the conjunction of two factors: the thrust of humanist thought and the advent of a new civilization, of a new form of democracy. The essential work of this synthesis will be to value and embody the sustaining foundation of life and the human beings whose effort now moves to the front ranks of history.

This developing phenomenon makes its presence felt in countless ways. Every day work appears more clearly as a font of creativity. Leaving aside its directly personal character, consider that property as an institution, once served as the basis for social power, order, and control. Now it is conceived more in terms of "function," not only in the bureaucracies of centralizing governments but also in the technocratic management of capitalist society. There power is not so much a matter of possessing as of administering.

Looking at work from another angle, we can see it in its most genuine and profound sense. It is not the effort of one single class but human activity in all its range and scope. It ranges from physical effort to pure investigation, from control over a machine to the administration of a modern business enterprise, be it public or private.

Here again we see a process of historical ascent, for knowledge is becoming more and more significant in the domination of nature and space. Those in the vanguard of humanity assert themselves, not by what they possess, but by what they know. The legitimacy of the new hierarchies lies in the level of their knowledge, which ultimately is to be put in the service of the entire community.

In a full and integral vision of humanism these facts acquire their due proportion and measure. At the same time the danger of new forms of domination are foreseen and forestalled. We do not want the new hierarchies based on knowledge to succumb to the temptation that tantalized earlier ruling sectors in history. We do not want them to fall prey to haughty pride and the thirst for domination. There can be no greater danger than unprincipled technocracies that are not balanced by countervailing controls. Often docile in the face of those who give orders, they may still try to apply their own dogmas coldly and blindly because they think those dogmas are bound up with science.

Only a real democracy can counterbalance such dangers. It places human and moral values above everything else, thus saving the realm of labor from a new kind of bondage. For technology could be used to construct a society more dehumanizing than any we have seen in the past.

The Integration of the Masses

Woven into the fabric of history, the democratic political and social philosophy calls for close attention to history's dynamic movement and for a whole and integral human personality. We must sustain and support certain truths, resisting the lure of surface events and passing fads. In short, there must be an ongoing link between theoretical thinking and practical action.

There were only two alternatives in Maritain's eyes. On the one hand the popular masses might succumb more and more to different forms of materialism. These seek to seduce the masses and vitiate their efforts toward historical progress. If the masses succumb to materialism, then the movement of history will go astray and take an abnormal term. On the other hand the masses may again look to Christianity for their philosophy of life and the world. They will then try to formulate a theocentric humanism of universal worth, which will be able to reconcile human beings of every condition, even in the temporal and cultural domains.

Their will for social renewal will be realized thereby, and they will achieve the freedom and personality of real human adults. This free personality will not belong to a class that absorbs its members and crushes other classes; rather it will be found in human individuals who impart their dignity to their class.

We must develop a broad-scale line of social and political action based on such a viewpoint. Two divergent trends have come to the fore in the last century. On the one hand we find the antagonism of the working class toward the Christian world, the latter having somehow become separated from the true wellsprings of its life. On the other hand we find a real effort to transform the temporal order and achieve social justice, but an effort based on the most fallacious sort of metaphysics.

Christians can hardly remain indifferent or tranquil in the face of this situation. It should pain them to see the masses of human beings filled with resentment over the offenses committed against their human dignity, to realize that they have never paid heed to the reserves of real humaneness, kindness, and heroism embodied in the daily efforts of the poor workers, peasants, and laborers.

The "high-minded" have handed this reserve of energy and human force over to the anti-Christian system. . . . I use "high-minded" here to refer to a web of illusions and inertia. In this framework we find many human beings who are fine people in their private lives. When it comes to social and political affairs, however, they close themselves up in a bitter, voluntary ignorance of both their neighbor and the most obvious realities. Feeling defeated even before they start, they refuse to put out any initiative to answer God's summons in the temporal order. Lamenting that the world escapes them and realizing that they do not know what to do with it, they lie encased in a coffin with their fine thoughts.[4]

Christians have even abandoned their good intentions. They realize that the world is slipping away from them, but they refuse to renounce their privileges. They reject those values that they once upheld, when those values were useful for maintaining the status quo. They have given themselves unreservedly to whoever can guarantee their security and privileges.

Rarely in history have we seen such a greater renunciation of truths held until they conflicted with self-interest. Christians prefer to remain in a "bitter and voluntary ignorance of the most certain facts." This sad spectacle can be observed in all societies, especially those of Latin America.

A Fatal Dilemma

Communism has undoubtedly taken the initiative in trying to represent the world of labor, the new tendencies of the middle class, and certain segments of the intelligentsia. It has managed to impose its view in countries of Europe, Asia, and Africa, as well as Cuba in Latin America. It also has considerable vote-getting power in many countries of the world.

Marxism as a philosophy and communism as a system clearly have influence in some of the advanced democracies of Europe. All the more reason, then, that it should crop up in those countries belonging to what is generally called the Third World. These countries can feel the impact of poverty and injustice more directly, and so they are even more desperately earnest in seeking out new ways of life, whatever they may be.

The traditional sectors have no real or valid response to offer these human masses, and hence they offer them no perspective at all. To maintain their "social order," they can offer only the answer of force. In their desperation they look around for someone to put an end to their insecurity and to forestall social shock.

Added to this is the fact that groups preaching violence as a practical method have arisen in recent years, even outside the bounds of communism. They go to such irrational extremes that they seem to be deliberately courting chaos.

These facts and others help the elements on the extreme Right. Well served by their adversaries at the opposite extreme, they raise doubts about the possibility of democracy surviving at all. Once we get down to the law of the jungle and class warfare, consensus and the possibility of living together in society seem to disappear.

The result is clear to see. Rightist authoritarian regimes appear, almost always ending up as more or less open forms of neo-fascism. These dictatorships, however, are not the same as the dictatorships of old. The classic old strongman has been replaced by elaborate governments who have learned all about the new technologies that can make systems of control and oppression even more effective. Once in power, therefore, these new regimes begin to employ the same methods as the totalitarian governments that they claim to be combatting. It is the same thing that happens in warfare. The discovery of some new weapon can give a temporary advantage to one side. Then the other side develops the same weapon, or an even more refined one, and the old advantage is lost.

To confront communist totalitarianism, then, the new dictatorships become more or less fascist. They seek to control all information. The apparatus of the secret police becomes more and more powerful, serving as a key element in the retention of power. Dissenters are discredited and destroyed morally or physically. Official pronouncements are presented as indisputable truth, and those who reject them are branded traitors. Those in power are exalted, and lying is used to serve whatever is proclaimed as the supreme good of the people. Needless to say, the people cannot say what they think is good for them. The self-perpetuating government decides that. Lacking all ideas, these regimes proclaim the "end of ideologies." To them ideologies are the sour vestiges of that abominable world where politics and "politicians" hold sway. If there is no room for minorities and dissent in communist society, there is no room for them in the new authoritarian societies either.

On the pretext that the danger is imminent, and that communism is the danger, these governments demand that everyone take a stand clearly in the struggle. Anyone who thinks differently is an enemy. Suppression is the fate for political parties, which attest to the decadence and corruption of democracy, as well as for social organizations generated at the grassroots by the people. Thus all institutional life based on consensus disappears. The only protagonists on the scene are those who hold power, dictate the law, and manipulate the instruments of control and repression against a silent and inorganic mass. They finally divide the nation into two irreconcilable factions. It is not surprising, then, that they would be equally or even more savage in persecuting democratic individuals and groups. The existence of some other alternative is abhorrent to them.

In acting thus, they do not realize that over the longer run they are abetting the cause of the very people they claim to be combatting. Once they destroy all the authentic structures of their society, the society is left defenseless. Communism or Marxism becomes the only real counterpart to the existing regime and the regime, by its very nature, cannot endure for long.

The basic, intrinsic weakness of such regimes lies in the fact that they essentially define themselves as "anticommunist." People cannot live solely in terms of negatives; they need hopes that will open their minds and hearts to the future. While they may copy the forms and practices of a real police state, these regimes can never mirror the perfection of the totalitarian regimes they are imitating. They may succumb to the same repressive methods, but they lack a global vision of life and history. They will always be merely a copy, and usually a bad copy. They have no authentic historical project to sustain them, no profound and coherent ideas to inspire their actions.

In the last analysis they are defensive regimes. They end up aligning with plutocratic minorities who support them to protect their own interests and to block social change. The plutocrats are afraid of such change because they see it as a threat to their own privileges.

That is why such regimes cannot win the support of the poorer classes even when they want to carry through certain reforms and improve the lot of those classes. Their support ultimately comes from segments that distrust the common people and the people, possessing their own secret intuition, mistrust the government in turn.

So force remains their basic recourse, and the maintenance of tranquillity and order their only argument. Now order and tranquillity are basic to the existence of any society. But they must arise out of some sound and deeper consensus based on the values that are recognized by that society. When they become the chief goal and supreme justification of a governmental regime, they lead to the worst sort of distortions. Ultimately they paralyze the life and progress of that society, building up pressures that only endanger stability more and more as time goes on.

Hence we cannot possibly salvage freedom, democracy, and a dignified way of life today if we accept the view that a country can be protected only by a dictatorial or "authoritarian" regime based on "integrism," i.e., one that suppresses all opposing parties and all forms of dissent. No regime will work if it tries to control all the media of expression, if it says nothing true or consistent, if it offers a set of distorted traditions from which all authentic values have been exorcised. Meanwhile, communism can withstand persecution because it does have a doctrine. It possesses dogmas, hierarchical structures, methods, and objectives that are not just local but worldwide. It can be overcome only by doctrines and actions that surpass it. So many contemporary societies are moving more and more toward two extremes. This is no idle conjecture. It is the reality to be found in various countries.

The greatest mistake would be for us to fall into that fatal trap. If we allow the whole issue to be posed in terms of those two extreme positions, the end result is clear enough—however many years it may take.

6

The Alternative

Breaking the Dilemma

But suppose we face the battle in positive terms. Suppose, instead of fighting *against* communism, we fight *for* freedom, justice, and a new society. Suppose we display a deeper vocation, a greater spirit of service, an attitude of confidence and trust in the human individual and the people. Suppose we display greater moral and doctrinal consistency, better organization, greater discipline, not prompted by fear but by conviction. Then perhaps we could truly flesh out in practice the humanism that is only partially represented in Marxism, but whose truths have helped Marxism to be the force it has been in history.

More than one person will say that this is "angelism," that it is much easier to rely on those who offer protection and silence. In such matters, however, the easy way out is always the way to utter defeat.

As I have indicated in previous chapters, Maritain proposed views and theses in the thirties and forties that have been gradually confirmed with the passage of time. As he predicted, Marxism has extended its ideological and political influence. To think that it can be stopped by the power of dictatorial or authoritarian regimes is to indulge in the sheerest illusion. Here is what he had to say in another publication:

If Christianity stands mute before the masses, we certainly are condemned to watch the advance of the communist ideology and its concomitant atheism. For the Communists possess a rigorous and consistent doctrine against which the liberal[1] ideology is helpless. Christians, however, can have a doctrine that is bold, solid, and rigorous enough to stop atheism and its postulates; to engage in open confrontation and challenge philosophy with philosophy, an atheistic philosophy with a faith-inspired philosophy, an atheistic humanism with an integral humanism.[2]

The confrontation in question here is between philosophies dealing with the temporal world. The philosophy he proposes has no claim to deal with the religious apostolate. Its aim is to find truth in practice, to serve the lives of human beings, and to work for a renewal of societal structures:

Such a philosophy has nothing to do with a purely decorative Christian order, one that merely labels certain principles and fomulas as "Christian" and then sticks them on a social and cultural regime that is essentially inhuman and chaotic.

It is here that humanism takes on its full and authentic significance. For it believes in democracy as a way of life. It is opposed to those who mockingly refer to "formal democracy" to ridicule it and destroy it. Its aim is to break the stubborn persistence with which the extremes play their vicious game, to cut through the dilemma of a debate argued on inadmissible and sterile grounds.

It is not true that the only response to hate is hate. It is not certain that tyranny can be opposed only by an equivalent tyranny at the other extreme.

It is not a matter of defending the status quo, of concealing the flaws and corruptions in democratic regimes. They are obvious in any case, the inevitable price exacted in all human activity. But they can be combated, precisely because they are open to view. That cannot be done in systems that suffocate freedom. With the passage of time they produce even greater corruption and flaws; but no one can keep check on them, and so they come to light only when the regime falls.

The aim of humanism is to correct, expand, and perfect the democratic process by looking for new forms of expression and new forms of organization. There is no other way for us to progress in our evolving history.

Opening up a Channel

At this very moment in history colonialism is disappearing, enlightenment is expanding, and a vast network of resources is available for providing people with information and instruction. At such a time it makes no sense at all to establish regimes that subject people and nations to the uncontrolled will of those in power, to prevent authority from being generated by the will of all those who make up the national community, to suppress labor and political organizations, and to turn the surviving organisms into mere conduits for the orders dictated by those in power.

It is clear enough what the democratic development of contemporary societies would entail. The value of all persons would have to be respected. They would have to enjoy the full exercise of their rights. Grassroots organizations would have to be alive and flourishing. With due respect for physical geography and the complex realities of modern society, the state would have to be properly decentralized. Institutions and political organizations would have to be respected.

This development can be held up for a time, but in the long run failure to heed it would lead to intolerable contradictions. No worse harm could be done to a people than to equate "order" with the status quo and the domination of its ruling groups. This is particularly true when they are trying to recoup or maintain their age-old influence and have nothing to offer but their own opportunism in a precarious situation.

The task is not to construct a wall athwart the current of history but to open up a channel that will let it run freely toward its full realization.

We must seek out the institutions and modes of expression that will allow for more real and authentic democracy. We must allow the common people and the great mass of workers to participate in society and shoulder their full share of responsibility, so that we can count on the rich backing of their support. To do that is to follow the authentic thrust and direction of history itself. That is what opening up a channel means.

The incorporation of the people does not mean the destruction of other classes and cadres. They will be integrated with administrative and technical sectors, with teachers and professionals, with the ever expanding ranks of the middle class who live by working and who cannot be equated with the European bourgeoisie of the nineteenth century as is done by certain superficial analysts.

We must remember that the current middle-class sectors are fluid and mobile. They are largely made up of people who are just emerging from the proletariat, who make enormous sacrifices in order to be able to rise to higher levels of economic and social life. They are also made up of skilled industrial workers who form part of the proletariat. All these are new segments of the middle class whose functions and human capital cannot be spurned without impunity.

In today's developed societies we find a similar process going on. New strata are being produced by the social process of upward mobility. Curiously enough, "new classes" can also be found in communist societies. They are composed of members of the party and the government; of the new techno-bureaucracy; of scientists, administrators, military officials; and of other privileged sectors. To say that there is only one class, the proletariat, in those countries is to utter an absurdity that deserves no further comment.

Integral humanism means building a social and political order with full confidence in each individual person and all human beings, in the people as a whole. It means that the true mark of history today is the full involvement of the popular masses in generating, discussing, and arriving at the decisions that will give shape to a given society. In this way we will not destroy the progress of the past but rather complement it. Capacity, quality, and hierarchy will not be denigrated; they will be appreciated and utilized without limitations imposed by class, group, or privilege.

Insofar as collectivization is concerned, we do well to recall the words of Lebret:

Extensive collectivization reduces human freedom to an excessive degree. It unduly restricts creative initiative and the elasticity that economic mechanisms need. It soon becomes fatally oppressive, overflowing the political realm to engulf the cultural and spiritual realm. It subjects people wholly to projects centered around material power and control. . . .

Complete private appropriation of all the means of production also clashes with the need for coordinated cooperation in order to achieve economic expansion. The latter, in turn, must be subordinated to the goal of satisfying the consumption needs of all the social classes and all human populations. . . .

The social and the economic cannot be separated. It is not a matter of applying some social corrective or palliative to an economic solution that in itself engenders a human evil. Instead we must advocate and look for some way to establish an economic regime that is integrally social and integrally pluralistic. . . . Its aim would be universal human ascent, which is, in the words of François Perroux, the ascent of "the whole person and all people. . . . "

Formulated thus, the problem of human economy poses more than purely economic problems. It poses the problem of our civilization.[3]

This new civilization must find moral, cultural, and political expression. It must also be translated into a truly human economy. In the process of creating, distributing, and using goods, the guiding principle will not be the concentration of economic power in the hands of the government, or, worse still, in the hands of a few individuals. The guiding principle will be to raise the standards of social and cultural life for all the sectors that go to make up the national society in particular and the world community in general.

Winning the Struggle for Survival

There are some people who will say that humanism is "very nice," but they say it disdainfully. Such a utopian view is inapplicable, they say, in our hard and violent world, in our world of superpowers and cold dogmas. With ideas alone you cannot exercise authority or tackle organized forces who possess instruments of stunning effectiveness.

It is an old debate, of course, a debate as old as humankind itself. It is a fact, however, that the great ideas that have transformed human life often appear vague, weak, and helpless at the start. But because they possess real content and some small measure of truth at least, they make their way irresistibly. By contrast we have hardly any memory left of the strong, practical human beings who mocked those ideas.

If this vision of humanism and democracy were nothing more than an impossible illusion, then we would be living in a world without hope. It would be a dead world. We would be crushed between those who proposed to build a new society by sacrificing human beings and freedom and those who imitated their tactics in order to eliminate that very threat.

In the last analysis the struggle on behalf of humanism and democracy is a fight for the survival of the human being as a person, as a subject of rights, as a people who can delegate but never renounce sovereignty because they are its source.

In other words, you cannot really refute the humanist and democratic view without falling into fallacies. But you can create images to suit your purpose, and the most often used tactic is to present democracy as a system that is fragile and unworkable in the present set of circumstances. Reason, serenity, patience, humility, and love of neighbor always seem weak in comparison with haughty cocksureness, bullying, and dominating ways.

There is no doubt that democracy often does seem to be ineffective. It looks so when there is a weakening of moral foundations, when civilization is going through a crisis, when people seem to lack the imagination they need to create new institutional forms or to keep the existing ones functioning.

At such a time it does not seem worthwhile to live in accordance with a system of rights and procedures dictated by law. It seems even more senseless when extremist factions lose all concern for the common welfare, aggravate passions, distort facts, and provoke violence in order to topple the institutional setup.

The image of power subject to no control rises to mind as an antidote. It is attractive to many for more than one reason. But one main reason is that it frees them of all responsibility. They do not have to think their own thoughts, wage earnest and difficult battles for ideas, and endure sacrifices to defend them. There is a real temptation to hand over responsibility to others, particularly if that will free one from the obligation to face dangers or make decisions. One might be willing to submit to enslavement for such benefits. It is appealing to other people besides those who want to see their special privileges guaranteed. Large masses of people may also find it attractive when they feel helpless or self-satisfied. When that happens, it is a sign that we are living through a period of decadence.

Historical experience, particularly in recent decades, has repeatedly proved that no real ideas or unity exist behind the facade of "authoritarian," "totalitarian," and "monolithic" governments. Frequently they are rife with corruption, and in the end they are always inefficient.

Nevertheless many people continue to hold the opposite impression. The overwhelming weight of proof to the contrary does not impress them for a long time, if ever. It is only after such regimes have disappeared for good that we learn what lay behind the brilliant facade. And even recently we have documented examples of the situation.[4]

But though we may know where false images lead us, such images often prove to be stronger than reasoning; and instincts often prove more overwhelming than intelligence. The whole process of evolution toward higher ground goes by way of a seemingly frail and fragile path; and every step backward entails the unleashing of the most primitive human impulses. The way upward entails moral effort and a process of overcoming in each human being. If the moral foundation is broken, then of course democracy will suffer the consequences. For ultimately a government based on freedom implies the existence of upright human beings, and that cannot be guaranteed by institutions alone.

Reform of democracy will not be possible without an ethical attitude of those who support it. If people begin to lose heart, then it should not surprise us if they go on to lose all dignity in their lives.

The system will crumble with the disappearance of the moral foundation and the common faith which find expression in a code of fundamental ideas that make societal living possible. If the most fundamental concepts are falsified, if democracy is turned into a hollow, lifeless system or a neutral ground where anything is permitted, then it is doomed from the very start. This is particularly true if people are even permitted to destroy it, if its detractors are highly active while some of its defenders act discouraged and frightened.

On this score Maritain is clear-sighted and far-seeing. He talks about the needs of a genuine democracy:

> A genuine democracy entails a basic consensus of opinions and wills that is grounded on a shared common life. It must also be conscious of itself and its principles and be capable of preserving and defending its own conception of political and social life. In short, it must contain a common human creed, the creed of freedom. . . .
>
> Bourgeois democracy of the nineteenth century was neutral, even with respect to freedom. As it had no common good, so it did not possess any authentic shared or common thinking. It should not surprise us, then, that even before World War II it should become a society without any idea of itself or any faith in itself, . . . particularly in those countries shaken by nazi, fascist, or communist propaganda. . . .

From another point of view, Maritain wrote:

> A genuine democracy cannot . . . impose on its citizens any religious or philosophical creed as a condition for living in its society. Such a conception was possible during the sacral period of our civilization, when a shared Christian faith was a prerequisite for the establishing of a political body. In our day we see its inhuman falsification in the now hypocritical, now violent, actions of the totalitarian states. They impose faith and obedience on human beings, asserting their belief in the spirit of the masses through the power of lies, propaganda, and the police force. . . .

The faith in question here for the survival of democracy is a secular or civic faith, not a religious one. As Maritain sees it, we come to it through basic precepts, through natural perception as the human mind progresses in its natural awareness:

Thus human beings can agree here even though they may hold very different or even opposed religious or metaphysical opinions. Their agreement does not come about by reason of any identity of doctrine but by virtue of analogical similarity in their practical principles. The latter leads them to the same practical conclusions, and so they can share the same practical secular faith. Though it may be for different reasons, they all can and should recognize truth, intelligence, human dignity, freedom, brotherly love, and the absolute value of the moral good. . . .

The state cannot create this faith. It is born in the conscience of the people, or better, in the conscience of each individual human being. To the extent that this faith grows weak, the democratic state grows weak and begins to disintegrate. It becomes paralyzed, an easy prey for all the forces that stand in opposition to freedom.[5]

Since Maritain put forward his thesis and unfolded his vision of an integrally human society, events have moved forward at a dizzying speed. The "secular faith" of which he spoke then has been steadily dissipating. The "absolute value of the moral good" has become a fiction in the face of unrestrained appetites. To a large extent, it seems to me, democratic societies have become hollow shells. Lacking any vital message, they are an easy prey for their enemies.

Maritain's humanist message, a message that could renew and revitalize democracy, is not dogmatic but open-ended. Its universal vision is philosophical. Its concept of the human being and history is clearly spelled out and defined, but it does not exclude anyone. As I indicated earlier, its projection, through democracy, into the temporal realm is not to be confused or equated with the religious mission of churches. The responsibility lies with those who undertake the task, not with anyone else.

There is clear and convincing witness to this fact. Consider the political organizations inspired in this doctrine. With all their defects and limitations, they have exercised governmental power in many different nations. And it can be stated unequivocally that they have never failed to respect the freedoms essential to democratic government and to avoid any confusion between the religious plane and the political plane. Indeed the problem has never even arisen.

Thus this humanist inspiration and its democratic project can accord with all those who have faith that respect for human beings and their rights can build a society for all people; that it can generate a new civilization based on inner personal reform and a sense of solidarity and justice rather than on hatred, class warfare, and lust for power.

Bearing Heroic Witness

This is not a dead faith. If it were to die, a new and dark Middle Ages like those that preceded the thirteenth century would cover the earth once again. But it is not dead. Everywhere voices are being raised and heroic witness is being given. Sometimes we do not register enough surprise at that fact, for want of reflection and sensitivity.

This witness is the consciousness of people today, which no one and nothing has been able to still. It is the expression of a moral courage that seeks to break the current dilemma. Those who have this courage are resisting the concerted attacks of the extremists against those who refuse to submit to them. They reject the use of illicit means to obtain licit ends. They refuse to focus on vengeance and the extermination of their adversaries. They reject hatred between classes, groups, and parties. Rather than taking the lives of others, they would risk their own lives and everything else to establish peace, justice, and freedom. All these attitudes are the finest proof of moral and physical integrity that a human being can give.

In a world where images shape so many opinions, the

"brave bulls" often seem to be those who practice violence in all its forms: Those who reject violence come across as timid milquetoasts. Yet it is the latter who are courageous enough not to be swayed by the fashion of the moment.

The "brave bulls" who go in for the new emphasis on force know in some way that they are protected. They may be part of a band. They may even be in the employ of an authoritarian structure that uses them, supports them, and covers up their atrocities.

In this confused tangle the real people of courage are the common people, the citizens without arms, whose taxes often pay for the weapons that are used against them. Their lives are not based on hatred, and they are disposed to reject all forms of coercion. Sometimes their only resources are their indomitable wills not to give in to lies and intimidation, to defend their dignity and rights, if only with silence.

This spirit and this kind of determination, of which we have many witnesses, are the preconditions for any liberative struggle. Now and in the future they are also preconditions for any authentic form of democracy.

A perfect example of this attitude is the witness of Sakharov, the Russian dissident. Solzhenitsyn writes about him, noting that the all-powerful totalitarian state in which he lived his life had made provisions for everything, but not for the occurrence of an unpredictable phenomenon, a miracle, such as Sakharov.[6] He helped to create the most terrible weapon of the twentieth century. He was three times declared to be a hero of Socialist labor. He was admitted into the narrow circles of the elite. Then he suddenly had the audacity to see his life as a mission to defend any and all human rights that had been trodden underfoot. He lost his villas, his privileges, his honors, and his influence. The dictate of conscience forced him to live in poverty, to see his family persecuted, to be under constant surveillance, and to be subjected to all sorts of threats and dangers. But he continued to fight on undismayed against an omnipotent hierarchy.

From whatever standpoint one may judge such a person, one cannot help but bow before someone who lives for an ideal, who for its sake renounces all privileges and risks everything, who expects nothing in return but insults and injuries. No one can accuse him of being a milquetoast, for his strength is stronger than any form of verbal or physical violence.

Another example I might cite here is Dr. Martin Luther King, Jr., who had so much to do with the course of events in the United States during the decade of the sixties. When Jimmy Carter was campaigning for president in the black districts of Los Angeles, he acknowledged that Doctor King had been the conscience of his generation, the healer of a sick society. More than anyone else, he realized that the power of love could topple the wall of racial segregation. Indeed, noted Carter, it was because of Doctor King that he, a Southerner, could campaign for the presidency in a black district.

The human race can save itself and keep moving upward only with the help of people like King and Sakharov; it cannot be helped by those who kill or imprison other human beings in order to have their way. And there are many more people like King and Sakharov than we sometimes believe. They can be found all over the earth, and some of them are well known to all. Countless people everywhere offer their silent, humble witness. For refusing to renounce their ideas, they lose their jobs, they feel exiled in their own homelands, and they are drowned in a sea of lies. And yet they refuse to give in or to be deceived.

Their story will probably never be written, their names never pronounced on anyone's lips. They are like the seed that grows in silence, without which people would die. For just as there is an economy of matter, so there is an economy of the spirit. It may not be reflected in the statistics, but it is even more essential.

Such testimonies are needed by every society, not just by those in which freedom has disappeared. They are also needed in open, pluralistic societies. There, too, it is sometimes hard to dissent from the established ways, to resist the compelling temptation of money, intellectual fashions, and various kinds of snobbism.

Overcoming Self-Doubt

This faith in humankind and freedom will have no future unless it is translated into works. No one could take democracy seriously if it comes down to nothing more than a pile of inapplicable aspirations.

Western Europe, North America, Japan, Australia, and the more advanced countries in general have proven that democratic government allows for unrivaled social and economic progress. Despite any existing errors, injustices, and flaws, there can be no doubt that the great masses of people in those countries today enjoy more freedom and well-being than they ever have in the past. Every day the democratic nations are moving toward greater justice and popular participation. We are centuries away from what the condition of the working classes was at the start of the industrial age. And yet we find division and hesitation in most democratic countries. As if some secret evil were gnawing away at them, they seem hesitant and doubtful in the face of their bold accusers, even in the very midst of a rate of progress undreamed of a few years ago.

Consumption as a goal does not bring fulfillment to life. There seems to be no answer to people's deeper uncertainties. Perhaps that is part of the human condition. Perhaps total satisfaction can never be attained. In any case that does seem to be typical of times when one historical epoch is ending and some new kind of societal life is coming to birth. Great contradictions seem to mark such periods, and we are certainly living through one now. Indeed the scope and magnitude of change has never been greater than that which we are now living through.

Perhaps that is why people who are living in free countries are gambling with their freedom, why people who are wealthy seem to admire others who dream of having such wealth. At bottom some democratic complexes do not seem to be held together by any faith or belief or moral standard. The growth of centrifugal forces is abetted by insecure, vacillating authorities, by continuing injustice and inequality, by the breakdown of family life, and by the presence of young people, most from the middle class, who scornfully reject the existing way of life. There seems to be no leadership in ideas and moral consciousness.

By a curious paradox we find artists, intellectuals, and the upper bourgeoisie claiming rights for pornography, drugs, the most sophisticated kinds of luxury, and the most bizarre deviations, while at the same time they express admiration for regimes where their works and lifestyles are unthinkable. The moral rigidity of such regimes rules out such works because they are regarded as a serious threat to the life and security of the government and the nation.

If that is the situation in countries that have attained a high level of prosperity, it is even more complex and difficult in the underdeveloped world. There a further argument is adduced to undermine and destroy democracy. The claim is made that democracy is a luxury that poor nations cannot afford.

Proponents of this view maintain that the existence of an operative legislative branch will bring the government to a standstill, that party factionalism does not allow for the degree of planning that is needed. Iron discipline is required, they say, to achieve satisfactory social solutions and rates of economic growth. Justice cannot be achieved, in other words, so long as complete freedom still reigns. Rulers cannot be effective if they are subject to counterbalancing institutional controls.

Not surprisingly, then, we see more doors being shut every day in societies that were open only a short time ago.

There are real reasons why such ideas gain headway. For large sectors of the proletariat freedom is an idle dream. It comes down to the theoretical freedom to express oneself and the practical freedom to cast a vote in an election every now and again. Large sectors of the populace live in dire poverty. Their children have no real opportunity to get an education. It is difficult, if not impossible, for them to get into a university. Often they can hardly form their bones and bodies properly because they increasingly suffer from malnutrition. Yet they patiently look on while tiny minorities indulge in extravagant waste.

The democratic system can scarcely survive unless it promptly carries out certain reforms and thereby corrects its drastic defects. But if we wish to save it, we can hardly begin by decapitating it. Yet some would apply a cure that is worse than the disease.

However formal or abstract a democracy may be, it is still preferable to other systems that do not even offer a faint resemblance of the guarantees it does. Some opponents of democracy prefer political upheaval and violence. Democracy, they suggest, is based on falsehood and alienation; it must be destroyed quickly and completely. No half-way measures will suffice. There must be a complete break, a total and violent revolution.

Roy A. Mevedev has experienced the results of such disdain for democracy. Here is what he has to say about it:

We have gotten used to talking disdainfully about "bourgeois democracy" as something false and ridiculous, . . . but this judgment is tendentious and mistaken. . . .

Bourgeois democracy is certainly a limited form of democracy, and hence readily open to criticism. It is easy enough to show that there is no equal opportunity for the laborer and the capitalist, the rich and the poor. . . .

Yet, with all the reservations we might make, we must take note of the fact that the sum total of varied socio-political institutions that gives shape to bourgeois democracy is no fiction, despite the assertions of many extremist groups in the past and in the present.... These institutions and mechanisms are the result of decades ... and centuries ... of hard effort by the people to win their rights. The democratic order prevailing in many western countries constitutes their most important tradition and their most precious political heritage.[7]

This testimony, which comes from the U.S.S.R., is not only correct but also profoundly representative. And yet there are many people today who have serious doubts about the future of democracy even though they want to live in freedom. They feel that there is no real democratic alternative at this particular juncture in history. Their outlook is a mixture of fear and resignation in the face of what seems inevitable. And it is reinforced when they see democracy defenseless, or equated with unsubstantial forms of populism, or less attractive to some people than the lure of violence and totalitarian discipline.

Taking Cognizance of the Situation

One might well wonder, then, if humanism has anything to say or offer now as a way of life. Can it inspire new faith in its underlying values and create structures that will express them? Can it bring about social and economic development of a truly human sort? Can it break down the old unjust molds and give new hope to the helpless masses?

We are living in a historical age that is different from the one in which the classic forms of liberal democracy arose. Can humanism imagine and give expression to the new demands of the day, translating the classic forms into relevant, updated institutions? Can it retain the perduring values of the earlier model and make them operative in a very different world? Even more importantly, can it awaken the common, shared faith in freedom that is needed, and inspire the heroic effort required to sustain that faith?

The project might well seem very difficult. But a close look at the whole situation should erase all doubts and defeatism from our minds. Time has brought many ideas and experiments to maturity. Today we can readily see how much error there was in certain theses that were propounded as infallible truths only a short time ago.

The present assault on democracy is not the first, and it will not be the last. As Pascal pointed out so well, humanity may progress with its inventions but the balance of good and evil remains the same. Yet we can also say that at every stage of advance or retrogression it is possible for human evolution to take new steps forward in the domination of the surrounding world and the recognition of certain values. Though offenses are still committed against these values, they are becoming more consolidated.

It is certainly true that never has a moment in history been more crucial for the whole world. Yet however obscure and beclouded the times may be, it is also true that more and more people are taking cognizance of alternatives. Awareness is not restricted to small groups or elites; it is shared by the average person.

No one in the world can fail to realize now where the various forms of nazism and fascism led their peoples: into confusion, weakness, and mad folly. The same has happened with other dictatorial regimes that once seemed impregnable. The witness to this fact is irrefutable.

Moreover, every day it is becoming clearer what really goes on in the communist world. Now we can see what happens when a government regime turns itself into the divine creator and dispenser of all truth, all work, all life, and even death itself. We now know what happens when people struggle desperately to attain and wield such all-pervasive power, not to serve the human community but to hold power for its own sake. We can now see that such immense power tends to move those who wield it to the edge of madness.

This is not to suggest that those living in the affluent nations of the West are not suffering from their own ills. While freedom certainly does exist there, there is no doubt that the prevailing conception is that of materialistic capitalism. Its economic successes cannot be denied, but it also produces deep wounds. It seems incapable of offering a civilization project that responds to the deeper aspirations that are part of human nature.

Just as I quoted a famous Soviet scientist above with reference to the flaws in his country, so I could quote many religious and rationalist thinkers who are critical of the situation in the West. There is an atmosphere of insecurity that cannot be denied. It has been created by many different factors: e.g., the unlimited appeal to appetites and the lack of moral restraints; the focus on production growth; measuring the standard of living by material goods alone; and the ongoing maintenance of a system that keeps the economy in high tension and allows for no slowing down in the pace of growth if equilibrium is to be maintained.

That is not all. It cannot be denied that in the democracies we generally find respect for human rights and open debate, so that healthy action and reaction is feasible. At the same time, however, we must recognize the profound chasm that has opened up insofar as people have come to disregard any notion of the supernatural and to overlook moral truths and norms that might give a center to human life and relate human beings themselves to something beyond their own temporal, biologically limited lives.

Confronted with the reality of the present-day world, many people may be opening their eyes and ears to things that they refused to heed before. Perhaps they will come to acknowledge the truths that they had forgotten. Perhaps they will consider where they are being led by those who base domination of the world on the omnipotent power of money or a deified state.

In short, the task of constructing a new civilization cannot be simply political. It must go down to the roots of the evils that now threaten us, as they have always threatened humanity in the past.

A new society, a free and humane society, must be grounded on faith, hope, and love. Skeptics, people without faith, cannot produce anything solid and stable. They cannot ensure progress, justice, and freedom. All their conceptions will be centered around their own lives here and now in the present. Without faith there can be no hope, and neither of the two can exist without love. Today love has a very clear connotation. It means nonviolence, and that goes far beyond acts of terrorism.

When wicked inequities exist in a society, that is violence. When some enjoy opportunities and others do not, that is violence. When people are denied the right to choose their rulers, that is violence. When people propose to transplant ways of living that destroy authentic cultures, that is violence.

As Garaudy puts it: "Without love neither a human being nor a society can exist, much less function. ... Love is the opposite of both individualism and totalitarianism, the two poles of oppression."

Surely that is true. There can be no doubt about it. But I should like to dwell on the point here, as I bring this first section to a close.

Those who practice hatred in any form make it impossible for human beings to live a reasonable existence. They destroy society. Hence one of the most urgent demands imposed on us today is to reject hatred in any and all of its forms. We must reject racism. We must reject class struggle as a tool and an end in itself. We must reject excessive and haughty nationalism. We must reject blind conservatism, which is concerned only to maintain its own prerogatives and which always leads to violence in the end.

By common consent we must destroy these tendencies. Only then will we be able to conceive a new society that is truly human, using methods that accord with human nature.

That is why the conception and philosophy of humanism has something to tell us today. Its values can give real meaning and thrust to democracy. The experiences through which we are living today may open our eyes to this reality, giving us the heart to create a real societal project within the overall perspective of a new civilization.

PART II

LATIN AMERICA
AT THE CROSSROADS

7

The Reality of Latin America

The Concept of Latin America

In Part I of this book I discussed the dangers facing democracy in the midst of a worldwide political crisis that threatens not just one ideological system but the very bases of a whole civilization. In many countries the threat is not just a possibility; it is already an actuality. In Latin America, for example, about 70 percent of the population already find themselves under regimes that are euphemistically labelled "authoritarian."

While similar events and processes are affecting other regions of the world, I think it is relevant and important to focus on Latin America specifically. There the facts appear in all their simple and brutal clarity. We can readily see the real consequences of certain ideas. We can readily appreciate the failures which result from the breakdown of certain values that allow people to live together in a democracy and that make representative democracy truly feasible in practice.

Europeans may find it of interest to consider the experiences we have gone through in Latin America. Many of their current experiences have been transplanted here and put to the test, so that one can consider where they lead. Other nations of the Third World may also be interested. Though their cultures may be very old, they have only recently attained political independence. They can follow the course of life in nations that have been sovereignly independent for a century and a half, noting the problems encountered both in the past and the present.

As is true of nowhere else in the world, Latin America is a projection of western civilization, of Europe to be quite specific. In more recent times it has also fallen under the influence of the United States, as have many countries.

Shaped by Catholic teaching under the tutelage of the Spanish and Portuguese empires, our countries emerged as sovereign during the republic-forming era of the early nineteenth century. In their own distinctive way they lived through the ideological liberalism, the theological disputes, and the evolving course of ideas and political processes that Europe experienced during the nineteenth and twentieth century. One might find it suggestive and worthwhile to follow the course of parliamentary debates in Latin America over the last century and a half. With a time lag of ten or twenty years, they used to mirror the debates that took place in Europe. Now, however, there is no time lag.

There can be no doubt that the political ideal traced out in our nations was that of representative democracy formed around the three classic branches of power described by Montesquieu. Within this basic framework they have fluctuated between an overly strong presidency of the North American type and a parliamentary supremacy of the European type.

Before we continue our analysis, however, we might well want to consider an objection that could be raised at this point. Some have asked whether it is correct to talk about Latin America as a complex of homogeneous countries. Is the term "Latin America" a fiction, since one can readily detect vast differences between some of the nations that supposedly are part of it? After all, the countries find themselves at different stages of development; some possess indigenous peoples and cultures, or groups of African origin.

Granting all that, it still seems that the dominant feature on the Latin American continent is the similarity of characteristics to be found in the different countries. Three centuries of colonial rule left them with a similar cultural physiognomy, a common religious faith, and only two dominant Romance languages. It also left them with the same basic type of administrative organization and of land ownership. This gave rise to a social dualism that still perdures. And the Ibero-Latin juridical system has left a deep imprint on the whole.

The political independence movement was rather uniform and occurred almost simultaneously throughout the continent. In an age when communication was difficult, the acts and pronouncements of the various revolutionary councils were almost identical in form and content, even down to details. So was the reaction of the people in various nations. Inspired by the same basic patriotism, they pursued the same objectives in their historical acts. The essential features that shaped our nations culturally and sociologically during the colonial period have not disappeared. They continue to exert an influence on the lives of our nations, giving them a common destiny.

It is certainly true that examples can readily be adduced to prove the contrary. Consider Mexico, Argentina, and Brazil. They seem to differ greatly in their racial composition and their political life. Yet despite these differences certain central tendencies seem to pervade all these nations. Today more than ever before they seem to be moving toward the same crises and turning points.

Hence it is not only possible but objectively correct to talk about "Latin America" as a real entity. Though divided up into more than twenty nations, it has more shared features than many other population complexes that appear to be politically united today. So true is this that the world at large tends to view them under one image, often in spite of themselves. From a distance it is easier to see the shared defining features than the differences between them.

The Cycle of Democracy and Dictatorship

With the exception of only two or three nations, the nations of Latin America have seen their democratic governments crumble in recent time and have fallen prey to dictatorships. This basic cycle of democracy-anarchy-dictatorship is an age-old experience here, recurring time and again. In the last century and a half only Chile had escaped it—along with Uruguay in this century.

For more than a century the nations of Latin America kept falling prey to dictatorial regimes. Liberal democracy would soon decline into anarchical forms. Undermined by demagoguery and the appeal of strongmen *(caudillos)*, it found itself unable to foster stable growth and to implement adequate forms of justice and peaceful coexistence. This would lead to the rule of some strongman, but again and again the rule by force proved to be a historical failure too. Once again the people would go back to a democratic regime based on real freedom. Then the cycle would begin again.

Today, however, that cycle is taking on a somewhat different cast and significance. Until recent decades the cycle took place on a rather restricted plane. The main actors were the ruling classes and the armies. The latter would restore "order," usually at the behest of the ruling classes. The dimensions of the cycle are not what they were, for there is now active intervention on the part of the proletariat and middle classes. In different degrees, but in line with a basic tendency to be found throughout the underdeveloped world, the peoples of

Latin America now find themselves assaulted by forces and factors that were hardly known a short time ago.

Today, however, that phenomenon has become decidedly complex. While democracy is being greatly perturbed in the older nations of the West, here it is suffering from a direct, frontal assault. And in Latin America democracy does not possess the structural defenses to be found in the older democratic nations of the western world.

In Latin America the political foundations that traditionally gave expression to democracy are being superseded by new formulas that do not fit into the classical molds. Consider Parliament (or Congress), for example. In our countries it has often been the principal or only representative body and organ of control. Today it has lost its importance. It holds no weight vis-à-vis new centers of power, and at times it is closed down by the dictatorship in power. Something similar is happening in European nations. Organized labor, for example, may have a direct impact on various policies, particularly economic ones. Congress frequently does no more than ratify agreements worked out directly between labor organizations and the executive branch. Not too long ago it was the debates held in the Latin American parliaments that exemplified or gave direction to public opinion, however restricted the latter might be. Now, however, far vaster influence can be exerted by the few people who have the mass communications media at their disposal.

This is a typical phenomenon that deserves notice. In a word, the boundaries of the old institutional order are being superseded. The members of a congress or parliament are elected periodically in accordance with laws and rules known to everyone. Their acts can be monitored, for the laws spell out what they can and cannot do. They must take on certain clear-cut responsibilities, debate opinions with their peers, and regularly go back to their electorate for renewed approval.

But what about those who control the mass media? No one votes them into their job. In a certain sense they are not answerable to anyone. No law clearly sets forth their responsibilities and limitations, except insofar as they may impugn the character and reputation of individuals. Even in such a case, the defamed person must have recourse to lengthy legal proceedings and the outcome is not certain.

Parliament finds itself similarly confronted with other new organisms and functionaries. There are those entrusted with the task of national planning. There is the institutional expansion of the state and the creation of numerous autonomous public entities. There are specialized techno-bureaucracies that enjoy great influence because they exercise real perduring functions. Faced with all this, the members of parliament find they lack adequate means to keep tabs on these entities. Indeed they lack the technical knowledge and advisory service that would allow them to pass judgment on the reports put out by these specialists and their organizations.

In Latin America the same thing is happening to political parties. They align themselves with sectors of opinion that correspond with their own ideologies. Their present structure is frequently inadequate to the task of letting them give real direction to public opinion. They lack the sources of regular financing that would enable them to meet their expenses. Their internal structure and party proceedings often paralyze them completely. In such circumstances they are often unduly subject to the influence of certain social and economic factions that exert pressure on behalf of their own positions.

For all these reasons we find that the political superstructure of Latin American political parties often does not mesh with the actions of the rulers who are elected to office. Nor does it mesh with the real-life problems that modern socio-economic development poses to those rulers. Real efficiency and effectiveness in this area often is bound up with technical data and information that grows increasingly important every day. All too often, then, conflict arises between different groups, even when they supposedly share the same party affiliation. Members of congress and labor-union leaders may dispute with the executive branch, while the latter must confront problems that go beyond the limits of party loyalty.

All these factors combine to break down the traditional molds to be found in a representative democracy. Yet the fundamental problem in Latin America does not derive solely from them. For various reasons it often stems from our people's loss of a common faith in democracy. Without such a faith, the system cannot survive; for along with it will disappear many intellectual values and the ethical standards that make it possible to perdure.

This faith is undermined by all those who are basically enemies of the democratic system, who use every means possible to throw democracy into crisis. Of course that includes violence and terrorism. This forces the democratic governments in our nations to defend themselves, to adopt a repressive approach even though they may not wish to. For in the wave of violence and terrorism it is hard to distinguish where an ideological conception, however misguided, leaves off and sheer criminality begins.

If a democratic government tries to avoid repressive measures, it will be accused of weakness; if it exercises repression, it will be accused of "fascism." The antidemocratic provocations hope to bring about the breakdown of the system. In so acting they actually play into the hands of those who want to establish an "authoritarian" regime. On our continent at least we can lay down one conclusion as axiomatic: The proponents of violence have achieved nothing but the downfall of many democratic governments and the triumph of the very dictatorships that they themselves abhor.

No less serious is the assault of those affiliated with Marxist-Leninism. Some, not all, socialist groups on our continent differ markedly from the Socialist parties of Europe in this respect. In theory and practice many maintain that they do not believe in the .democratic system. They may make concessions for tactical reasons, "if the situation calls for it," but in the last analysis their imagined model of society would entail the end of freedom.

This extreme provokes a reaction from the other extreme. It spurs into action what Maritain called "the desperate blindness of the older ruling classes." They see such movements as a threat to their privileges, their accustomed habits, and their deep-rooted forms of living and being.

In recent years, in fact, some democratic regimes in Latin America have put through reforms that positively advanced economic and social development. The advances were real and meaningful, and the results can be measured in the countries where they took place. Almost always, however, these steps were impeded or blocked completely at some point by the incomprehension and resistance of rightist groups. The latter are unwilling to lose their position, to accept regimes that will put an end to their social, economic, and political domination. These reforms have also been blocked by implacable assaults from extreme leftists, however. In their eyes the reforms smacked of mere "reformism" rather than "revolution."

Thus both extremes have tended to bring attempted social reforms to nought. Our "political underdevelopment" has manifested itself once again, having a negative impact on the continuity of democracy. One extreme views the reforms implemented as excessive and revolutionary; the other extreme, whose impatience has with some justification been called a display of "revolutionary infantilism" and "political fantasy," views the reforms as too slow-paced and inadequate. At bottom we find two opposing minorities who, for different reasons, have ceased to believe in freedom and democracy.

We must face up to the fact that many democratic governments and political forces have failed to provide a solid line of conduct that would deal with these extremes. Some fail because they seek to cajole one side or the other in the hope of using it for their own purposes; the result is always quite the opposite. Other democratic sources, divided by internal party squabbles, have not shown the vision needed to effect unity and salvage democracy; instead they have opened the door to those who seek its fall.

Facile Explanations

Frequently attempts are made to look for facile or self-serving explanations. People try to play down the real facts, to ignore the underlying reasons for the present crisis of democracy in Latin America. Yet the crisis now affects many of our nations and about two-thirds of the Latin American population.

Some try to place most of the blame on outside causes. It is not the fault of those within the country, they say. Our nations are the victims of imperialism from one source or another. Secret agencies are at work, and the superpowers are interfering openly or surreptitiously. Depending on one's own ideology, one blames one side or the other as the enemy.

It would be senseless to deny that such outside influences exist. They become more apparent every day throughout the world. One need only look at Angola, South Africa, or the Middle East to be convinced on this point. Such outside interventions have taken place quite openly in other countries of Asia and Europe, for example. It has been prompted by an appeal to military security, by the presence of international ideologies (e.g., those of the Social Democrats and the Christian

Democrats), and of course by the U.S.S.R. and the United States.

There is no doubt that ideological currents and the international organizations that uphold them do exert influence and intervene around the world in the present-day context. In Europe, for example, the leaders of various currents have stepped in to support parties with similar beliefs in Spain, Portugal, and Italy. It is not a matter of political or strategic indifference that a nation leans toward one option or another.

These influences operate in accordance with the peculiar features of a given nation. They do not take the same form in East Germany, Lebanon, and those countries that have free elections.

Given this context, we cannot ignore the fact that the superpowers and even lesser nations have operative networks around the world. To ignore that fact would be as ridiculous as to maintain that one side operates that way while the other side is innocent. The fact of such influence is one of the greatest dangers facing the freedom and independence of any given nation. As we have witnessed, nations may turn into little more than electoral and ideological battlegrounds, or markets for the weapons industry.

These factors do have to be considered, then. But we would be trying to evade the truth if we concluded that what happens in Latin America is always the result of such intervention. To say that is to assume that our nations and peoples are so insignificant that they are merely the passive victims of outside influences.

Consider Portugal and Italy, for example. Important international influences were at work in the recent events that took place in those countries. But it is clear that those influences were not the determining ones. It was those peoples themselves who have proved to be decisive.

Now consider what happened in recent years in various nations of Latin America. Some nations were already on the point of collapse when the death-blow came. While outside influences were clearly present, the main cause of their collapse was their own internal decomposition. Even if no outside influence had been present, those regimes would have ultimately collapsed from internal decay. It is akin to what happens in the biological world. The human organism carries certain latent germs and pathogenic viruses within it. If the organism grows weak, if it is incapable of defending itself, those germs and viruses will grow more active and take over.

To cite two examples among many, Argentina and Chile prove this assertion. In them democracy had been subjected to such extreme tensions that consensus had disappeared. Indeed much more than that had disappeared, namely, the most elementary preconditions for a viable form of societal life.

In such circumstances we usually find the same set of general features: a disorganized economy on the point of bankruptcy; authorities without leadership who are undermined from within by the very groups who claim to support them; general insecurity and a growing feeling of mutual distrust; armed bands and extremist elements of various affiliations who try to influence the course of events to their own advantage. In such circumstances no institution can escape the process of disintegration. The universities cease to be institutes of study and research, turning into centers of ongoing political warfare. The communications media lose all their objectivity in providing information and critical judgment, openly serving the interests of the group they represent. Thus all dialogue disappears. There is no possibility for public opinion to see and evaluate events with a clear eye. Those in power end up trying to make their power total, while those in opposition feel threatened and sharpen their attacks.

Some groups from within the Christian churches have fallen prey to this process. Certain priests and ministers, exasperated by the misery they found around them, have moved away from their hierarchies, discovered political action, altered the thrust of their mission, and found a "scientific interpretation" in Marxism. Now they are turning this interpretation into dogma, to replace the faith in their own doctrine that they have lost. With all the passion of neophytes they offer a politicized interpretation of the gospel message and hurl anathemas at those who dare to dispute their statements.

Certain forms of populism have also helped to undermine democratic regimes in Latin America. They propose to restore stability by catering to people's most primitive passions and by distributing without creating anything. In such a setup the governing authority abdicates its authentic function. It renounces the exercise of discipline and real effort, replacing the void with the constant agitation of the masses. As a result they receive no support at critical moments, for the people can see through the game. They may readily join in the festivities offered them for a while, but they know that in the end they are being led up a blind alley. As Ribeiro incisively puts it: "What differentiates populist leaders from reformist or patriarchal leaders is their intrinsically demagogic attitude, which is combined with an air of political opportunism that causes them to fight openly and directly for their own personal power."[1]

Such, then, were the factors at work in the case of Argentina and Chile. They produced such extreme tensions and such a pervasive lack of prudent judgment that democracy was unable to survive. This gave rise to a feeling that things could not be allowed to continue as they were. So pervasive was the feeling of frustration that it was even shared by those in power, not to mention those outside.

Now the Communist parties fully realize that people have a negative reaction toward such anarchy. In many countries of the world they are advocating the order, discipline, and security that vacillating democratic governments have been unable to ensure. But in Latin America at least this field of competence has already been pre-empted. In Latin America the armed forces are the professional advocates of these three objectives.

So various nations in Latin America are now going through a great trial, some suffering worse than others. Authoritarian regimes have been installed, the most basic human rights have been suppressed, and the injustice affecting people's lives has been intensified. But they are pondering what has happened to them, even though they may not be talking about it. In the future they surely will not choose to repeat the mistake that led them into this strait, which took away their freedom, however limited it may have been, and subjected them to unlimited bondage.

We must work, then, for the restoration of democracy among the peoples of this continent. It is a difficult task, of course. But for all the reasons cited above, our quest for a restored democracy must be grounded on truth, not on deceit or the mere mouthing of false and sterile slogans. Otherwise we may fall prey once again to different forms of vengeance and hatred and never find a democratic way out. Only a prior effort and reflection and sincerity will enable us to acquire new perspectives and to break the tragic cycle that has dominated our history for centuries.

Moral Factors

If we examine these processes more carefully, we will detect human failings that simply have to be corrected. It is not just that the older institutions have been overtaken by new realities. What we now find is an absence of a moral framework to serve as a support for action. If there are reserves of virtue and resourcefulness in the people of Latin America that give cause for hope, there are also hollow spaces that account for many failures.

The ruling classes have clung blindly and egotistically

to their privileges. The growing sectors of the middle class, upon attaining power, have not displayed the solvency and spirit of service expected of them. In 1940 Gabriela Mistral described the situation in masterful terms:

We cannot resist success in any field. Like alcohol . . . it inebriates us and robs us of clear-headedness. It dispels our flabby convictions and makes mince-meat of us. The cult of success in Latin America is monstrous. I am fully acquainted with its vulgar face. I have seen it in people's submissiveness to money, to government power, and to personal mediocrity that has been blessed by fortune. The victory of one or another regime is as convincing to us as a club or a punch in the nose would be. It paralyzes our ability to react. . . .

Military dictatorship is nothing new to us. It is one part of our two-edged tradition. The history of Hispano-America is . . . the pageant of freedom as a passion play, of what Unamuno would call an "agonic freedom." It is a freedom that makes its own *via crucis*, falling down and then rising up again. The time for merrymaking, for eating and drinking well, has been translated into a political doctrine. The young braves who once swore their allegiance to the ministry of agony are now abandoning their Christ-Freedom, who cannot give them the wine of power and the fatlings of fiscal profit.[2]

In a personal letter to me around the same time, her prophetic and poetic vision provided an even more poignant and bitter X-ray of the Latin American scene:

I travelled from Chile up the coast, and I have seen enough foulness, political corruption, and bullying to make me weep for the Pacific America I love so much. This experience . . . has forced me to abandon the notion that there is some policy or politics at all. What I find is the corruption of people by envy, stupidity, and the lack of Christianity. What I find is a teaching without Christ and without the Greeks. What I find is our lack of history, tradition, and maturity, as Reyes says. Cuba is bleeding to death on this account, and Cuba is not alone. But its friend has no hope of convincing friend or foe that the real battle is there, not among political groups. . . . Without humanity there is no human being. . . . Good God, we must begin to do something![3]

If she were to take the same trip today, what could she add to those earlier comments? Alas, only that some of those features have become more accentuated in many countries, and that the evil has become even more extensive. In the establishment of many regimes we certainly have not seen "some policy" or "politics." All we can see in them is the weakness which Gabriela Mistral pointed up, and which seems to recur periodically.

If Latin America is to find its way, it will not be with political formulas alone. First and foremost we need an inner reform to brighten and cleanse the murky atmosphere in which we now live, for the systems of oppressing and destroying human values have been refined to a point scarcely conceivable a few decades ago.

It is not enough to ponder new lines of conduct that will allow for real, operative democracy. We must also develop a new attitude toward problems, so that we can tackle them with seriousness, uprightness, and effectiveness.

The absence of an authentic humanism is reflected in a false vision, not only of ourselves, but also of the world in which we live and which has such a profound impact on us. This lack of solid formation in Latin American life today has also led to a lack of real creativity. We have been unable to find our own authentic models for living, and this has led to much frustration.

Few have taken the trouble to ask why all this has happened on our continent. There are different interpretations, to be sure, but none has focused on the conscious awareness of our people as a factor that might make them reconsider the causes of their failures. Still less is there any realization that the breakdown of moral supports may have a great deal to do with it all.

8

A Splintered Continent

Two Different Courses

There is a question that weighs heavily on the subconscious of the people and nations of Latin America; indeed it should weigh even more heavily on them. It is this: Why has their destiny been so different from that of North America and the United States in particular?

More than one study has broached this question.[1] More than one has noted the advantage held by Latin America around the time that political independence was won. All the odds in favor of fruitful development seemed to lie with the latter, whose population was six times that of the United States.

In the 1770s there were no more than five cities in the future United States: Boston, Philadelphia, New York, Baltimore, and Charleston. Their population ranged from 5,000 to 15,000. By contrast Latin America already possessed many active centers of urban life with much larger populations. To name just a few: Mexico City, population 90,000; Havana, population 76,000; Lima, population 50,000; Santiago de Chile, population 30,000; Bogotá, population 25,000; Buenos Aires, population 20,000.

Even as far back as 1576, Spanish America seemed to be way ahead of North America. There were 9 *audi-*

encias, 30 governerships, 25 comptrollerships, 3 mints, 4 archbishoprics, 24 bishoprics, and 360 monasteries with distinguished schools, workshops, and art centers. There were also many universities and printing plants. All these institutions, along with the residences of the viceroys, were housed in imposing edifices that still stand today.

By contrast Boston was established only in 1630. Even at the end of the eighteenth century it was inferior to the viceregal cities of Spanish America. The same holds true for New York and Philadelphia.

What happened so that in a relatively short space of time the status and importance of the two continents should shift so dramatically and completely? Countless answers have been given to the question. Some are racial, explaining everything in terms of Anglo-Saxon dominance. Others focus on the link between religion and economics, contrasting Protestantism and its favorable impact on the economy with the Catholic church and its paralytic effect on economic development.

I do not intend to discuss these varied answers as such. It would take volumes to analyze and evaluate them. I shall simply dwell on certain facts that seem relevant here because they had a direct impact on the past and continue to influence our present.

United Versus Disunited States

The first thing that strikes us is that we find "united" states in the North and "disunited" states in the South. Much of this is obvious, of course, but the point bears repeating. The fact is that Latin America has been divided up into numerous parcels of land, each succumbing to a haughty and narrow-minded nationalism.

Since the birth of independence more than a century and a half ago, not one generation has failed to point up the need for unity between the nations of Latin

America. Indeed all the arguments are well known by now. Yet the sad fact remains that this is the most balkanized continent of all. The European countries have increasingly joined their destinies. In the Third World, the African continent already has its own unified organization, its own leaders, its own vision and motivations. It carries on a privileged dialogue with the European nations. Despite its regressive tendencies and its tribal problems, it finds expression in the international sphere. Asia and Oceania are represented by countries that are really subcontinents in themselves.

By comparison Latin America seems to be a splintered continent. Each of its many governments has been constantly looking for its own bilateral deal and its own little piece of success, often living without glory or honor. To distract its people from political problems each has tried to foment border disputes when it has nothing to show but a lot of unoccupied land. For these and many other reasons, the nations of Latin America have been unable to present an organized front vis-à-vis the rest of the world.

There have been many attempts to consolidate the continent but they have either languished or failed utterly. It is not that the need for consolidation and a united front vis-à-vis other nations has not been recognized. It is not that there are technical objections, or that the advantages of such consolidation have not been seen. It is not that the need for Latin America to create some area of continental dimensions is not seen to be even more important today for further development and the use of modern technology. The plain fact is that we have lacked a common vision and failed to make the necessary political decisions. Personal position and exaggerated nationalism have won out over unity.

The many efforts at integration and unification in the world have clearly been the result of political decisions on a grand scale. Consider the unification of Germany or Italy, which brought together peoples who differed even more from each other than do those of Latin America today. The organization of the European Community was also the fruit of clearsighted vision and political will, which managed to supersede the accumulated antagonisms of centuries. The Civil War in the United States was fought, not only to free the slaves, but also to prevent the secession of the Southern States. The U.S.S.R. is another example worthy of mention, though here again the historical and political differences were real.

It is this kind of decision-making that has been lacking on the South American continent. It is made up of splintered, isolated countries that lack the gravitational pull, the power, and the scope demanded by present world conditions relating to politics and economics. In short, our mental horizon is characterized by narrow localism and provincialism.

This historical failing continues to have a serious impact on the life of our continent. However much we may try to avoid invidious comparisons with the North, a thousand negative ones float into our minds. Worse still, the differences between the United States and the nations south of the Rio Grande, grow greater every day, and with increasing speed. The problem is only compounded when we note our lack of influence in the international sphere. All other nations seem to play a better hand of cards than our divided, talk-prone nations, who seem to be quite ineffective.

The only exception on our continent, perhaps, is Brazil. Its history has taken a slightly different course. By virtue of its size and its population, it is capable of representing a real integration of different states.

Since the fact is clear and can hardly be doubted, we must try to understand why and how this disunity has come about. I think it is easy enough to offer an interpretation that explains one of the fundamental causes of our lack of political unity.

The ruling minorities have been uprooted from their

own nations and peoples. Moreover the regimes based on force, which also look to those minorities for support, have proved incapable of envisioning a grand historical design and laying the bases for an effective community of nations in Latin America.

Such a community, of course, would have to be more open and decentralized. It would require a different representative system and greater fluidity between the various social classes. That in turn would threaten the age-old forms of dominance and superiority. For the ruling powers and minorities, the important thing is to maintain themselves in power. They feel an instinctive animosity toward any thought of integration and unity. By opening up the geographical boundaries that now encircle people, integration would create markets and human spaces that would accelerate the process of social change in Latin America. It is much easier for those who now hold a privileged place to maintain the present setup and to operate within its narrow boundaries. Any change toward greater continental unity would upset the status quo in which they now live so nicely.

That is why the already "established" interests have not shown any enthusiasm for greater continental unity. They are used to the rules of the game as they have formulated and known them. Those rules allow them to maintain their privileged position. They could not do it so easily if the ground rules were changed.

The new "authoritarian" governments, who for the most part base their actions on the doctrine of "security," are not favorable to unifying movements either. They are essentially "nationalist" in outlook and their frame of mind ultimately coincides with that of the traditional ruling groups.

Recently some enterprising businessmen, more modern and aggressive in outlook, have come to see the value of working for an expanded sphere of human activity and geographical space. They have come to realize that such an expansion would benefit both them and their nations, broadening an otherwise limited future. But if we are to achieve a union of nations that will really benefit the interests of our countries, we need governments with vision and political will power. They must be able to look beyond their own short-term existence and convenience, to consider the future of the Latin American peoples and their place in the decisions that are made by the great power centers.

The policies of individuals or groups who lack popular support and lofty objectives can hardly contain broad-ranging visions. The common people, in turn, can hardly show an interest in such policies when they are not allowed to participate in the decision-making process.

The conduct of labor affairs has failed to promote continental integration here. Effective solutions to such issues would open up new horizons to our laborers. Now, for want of such solutions and horizons, they restrict themselves to demands for immediate gains and narrow questions of self-interest.

All, then, are caught up in internal quarrels and the immediate needs of survival. They do not see that the future is slipping away from them, that their own problems will not be solved unless they place their own concerns and views in a broader frame of reference.

Internal and External Conflicts

Those who advocate integration usually stress the logic of their position and the benefits to be attained. They rarely stress the adverse consequences stemming from disintegration.

Divisiveness has not just reduced our nations to small size. It has also provoked upheavals that have squandered their energy and wasted their resources. There have been wars between countries to settle boundary disputes and fierce domestic struggles to consolidate government rule in countries whose contours were ill defined at best.

Once political independence and unity were established in the United States, border skirmishes eventually arose with Mexico and ended up in a war that was quickly finished. But more local quarrels, which are often more savage because they are confined to a relatively restricted area, were kept down to a minimum. Moreover, from the very first its ruling figures seemed to have a continental vision. Soon this broadened into a worldwide vision, though this became apparent only in the early decades of this present century. In Latin America, by contrast, the independence movement did not end with a revolution to expel the colonizers. It was prolonged for decades in civil wars and domestic conflicts, some of which came to an end only a few decades ago.

In Venezuela, for example, these disputes brought about the death of almost half its population. The so-called "Goths" were exterminated. Bolívar predicted that it would fall into the hands of a desperate mob and then all sorts of ravagers, a victim of every sort of savagery and crime. His words were prophetic. With brief respites the internecine quarrels continued up to the dictatorship of Juan Vicente Gómez. His reign, which lasted from 1908 to 1935, put an end to anarchy and *caudillo* rule. It should be noted that the present president of that country is the fourth to be elected by the people in the period of constitutional continuity inaugurated by Rómulo Betancourt in 1959.

The same sort of conflict took place in other Latin American nations. Consider the turbulent internal and external conflicts that mark the history of Mexico. Consider the bloody disputes between centralists and federalists in Argentina, which reached extremes of inhuman ferocity. In Colombia liberals and conservatives carried on their bloody quarrels into the middle of this century. In their last phase these disputes killed proportionately as many people as did the Spanish Civil War. These conflicts ended only in 1957, when peace was restored between the two factions and it became possible to stabilize the democratic way of life.

In Uruguay the conflicts were just as bloody during the nineteenth century. It consolidated its democratic system only in 1903, under the presidency of José Batlle y Ordóñez. It would take too much space to recount all the guerrilla wars, *caudillos*, coups d'état, and dictatorships that have plagued Bolivia, Ecuador, Paraguay, and Peru. All this is quite apart from the history of those countries to be found in Central America and the Caribbean area.

In the past the only exception to this general picture was Chile. It brought an end to anarchy and civil war in 1833, organizing a solid democratic government and juridical setup that lasted substantially for almost 140 years.

So if we compare the unfolding history of the two Americas, we find that the United States experienced only one civil war while our nations have a long history of chronic violence and destruction. This trend has disrupted cities and towns that were secure and prosperous during the colonial era.

Symptomatic and revealing is the differing fate of the heroes of the independence movement in the United States and in Latin America. San Martín died an impoverished exile in France. O'Higgins longed to return to Chile in his last years; he finally died outside his homeland after an exile of more than twenty years. Sucre was assassinated far from his birthplace, in Peru. Artigas spent his last days as an exile in Paraguay. Iturbide was thrown out of Mexico and executed upon his return. Bolívar, the greatest and best known of these figures in history, barely escaped various assaults on his life. He died far from his homeland, in poverty and abandonment, feeling that he had tried to "plow the sea." This brief chronicle, which could be extended indefinitely, speaks volumes about the character and shape of our nations and the course they have taken.

The way they treated their legendary heroes might serve as an instructive lesson for those who have done much less but who clamor for the applause and gratitude of their people.

One cannot help but feel pain when one compares the lives of our illustrious figures with those of Washington, Jefferson, and other North Americans. They did not have to die for their merits to be recognized. One can even admire the residences where they ended their days in peaceful splendor, surrounded by the admiration and respect of their people.

From the very outset we can detect undesirable traits in the conduct of our peoples and nations: fickleness and envy, the desire to obstruct and topple anyone out of the ordinary, and the lack of moderation in words and actions that has marked the course of our history.

Equally influential in the developing course of our southern nations have been the recurring border disputes. It is not surprising that some confusion should arise about boundaries when independence was won. South America is a vast area, and knowledge of its geography was somewhat vague. But these disputes were translated into bloody, exhausting wars that have continued right down to our own day. Much time and energy have been wasted in them. They have led to exacerbated nationalist feelings and disproportionately large expenditures in armaments. Often they were used by precarious governments to consolidate their hold on power. And one need scarcely mention the human, political, and economic cost of these disputes, which are responsible for so much backwardness and poverty.

Recall the different warlike interventions of Brazil and Argentina vis-à-vis Uruguay; and of those three nations with Paraguay, which was practically dismembered in the process of reshaping the central core of the continent. Recall the prolonged dispute between Argentina and Chile over Patagonia and the extreme South; the wars between Chile, Peru, and Bolivia; Peru's conflicts with Colombia, Bolivia, and Ecuador; Ecuador's disputes with Colombia; Colombia's disputes with Venezuela; and the Chaco War between Bolivia and Paraguay. This is aside from the wars in Central America and Mexico, which despoiled large expanses of territory.

This "balkanization," as I have called it, has cost our continent a heavy price. We tend to hide that fact when we study the historical course of Latin America. We try to hide the truth and its consequences under a cloak of gilded romanticism.

Now of course one could say that in the past and present centuries the nation-states of Europe had conflicts that were far greater in scope and magnitude. That is true, and no one can fail to reckon the human and economic cost of those wars. In their wake the nations of Europe ceased to be the great governing powers and were forced to hand the scepter over to the United States and the Soviet Union.

But when historians and analysts examine the history of Europe, none of them fails to point up the effect of those tragic events on Europe itself. Here on our continent, by contrast, we rarely measure the impact of our internecine conflicts on our newly developing nations.

Now we seem to have gotten beyond the warfare phase. There is reason to hope that this factor, which has weighed so heavily on our past, will not continue to penalize us in the future.

9

Weighty Internal Factors

Social Dualism

The facts related earlier have had a decisive impact on the birth and growth of Latin America. But other facts may well go even deeper, explaining why the course of development on the two American continents has gone in two different, if not directly opposed, directions.

The first thing that strikes the reflective observer is that democratic institutions have operated from the very start on the North American continent, and they have always entailed the active participation of the populace. Some of their essential notes have been the existence of jurors; direct election of local authorities, from the sheriff to the judge; an ongoing community life; the drive toward equality and open-ended opportunity; social mobility; freedom of inquiry; and the quasi-religious force of the Constitution and its provisions, shared and deeply felt by the people. To all this we might add that a dose of pragmatism has kept them from falling prey to intoxicated rhetoric and outlandish promises on either the social, economic, or political level.

As is often the case in human undertakings, these lofty principles have not always operated in perfect fashion or in a completely continuous way. The important point is that they have habitually served as the inspiration for the course that the United States has taken; and also that they have been at the root of reform movements when they were being violated.

In stressing the positive features of North American society, I am not trying to idealize the situation. No one can be unaware of its internal imbalances, its latent and effective violence and criminality. People on our continent could hardly overlook its actions abroad, which have not always corresponded with its initial principles in the conduct of foreign affairs. Consider Mexico, Central America, and the Caribbean area, for example.

Moreover, there is no doubt that the United States was deeply wounded by the race problem, which was not fully resolved by the Civil War. Yet in this century, and particularly in the last two decades, the process of racial integration has made real steps forward. Once again we have witnessed how an open society can address its problems. Thanks to people who were able to face issues squarely and work out solutions, the country has been moving toward the solution of a crisis that once seemed insoluble.

Whatever one's overall estimate may be, then, it seems incontrovertibly true that democracy in the United States has involved the participation of the people and has been concerned about equal opportunity. This has given it quite a different character than democratic regimes in Latin America.

In any case it is not my purpose here to delve into the positive and negative features of differing conceptions of life or of different human qualities. My main point is to point up two social models that were, and still continue to be, different, and to show the historical consequences of the course they have taken.

In our nations the independence movement was spawned by the thoughts and actions of people who in many instances had been inspired by the ideals of the French Revolution. But they did not relate those ideals sufficiently to the specific and peculiar reality of people's lives in our colonies. Rather than being a mass movement, revolt was a movement of the Creole class. Only some segments of the common people participated in it because many remained loyal to Spain. From the very first the revolt took the form of cruel civil wars that were prolonged over a long period of time. Once our nations had dissociated themselves from Spain and Portugal, they still retained practically all of the structures of the older colonial system. The lot of the people was not basically changed. Society was organized along vertical lines. A ruling class, in part the same one as before, argued over power for a long period of time—down to this very day in some countries. Republican sovereignty brought no essential change to the social and economic structure that had prevailed earlier in Latin America.

The agrarian structure perpetuated the old *encomienda* system. Now there was the *fundo, latifundio, hacienda,* and *fazenda.* This gave rise to a new type of feudalism, which sometimes was even more rigid than that of the colonial era. It left a profound imprint on the politics, family life, and even the military setup of our nations.

Consider the case of agriculture in both regions. In preceding centuries it was the basis of the social order and the economy. In the United States the farmer was the prototype of rural life. The move westward toward the Pacific Ocean was the move of people in search of land and a better future. Here in South America, by contrast, complete private appropriation of land, generally in compensation for military or political considerations, took priority over its practical cultivation.

In 1884 Augusto Orrego Luco published a series of articles in which he dealt with the situation of common Chilean laborers, of the peasants in particular. Here is what he had to say:

The daily wage goes down while the farm product goes up. Thus the owning class grows rich while the common people sink into poverty. In a manner visible to all, this has given rise to the upper classes who bathe in opulence and the lower classes who drown in misery. The former wield power while the latter fall prey to a servile atmosphere that cannot help but be enervating.[1]

Helio Jaguaribe, the Brazilian expert, has offered a basic explanation:

Latin American societies remained underdeveloped from the time of independence to the early decades of the twentieth century because they ended up as dualistic societies. Complete emphasis on the objectives of the elite was not compatible with the interests of the masses. It prevented social integration . . . and fostered the establishment of a social system (i.e., a system of values, participation, power, and ownership) which did not favor national development.[2]

This social dualism has characterized Latin American life to the present day. Elites have dominated the masses of people without any countervailing force. They are strangers to each other, the masses being forced to live in tightly vertical regimes. In the colonial era everything emanated from a central authority in Spain or Portugal; since that time everything operates through rigid, pre-established hierarchies. Such has been the case in agriculture, which for years has represented about 80 percent of our total production. For decades, and even up to today in some places, it is a system based on the servitude of the laborer, who has no real opportunity to ever become a landowner.

To this must be added the fact that the Spanish and Portuguese found a large population of natives here, and also ancient civilizations that had deep roots. The native masses were not eliminated by Spanish and Portuguese colonization. So two well-defined strata lived side by side, intermixing more and more as time went on. In many nations this has been another factor intensifying social dualism. Moreover, in certain areas groups of African origin were to be found. José Medina Echavarría has this to say:

The whole economic, social, and political history of Latin America is largely that of consolidating and transforming the *hacienda* as a socio-economic unit. The decline of the traditional structure goes hand in hand with the gradual decline of this older organization. . . .

The *hacienda* was engaged in much more than economic exploitation alone. It was also a political power. In some countries, with a nod from the government, it also became a military power. The *hacienda* was the cornerstone of the domestic structure, a fairly closed social unit that embraced the landowner, his family, and his clients. All came under his authority. He was both protector and oppressor, both a paternal and an authoritarian power center. . . .

This family-like structure has lasted down to the present, where the weight of kinship can still be seen and felt. . . . We might well consider to what extent the seignorial values of the *hacienda* have shaped the economic ethics of the Ibero-American people.

One could hardly find a better description of the feudal system: "both protector and oppressor, both a paternal and an authoritarian power center."

But even though this system does persist still in some countries, as I have indicated, it has been undergoing alterations in recent years. I shall consider that point a bit more fully later on. Still it must be stressed that real changes are needed to alter this structure, and quite the contrary took place during the nineteenth century. The social organization of agriculture became even more rigid. The air of servile work has profoundly affected the past and present setup of society. This gave rise to manifest contradictions that now cannot be tolerated with the rise of an industrial society and an expanded middle class.

This reality has been recognized and acknowledged by all who have tried to look squarely at the facts. The Peruvian Mariátegui put it this way:

The Creole feudal setup has been harsher and greedier than the Spanish one. The Spanish *encomendero* generally had some of the noble habits of the *seigneur*. The Creole *enco-mendero* has all the defects of the plebeian and none of the virtues of the *hidalgo*. The servitude of the Indian has not diminished under the Republic. . . .

The individualistic character of republican legislation has unquestionably promoted the absorption of native property by the latifundist system. In this respect the situation of the Indian was viewed more realistically by the Spanish laws.[3]

Mariátegui's description applies in varying degrees to other countries as well. It confirms the view that there was a retrogression at the start of the republican era. For during the colonial period there existed countervailing forces: Spanish legislation, some sectors of the church, and the ongoing vigilance of the Crown. In some instances at least, they could make their presence felt.

Another Peruvian, Víctor Andrés Belaúnde, held a very different ideology from that of Mariátegui. Yet he, too, pointed out that the Indian had been forced to remain tied to the land, ensnared in a feudal system without religion, poetry, or glory.[4] What was forced enlistment in one country became tenancy in others, but the situation was basically similar in all. Thus was created a dual society, two classes separated by an abyss. They were kept apart by money, by culture, by habits and customs, by language and topics of conversation, and of course by the code of behavior governing landlord on the one hand and worker on the other.

The seed of democracy could only grow with difficulty in such soil. Most people could hardly have any thought of independence or of popular organization. The masses who labored in the fields were completely dependent. Freedom was a chimera upheld by the ruling minorities in the upper classes. Political liberalism did not penetrate economic structures, and individualism consolidated the differences.

Thus the exercise of rights quickly degenerated into inefficiency and anarchy, creating the conditions for the rise of strongmen and dictators. Once these were established in power, the people who yearned for freedom began to resist once again. They could always find someone to embody their aspirations, and he quickly turned into a new strong man or messiah. The people invested too much hope in such figures, thinking that all problems would be resolved magically once their heroes were installed in power. But the underlying constants of political, social, and economic power were not touched, so disillusionment and failure soon set in. Those who had plumped for the protecting *caudillo* now began to clamor for "order." There was always another messiah waiting to heed this clamor. Some of these "saviors" even conveyed an impression of efficiency and effectiveness by building bridges, buildings, and roads—tangible things that people could see and appreciate. The memory of such public works restored more than one fallen dictator to power after a period of anarchy.

Many examples could be given. The central fact, however, is that none of these leaders ever tried seriously to alter the social bases of the system, the existing foundations that represented such a serious and perduring obstacle to democracy. Vasconcelos has a memorable commentary on this point:

In the economic arena the *caudillo* is ever the chief bulwark of the *latifundio* system. Though some of them were declared enemies of property, almost every *caudillo* ended up as a landowner himself. The fact is that the possession of military power inevitably entails the exclusive appropriation of land. When one is called a soldier, a *caudillo*, a king, or an emperor, despotism and landownership are correlative terms. That is to be expected. Like political rights, economic rights can be preserved and defended only in a regime based on freedom. Absolutism leads inevitably to the impoverishment of the many and the abusive luxury of the few.[5]

Thus there has been no real mobility in Latin America. Social rigidity and sharp social contrasts have been the dominant feature. Though they have been lessening in some countries in recent decades, in other countries people have been trying to intensify and solidify them.

There can be no basic consensus and no real socioeconomic development if that situation does not change. Social peace cannot be attained or bolstered unless the sources of obvious conflict are removed. The discontented may be silenced forcefully for a time, but the reasons for their protest will remain. The more they are stifled, the deeper will grow their resentment.

Of course it is extremely difficult to solve all the problems that exist in a human society. But our nations will not achieve basic stability until they face up to the primordial issue of "social dualism." To live amid such dualism is to live in insecurity, and no ideology of "security" will solve the problem. Security will be born only of consensus; and we will not achieve consensus unless we realize that a country cannot contain two widely separated classes, two different kinds of people with different status and different opportunities.

Latin American Imitativeness

One of the economic and psycho-cultural origins and results of social dualism is Herodianism on the part of the ruling minorities. Part cause and part effect of that, in turn, is an excessive imitativeness that is a caricature of real information-gathering and universality.

For a long time our nations have been deeply influenced and guided by these Herodian minorities, whose whole way of life is separated from their people and based on foreign cultural patterns. This process has reached its ultimate extreme in certain countries of Central America. At the root of their political underdevelopment is the fact that they have not thought and lived in terms of themselves, but in terms of foreign influences that had penetrated them deeply. They have not utilized their own strengths and resources to find their own way.

Latin American imitativeness has been all out of

proportion. In the past the upper classes imported from Europe their ideas, their lifestyle, their way of thinking, their fashions, and even their furniture. Once their countries became independent from Spain and Portugal, these classes became so "Frenchified" that they were uprooted from their own soil. The "transplanted" as a type has been masterfully depicted in our literature by various authors.[6]

This imitativeness has not lessened in the present. Not only fashions but also new "ideological" and "revolutionary" models are imported without any consideration being given to the distinctive character and reality of Latin America. Our countries end up being "echo chambers," because our people do not seem capable of thinking for themselves.

Of course there are ideas that know no frontiers. But if we are going to borrow ideologies, the least we can do now is show some imagination. We should be able to adapt them to the features of our own native soil so that they can bear fruit with a flavor of its own.

Some time ago Gabriela Mistral spoke about the stunted body of the newborn innocent known as America, our America:

It is not due to the organism itself. The continent is a formidable mass, and Chile is a solid body of metal. Hence our inability to create our own model of life raises surprise and then indignation. After so much reading of politics, . . . after so many years of living a distinctive life here in America, . . . after so much stress on its course in scholarly textbooks, . . . we can find nothing to save us except the recipe of fascism, nazism, communism, Portuguese corporatism, or the cave dweller—anything but our own.[7]

This has not happened in literature or the arts, to be sure. There we have found vigorous, original expression of universal transcendence. But that only makes the basic phenomenon all the more disconcerting. The over-hasty importation of customs, ideas and, above all, political models has been a perduring trait in Latin America.

Bolívar saw this lack of practical wisdom and this imitativeness as the root of many of our troubles. Offering advice to the Venezuelan Congress, he told its members that their country needed a Constitution that would accord with its history, its immaturity, and its sociology:

Our lot has always been a purely passive one. Our political life has been crude. It was all the more difficult for us to achieve freedom because we had been situated in a state lower than bondage. . . .

Devoid of political, economic, and civil knowledge, people are adopting pure illusions as if they were realities. . . .

I must say that I never had the least notion of equating the situation and nature of two such different entities as the Anglo-American state and the Hispano-American ones. Wouldn't it be very difficult to apply the English political, civil, and religious code to Spain? Well it would be even more difficult to apply the laws of North America to Venezuela. Doesn't the spirit of the laws tell us that they must be appropriate to the people making them? That only chance could account for the suitability of one nation's laws to the conditions of another country? That laws must relate to the physical makeup of a country, its climate, its soil, its situation, its size, and its people's way of life? That they must relate to the degree of freedom that the Constitution can tolerate, to the religion of the inhabitants, to their inclinations, their wealth, their numbers, their commerce, their manners, and their customs? That is the code we must consult, not that of Washington!

Seventy years later we can hear another hero of Spanish America, the Cuban José Martí, speaking in similar tones:

The inability of Spanish America to govern itself lies in the fact that . . . some want to govern a distinctive group of peoples, with their own singular and violent temperament, by laws inherited from four centuries of practiced freedom in the United States and from nineteen centuries of monarchy in

France. But a decree of Hamilton will not stop the torture of
the plainsman and a phrase of Liegés will not stop the coagu-
lated blood of the Indian race. . . . Government must be born of
a nation. Its spirit must be that of the nation. The form of
government must be reconciled with the constitution of the
nation.

These remarks are quoted in a book by Carlos Rangel,
with this concluding comment:

The tyrants of Latin America have been . . . the revenge of
historical and sociological reality on the attempt to construct
"airy republics" on the foundations inherited from the
Spanish Empire. This attempt was all the more senseless because a bloody war of emancipation intervened between the
shipwreck of the empire and the birth of independent republics. Bolívar describes that episode . . . in terms of his own
country: "The living have disappeared. The works of man, the
houses of God, and even the fields have experienced the formidable devastation. . . . The fields irrigated with the sweat of
three hundred years have been parched by a fatal combination
of earthquakes and crimes. Where is Caracas? . . . Caracas does
not exist."[8]

A century after Bolívar delivered this message, Víctor
Andrés Belaúnde, an expert on Peru, had this to say:

The national reality has not been recognized or deeply sensed.
Our universities . . . have gone astray by failing to study the
reality of Peru, by wholeheartedly accepting fashionable scientific doctrines without seeking their verification in Peru. . . .
Our sickness is mainly psychic. Our national ideals have
been on the wrong track, inspired by an imitative culture
rather than illuminated by a direct look at the world around
us. They have not had the pulse and sap of reality. . . .
All our enthusiasm and applause has been reserved for
high-sounding or aggressive phrases. . . . Underneath this
bawling runs only spiteful backbiting and tendentious-
ness. . . . We do not express hates which, even though censura-
ble, are the product of a lofty passion. What we have are lifeless
grudges that betray the absence of an ideal of our own. . . .

And if our political reality has been poor, our political ideology has been even worse.[9]

The Bolivian scholar Carlos Medinacelli writes:

If we want to be a nation we must first learn to think and express ourselves in accord with the national genius, the soul of the race, the territorial spirit, because this is our own. And it does not matter how mestizo or indigenous this spirit is. Let us be genuine! Let us dare to be Bolivians![10]

Various other analysts have expressed similar sentiments. Though not the only cause, this excessive imitativeness has been one of the causes of the ongoing instability in Latin America. Since our ideas and institutions lack real roots, they bend like reeds before the first gust of wind.

The European nations and their institutions have deep roots. They are the fruit of years and even centuries of experience. Their people rarely act precipitately, or allow themselves to be dazzled by the first ripple from outside. We, on the contrary, are quick to take in any novelty. Without analyzing it at all, we try to take it in at once and put it into practice.

Recent events in Europe confirm the difference between those nations and ours. France, for example, was jolted by student unrest in 1968. Soon, however, calm was restored to the universities. After careful discussion and consideration, certain reform measures were passed and the academic centers returned to their strict discipline of study, investigation, and work. In West Germany terrorist groups found themselves repudiated by the whole country: by labor unions, the courts, and the diet. They were dealt with quickly and energetically. The case is the same in the United States. Though it has enjoyed independence for only two centuries, it possesses a political maturity and poise that cannot easily be upset. The university unrest and racial agitation of a few years ago, which were very like that which took place in other countries, as well as the drama of Watergate and the defeat in Vietnam, were not only controlled and absorbed, but actually superseded. In all these countries, then, rebellious and violent factions can make noise and raise a ruckus, but the socio-political body is more solid. It takes more than that to topple it.

In Latin America we are quick to take in any "imported merchandise." That label alone is enough to open the gates and win our acceptance. Many foreign ideas are accepted here with the same dazzled enthusiasm that the indigenous inhabitants of America welcomed the conquistadors' trinkets. It would be absurd to think that ideological currents do not influence or inspire our way of life. Ideologies have never known frontiers. Conceptions of the human being and society, whether on the philosophical, religious, or politico-social plane, are universal and impossible to ignore. The problem, however, arises when we precipitously import concrete formulas and try to apply them through laws and institutions that are alien to the character, resources, and degree of evolution of our people.

Just because these ideas exist elsewhere, there are those who want to implement them without reflection. This is even more serious when they are the product of unrealistic lucubrations rejected even in their countries of origin.

This immaturity has been the underlying cause of many of our failures. It has allowed the world to form a very negative image of many of our republics, and of course of their dictatorships.

The Changing Physiognomy of Latin America

The factors discussed above do a lot to explain the trajectory of our South American nations. Yet, despite the political problems and the ongoing social dualism, some countries in Latin America have made real social and economic progress in recent decades. That has to be pointed out also.

Starting in the thirties, some real industrial development began to take place, thanks to a protectionist policy and increased government activity in favor of production and social progress in some areas. Both factors helped to create an expanded middle-class sector of increasing scope and importance. In almost every country the administrative and technical personnel in that class have acquired preponderant influence. At the same time, of course, a strong and well organized industrial proletariat has appeared on the scene.

International organizations and university centers have also been active in providing extensive, up-to-date information on what is happening in each country. Now we can count on an increasingly refined analysis of the factors at work, of their causes and effects. This provides us with a broader and more satisfactory overview of our nations as a whole, and with trained cadres who have a more comprehensive understanding of the problems.

Other changes are taking place in Latin America at the same time. Some are the outcome of worldwide phenomena, whose effects can readily be seen here. Education has clearly made strides. Illiteracy has decreased rapidly, and it has disappeared in some areas. University centers, some of indisputably high quality, are proliferating. Communication is broad and widespread, thanks in part to the uniformity of language.

One of the most characteristic features has been the rapid growth of urbanization. It has been so rapid that it has given rise to many megalopolises, radiant with energy and enterprise. They undoubtedly symbolize a new phase in the life of our nations. Once again, however, social dualism makes its presence felt. On the one hand the urban conglomerates contain districts that are ultramodern and neighborhoods that are as luxurious and well off as any in the world. On the other hand they are ringed by marginal districts filled with poverty and families who have recently come from rural areas. Two examples are São Paulo with eleven million inhabitants and Mexico City with twelve million. In one year the latter city took in 500,000 peasants. These people are not just abandoning the land. They are giving up a whole way of life, the societal relations with which they had been familiar, to plunge into a dehumanized underworld where they lack even the bare necessities. This is a very specific kind of reality, now found throughout the continent.

Secularization is another factor which has affected the political and social physiognomy of Latin America. In all our countries the Catholic church was traditionally linked up with the state. This linkage created problems and controversies that occasioned many bitter fights in the past. The interference of the state in the church helped to corrupt the latter; and the interference of the church in the state and partisan politics was extremely disrupting and negative.

In Latin American nations the church found itself allied with political parties that were almost always conservative. Linked with those who opposed all innovation, it had to fend off the attacks of parties who favored liberalism. This was the normal situation, which to some extent had been inherited from the colonial era. Thus the church seemed to be a focal point of opposition to change and a bosom ally of those who were socially and economically powerful.

The transformation that has taken place in the church in recent decades is thus of the utmost importance. It now advocates a social philosophy that calls for the most thoroughgoing changes. Not only must the attitude of individual Christians change. They must also assume their obligations toward the larger community and work for a new order in which social justice will be a central objective.

In various countries, then, the church has been moving away from its earlier involvements, from the tutelage of the state and the dominant classes. It has revived the full gospel message, and in many countries it has become the chief defender of human rights and of the poor in particular. This represents a substantial change in one of the bases of the traditional order. At the same time, curiously enough, other religious denominations have arrived on the scene and increased the number of their adherents. Yet this has not led to conflicts, as often happened in the past. Instead understanding seems to grow daily between the various religious creeds.

On the economic front there has been a notable advance in development in recent years. The same holds true for the construction and improvement of the physical infrastructures, particularly in the case of transportation and the mass communications media. The growth of the industrial sector has been quick, even explosive in some countries. Its contribution to the national product has overtaken that of agriculture. The *hacienda* and the farm product are no longer the most important social or economic unit. The integration of our economies on the regional and continental level has continued to proceed slowly, despite obstacles and the irresoluteness or downright hostility of our governments.

There has been a growth in education. Universities have spread and expanded. Parties and ideological currents of different stripes have been actively at work. And the labor movement has intensified where it has been allowed to exist and express itself. All these factors have bolstered the tendency toward greater participation of the people and greater notice of their presence. New legislation has also worked toward these same objectives.

Another major fact in altering the physiognomy of Latin America has been the ongoing conquest of the hinterlands. There can be no doubt that we have been a seashore civilization up to now. By contrast the winning of the West was one of the dominant features of nineteenth-century life in the United States. It truly was the march of people in search of new lands and new

horizons. In South America this project is still of recent
vintage. Backed principally by the state, it is well under
way by now. Brazil is the most obvious case. Gradually
we are making our way into the interior, discovering
and in a sense "conquering" a wide expanse of almost
uninhabited territory.

So we find ourselves faced with a wide range of new
problems and a host of great possibilities: explosive
population growth; masses of young people, since half of
the population is under twenty-five years of age; and
unlimited reserves of water, land, woods, and minerals
of every sort. Our human resources are not any less.
When they have been given the opportunity, they have
shown that our people possess unsuspected reserves of
intelligence and creative ability.

In this connection it is worth pointing out that notable
figures have appeared in our political life, despite all the
convulsions going on. Their deeds light up the various
epochs of our history. In the midst of their struggles
they have not given way to despair. They have kept the
conviction that we can arrive at real progress only
through a free, democratic system.

Thus a cursory examination of the evidence leads us
to the inescapable conclusion that the balance sheet for
the period is not wholly negative. There has been a wide
variety of intellectual creations and social and economic
changes. The life of our peoples has advanced on many
fronts. This is evident in the history of each of our nations, which could not be explained otherwise. It is evident on the plane of political conduct. It is also evident in
the contribution of the daily increasing number of professionals, university students, researchers, technicians, painters, poets, novelists, musicians, artists, and
artisans.

And yet, despite all these favorable indices, our nations have not taken off in any clear and definitive way.
They live under the threat of instability, which is the
result of causes already noted and ever new circum-

stances. Every day the gap grows wider between them and the more developed countries. Their life is corroded by the presence of injustices. The clearest witness to this is the fact that more than one hundred million people, one-third of the population, live on the margin of life in dire poverty. The disproportion between what has been achieved and what might be achieved is certainly well known and obvious. It is not a supposition. It is a fact that cannot be disputed or hidden. One journal in the United States had this to say in discussing Mexico, a country whose political setup is seemingly stable:

A small percentage of the population is comfortably rich; a large portion is lamentably poor. Lavish playgrounds for international jet-setters exist almost side by side with villages still run by caciques, or chieftains, who seem to belong to the last century. The nation has long suffered from lack of education, poor communications, inefficient bureaucracy, and outright political corruption—all of which, in spite of the wealth of its natural resources, have kept Mexico from being as great or as well developed as it ought to be.[11]

São Paulo, the driving force behind Brazilian development, is another good example. It almost seems to stand in direct contrast to the plight of the Northeast region of Brazil as a whole. Basing its estimate on official documents, the university of that city has concluded that "the economic growth of greater São Paulo is directly bound up with a deterioration in the living conditions of vast segments of the population."

These descriptions are valid for almost all of our countries. They reflect the dualism that exists in societies not yet well integrated. There is a sharp contrast between the rich and the poor, between what has been achieved and remains unachieved as yet.

No false optimism can be allowed to stand in the way of the truth. Only by heeding the truth will we be able to appreciate the dimensions of the task ahead of us. To put it briefly once more, we find marked advances on the one hand, terrible steps backward on the other; blatant opulence on the one hand, intolerable poverty on the other. This produces social and economic pressures that cannot be concealed, that continue to grow slowly but surely.

The picture of Latin America, then, begins to emerge clearly. It is a land full of contrasts and full of life; a kind of world "middle class" that looks more like a "poor relative." It has no real personality and influence of its own, though it pains one to admit that. It bears the wounds of terrible social differences and political instability. Its conduct and leadership does not seem to measure up to its rich human potential, its physical and geographical size, and its incalculable possibilities.

This is the general context in which Latin America now confronts one of its most critical junctures in history. The way in which our nations channeled their life after independence has cost them a century or more of convulsions, alternate anarchy and dictatorship, internal warfare, and external boundary disputes.

The question today is whether they will recognize the lessons of experience and show more clear-sightedness or keep on repeating the mistakes of the past.

Today it is not a matter of starting life over again and inaugurating new republics. Today's challenges are more complicated, varied, and widespread. The decisions to be made and the lives to be led by people cannot be subjected to the limited decision of small minorities. Nor is the existence of democracies enough, if that simply means the sporadic involvement of the people in elections. The right to participate in elections was undoubtedly a major achievement. But that does not necessarily mean that all the people will have a real share in the life of their countries, in the decision-making process and the sharing of societal life. The act of voting, however decisive it may be in a democracy, is only sporadic and occasional. By contrast the real centers of power, be they financial, economic, political, or informational, are permanent and ongoing.

The phenomenon of extreme poverty exacerbates the picture. When this poverty touches broad sectors of the populace, and when they are keenly aware of it, it can only intensify bitterness, resistance, and rebelliousness.

Then there are various groups who are active pressure groups. Unknown even quite recently, they are active centers of pressure and power that exceed the boundaries of the older structures. They would include labor leaders, professional groups, technobureaucrats, intellectuals, radicalized sectors of the middle class, and young people in particular.

Finally, Latin America does not confront solely a new internal reality. It also confronts an external reality that grows more important every day. To that we shall turn our attention now.

10

The World Outside

Interdependence and Dependence

Now we will consider the foreign policy front. In the eyes of much of the outside world Latin America is a kind of backyard naturally linked with the United States. Cuba, the exception, does not really alter that basic image because its importance rests to a great extent on the support it gets from another superpower.

In a world that has now become one interconnected planet, Latin America has established relations with every continent; but its relationship with the United States is a decisive element at present and will remain so in the future. The whole subject is one of great importance and has always aroused much debate. Fifty years ago, in 1928, Haya de la Torre incisively described the situation. In some respects his words are even truer today:

From a strictly economic standpoint the two Anglo-Saxon empires that dominate our nations now balance each other. Because of more favorable objective circumstances and an elastic interpretation of the Monroe Doctrine, however, Yankee imperialism now clearly reigns supreme in most Indo-American States....

Thus the alleged autonomy of our republics is only apparent.

They are really economic vassals of the great empires. It is these that control our production, quote prices on our money, fix prices for our products, manage our finances . . . and regulate our pay scales. . . .

And since those who govern the economy also rule politics, the imperialism that controls the circulatory system of our nations also directly or indirectly dominates its nervous system.[1]

In this statement we have the basic outline of what has come to be called the "theory of dependence." It was formulated explicitly in the sixties by such people as Cardoso and Faletto,[2] and it has exerted considerable influence on many Latin American sociologists and economists as well as European and North American writers. It has been further elaborated and applied in different ways. Its basic premise is that external economic factors exert such an essential influence on our countries that they determine our political, social, and cultural life. As one discussion puts it:

The two economies are structurally different. The center is integrated and diversified; the periphery is specialized, one-sidedly developed, or dualistically divided by the existence of highly developed technologies alongside very backward ones. The rhythm of importation by the center is based on the rhythm of its own internal development; that of the periphery depends on its exports to the center.[3]

Thus the center, which has a life of its own, considerably conditions the life of the periphery. The development of the latter always stands in a disadvantageous position with relation to the former, whether it be a question of the value of its basic products or of their differences in technical progress. In addition, the nations of the center occasionally transfer their own crises to those of the periphery. Some proponents of this theory go so far as to say that dependence has been so deeply "internalized" that it radically distorts the socio-economic structures of the dependent countries.

For Cardoso and Faletto underdevelopment arose when "the expansion of commercial and industrial capital brought together into one market economies that showed different degrees of differentiation in their production system and had therefore come to occupy different places in the global structure of the capitalist system."[4] Thus the two economies have different positions and functions within the same international economic structure of production and distribution; and their structural relationship entails the domination of one by the other, not only economically but politically.

The value of this new kind of analysis lies in its attempt to see the stages of Latin American development in historical perspective. This is done by examining the potentialities and the obstacles that face Latin America in the light of its dependence, paying due attention to the changing situation of the nation-states in the region.

In the case of Marxist analysts, the theory of "dependence" is linked with the Leninist definition of imperialism: "a form of international domination in which certain countries exercise control over other regions of the world. Through the exercise of this domination they obtain certain benefits of an economic nature."[5]

This is not the only interpretation of dependence, however. In recent years many contrasting views have arisen. Some deny that dependent countries have any possibility of spontaneous development; others, such as Helio Jaguaribe, Celso Furtado, and F. H. Cardoso, offer more nuanced views. All tend to feel that in their foreign relations our dependent countries also are influenced by particular and varied domestic situations.

Whatever be the basic postulates of those who deal with this theme, their explicit or implicit intention is to provoke political action that will lead to the liberation of Latin America. Without such "liberation," it is felt, Latin America can never reach its full development. Such a general formulation can hardly be questioned. Every regime declares that it is looking for independence, and the existence of "dependence" can hardly be denied. Moreover, we are living in an increasingly dependent world, and foreign powers do exert pressure on governments. Sectional influences also affect cultural, social, economic, and political mechanisms. But these influences and pressures operate differently on the social groups within different countries. Their impact on development is conditioned by historical factors that link the foreign and domestic factors at work in each particular nation of Latin America.

It is inevitable that the more powerful centers will have a preponderant influence on developing countries. That was the case in the past, and it will be the case in the near future. It applies equally to the capitalist world, the socialist world, and any other that may arise. It is something akin to the law of gravity.

It is not enough to recognize the fact of dependence and the impact of the great powers. We must move on to find ways to diminish this dependence and acquire autonomous forms of growth within an increasingly interdependent world. For interdependence affects not only the peripheral countries but also the great industrialized centers themselves, however great their potential may be.

The theory of "dependence" undoubtedly helps us to gain a better understanding of the whole Latin American process. But it has been found to be of very limited usefulness when used politically as an instrument for liberative action on our continent. We must know the detailed mechanisms of dependent relations in the various fields where they show up. Only in that way can we overcome the obstacles to development on the practical front. We want to know the key areas and the kinds of cultural, political, social, and economic action that would foster autonomy.

It obviously makes no sense at all to answer with the one word "revolution." That would only bring us back to the problems and political options that we have been considering in previous chapters.

In fact the theory of "dependence" is somewhat confused with the struggle against imperialism. Those who go to extremes with the theory end up mouthing slogans. They provoke new alienations without eliminating the old ones. Such is the case with Theotonio Dos Santos and André Gunder Frank, who try to explain the whole history of Latin America and its underdevelopment in terms of that theory.

Dependence certainly is a reality, but one can hardly posit that it exists only between capitalist nations and the underdeveloped nations. The relation of dependence exists between the whole industrialized Northern hemisphere and the underdeveloped Southern hemisphere. The Marxist theoreticians of "dependence" neglect to tell us that the Northern hemisphere includes not only the United States and Western Europe but also the U.S.S.R.

Worldwide capitalism does not constitute the whole economic picture. It interacts positively and negatively with its industrialized counterparts in the socialist world. The overall economic system now takes in more than capitalism alone. For the socialist countries of the Northern hemisphere take part in it and often share its assumptions, even though they may repudiate it verbally.

Foreign Relations

That is why it is very important for us to define the parameters of our relationship with the outside world. Within the overall picture it is obvious that the relationship of our nations with the United States is of critical importance. It is the epicenter of power in economic relations for much of the capitalist and socialist world, and therefore for Latin America.

To many the United States is the enemy, the source of all ills. There is a propensity here to assume always that the blame lies with the outside world. It is our way of finding excuses for internal inefficiency and failure.

So long as the objective conditions of the present economic relationships between the United States and the Latin American countries do not change, mere complaining will not help matters. It is not enough for intelligent people to provide keen analyses of reality. That is important, of course, but it is still more important not to distort the truth by indulging in exaggeration and unreal fancies.

Paradoxically enough, in the eyes of other Latin Americans the United States is the bulwark of freedom, the guarantee against communism. As the nation of capitalism par excellence, it is an object of unreserved admiration; it offers the only formula for economic progress and the hope of financial aid. Those who see the United States in this light tend to belong to the upper classes. They are not interested in the open democracy and the social mobility to be found in the United States. What intrigues and entices them is the material consumption of goods that we are not capable of producing. From some distance behind they want to take over a form of capitalism based on closed strata and narrow markets, one from which the masses in Latin America are excluded. Monopolies and oligopolies would prevail in such a setup.

Under such a system there is no spirit of creative effort and adventure combined with broad-based competence. Nor are there any controlling counterweights as is the case in the United States, where labor organizations exist and the public authorities are subject to ongoing criticism and control by an alert public opinion.

In our nations, then, some foster hatred while others surrender to outside influence. Meanwhile the democracy in North America has always ended up allying itself with the privileged groups or dictatorships in Latin America that have little to do with democracy.

We cannot prescind from a relationship with the United States. That would be a mistake, to say the least, because there are many good reasons for such a relationship. One need only look at a map to see that. But we will always end up in frustration and dependence if we try to build that relationship on the basis of a splintered, self-negating Latin America.

In our relations with the United States our rulers have always gone from one extreme to the other without ever finding a proper balance. Their conduct has been erratic, with occasional verbal displays of independence. They have been unable to get together and form their own version of what would constitute a policy of authentic cooperation. Those who can only criticize or advocate the "strategy of hate" sacrifice the real interests of our nations to dogmatism or the play of world powers. Those who surrender to others cannot be friends or allies; they can be only employees or commissioned agents. They use their opportunities to do their own business. They are not concerned about the plight of our peoples.

Our peoples do not hate the people of the United States. On the contrary, they feel admiration for their high standard of living and their technological feats. At times we can be harshly critical, but we are not enemies, for our peoples have a large fund of good common sense. They are not easily carried away by shibboleths. But they notice that it is often the privileged minorities of Latin America who make contact with the United States. And so they cannot help but think of the old adage about birds of a feather. Despite their good will toward the United States, and despite the many cooperative foundations that offer real, disinterested aid, they cannot help but feel growing sentiments of opposition and mistrust.

Impressed by what was going on in his native Mexico and other countries, Daniel Cosio Villegas pointed this out some time ago: "Throughout Latin America we can see the traces of United States violence and assault. These were perpetrated by its rulers and its capitalist enterprises. . . . Like a pool of stagnant water, a thick layer of suspicion and mistrust vis-à-vis the United States encrusts the surface of Spanish America."[6]

In varying degrees this mistrust does exist because the United States has not lived up to the principles in its fundamental charter when it has dealt with its neighbors to the south. It has committed many mistakes in Latin America. Today many of its own leaders are beginning to recognize and acknowledge that fact. Unfortunately the international image of a country is not shaped by its people but by those who make its policy or engage in business.

It is essential to the future of Latin America that we discover our true role in foreign politics; and our first task is to decide what the nature of our relationship to the United States should be. Perhaps the fundamental lesson here is that our lack of cohesion and other factors have turned us into basically passive entities. We have not shown any real initiative in our dealings with an active United States.

This has been the case for a long time. Ever since the Monroe Doctrine was promulgated, the initiative has been with the United States. There was Theodore Roosevelt's policy of the "big stick." Then there was F. D. Roosevelt's "good neighbor" policy, a felicitous phrase and a fine intention with meager content and results. Then came the now defunct Alliance for Progress. This was perhaps the most serious effort by the United States on both the theoretical and practical level to formulate a program of cooperation; but it was followed by silence and a void.

Now what has been the response of Latin America to each of these initiatives? Has it rejected them, modified them, or actively cooperated in the task of creating a satisfactory formula? Whatever criticism might be made, the Alliance for Progress was an important proposal. Unfortunately its philosophy and its implementation were not the result of joint elaboration. Perhaps that is why there was no real response to it here, neither a positive nor a critical one. The truth is that most governments in Latin America saw it as a way of getting loans to overcome the crisis of the moment and stay in power. This passivity is the basic fact about Latin America, even though there have been such things as the Drago Doctrine, the Estrada Doctrine, and Kubitschek's "Panamerican Operation." It accentuates our dependence, and it cannot be resolved by simply complaining or letting resentment build up. We must be able to project our own vision of the proper way to carry on a relationship with the United States. Then we must be able to implement our vision in a sustained, coherent policy that is shared jointly by all. Without these ingredients we cannot have fair and effective treatment from the United States. In the past and present century, particularly since the 1940s, the struggle for autonomy and politico-economic independence has been linked up with projects for continental integration. This was the view propounded by Haya de la Torre and many others. Such integration, it is felt, can overcome many of the causes of dependence. That is the thinking that underlies such proposals as the Latin American Free Trade Association and the Andean Pact, which links the Pacific nations of Latin America. The stagnation of the former and the slow progress of the latter have frustrated these efforts.

Failure to promote effective unification makes it difficult for our peoples to act in concert and to develop a common policy vis-à-vis the United States. This failure is due to the fact that many of our governments have no solid base of support and live from day to day, preferring bilateral relations with the United States that will provide them with the aid they need to survive.

All this is very convenient for the rulers and business interests of the United States. When it is a matter of an agreement being worked out between one very powerful party and weak, divided republics, it is clear to see whose interests will be served best. It obviously suits certain business interests. They can do business with governments who will open the door wide to them and also ensure silence and order.

In all these respects Latin America is far behind other countries. As I noted earlier, that includes the nations of Asia and Africa. These seem to have a better defined personality of their own and act with greater independence. They can even define their own objectives more clearly than we can. Their Pan-Asian or Pan-African organizations do not have their headquarters in Washington, London, or Paris. Their international institutions for political policy and economic defense are truly their own. They get more respect from Washington than our own Organization of American States does, for the North American character tends to have more respect for those who know how to defend their own interests than for passive adulators.

For all these reasons we must fashion a policy that looks to our own interests. No power is innately generous. If we are to formulate such a policy in vigorous terms, we must reject submissiveness and its counterpart, strategic hatred; they lead nowhere.

Latin America must be capable of acting in concert. It must define what it regards as its legitimate interests and explain how it sees them. It must specify its goals and the proper ways to reach them. Only then will we see the beginning of a real dialogue that can lead to real cooperation; for such dialogue and cooperation cannot exist if one party is utterly dependent on the other.

This is where the true advantage lies for our nations. It is also where the true advantage of the United States lies, though this is not understood by the flatterers and others who seek personal advantage. In today's world the United States needs friends and allies. If we do not take this course, then the differences will grow greater every day. Mistrust and rancor will intensify below the surface. So will the other negative factors which some would like to use to their own advantage.

I should add here that there have been encouraging signs in recent months. Pronouncements by government officials and various reports[7] hint at a promising change in outlook with regard to relations between North America and Latin America. As one group of Latin American representatives has noted: "One positive sign is the way in which the new administration in Washington has stressed the need to thoroughly reexamine hemispheric relationships on the basis of new concepts. These diverge sharply from older forms which no longer have any meaning."[8]

The very recognition that these relationships must be reshaped now suggests closer attention to the problem that is preoccupying our countries. This recognition is particularly significant because it is not just the result of a government statement. It is part of a broader and deeper trend that takes in the press, Congress, universities, and labor unions.

Of course all acknowledge that hemispheric relationships must be considered in terms of the whole international context; that it is necessary to maintain relations with all states, whatever form of government they may embody.

But the important point is that they now recognize that the people of Latin America have taken conscious note of the fact that they have often been victims of coercion and exploitation from North America. They now want to see friendship between our peoples as well as ties between governments. They also realize that this cannot be achieved if in practice the United States continues to appear as the ally of those who advocate alienating social systems and those who propose developmental models that are at odd with the needs and nature of our people. For such systems and models have always ended up favoring a small minority to the detriment of the vast majority.

People are also putting forth the proposition that our nations must seek integral development. That would include "economic and social growth, political participation, and respect of individual freedom and human rights."[9]

The gradual shaping of this new policy is obviously a step forward in itself. But it cannot remain at the level of high moral judgments or mere statements. It must be translated into forms that will make it operative.

Thus a great opportunity has presented itself. A positive result, of course, will depend on several essential factors. First of all the new tendency, which is evident in intellectual circles, among liberals, and in public opinion, must be able to sustain a course of pragmatic and resolute action in the face of older tendencies that have always regarded Latin America as a "dependent" zone. The second essential factor is the stance of the Latin American people themselves. The forces here opposing social reform and respect for human rights are still strong. They condemn any and all innovation and try to enshrine their view in "authoritarian" regimes. Such regimes are socially regressive, mistrustful of change, and look everywhere for allies to defend their policy of "security." Undoubtedly they have allies in North America, who may be close-mouthed but who are nevertheless effective.

To repeat it once again, the problem cannot be solved simply through action on the governmental level. The attitude of young people, universities, and varied social forces is most important. They must promote a new kind of relationship between the two hemispheres, a relationship grounded on democracy within each nation and within the whole international community. Full solidarity between our peoples must be based on a fairer balance between North America and Latin America.

Of course I have hardly exhausted the issue in question. We no longer live in the relatively closed world of President Monroe. It is an open world with much contact between peoples of the East and the West, of the North and the South. States have learned to engage in dialogue, no matter what their form of government or ideological affiliation may be. The relationship between the two Americas, as was noted, must now be viewed in this world context where the United States is a major power and Latin America must increase its political and economic ties every day.

Latin America could hardly fail to have such ties with Europe. The two regions are linked by strong bonds, quite aside from the interests and weight of the Common Market. Latin America can hardly ignore the socialist world and other continents. Communication with them grows more active every day, particularly through organizations of people in the Third World.

Each of the other regions of the earth has worldwide relations and relations of a more special type. The African nations, as an example, have such ties with Europe, as the Lomé Accords show. These were signed by the nine countries of the European Community, forty-three African states, and the Bahamas, Barbados, Jamaica, and Trinidad and Tobago. They reached agreement on formulas that are far more advanced than those we find in the Inter-American system. Relations of a more special type are exemplified by those existing among the nations who belong to the Warsaw Pact. Those nations are certainly far more "dependent" than any others. Similar relations exist among the Arab nations. These accords and special relations offer concrete, positive opportunities to the parties involved.

By contrast Latin America seems to grow more isolated every day, and little is to be gained from simply bemoaning that fact.

Some say that we are weak because we are dependent. I think we could just as well say that our dependence stems from our weakness, from our inability to organize ourselves as an integrated unit within the overall world picture. Every day we find that the large regional power blocs have more weight within that context.

Some can entertain the illusion of localized success within the superstructure of international diplomacy. In each country the communications media reflect the worldwide scene in terms of the public for whom they operate. Each country, and of course the government in power, is depicted as the epicenter of diplomatic life. Some are past masters of the art of indulging in petty vanities about themselves and their countries. In the end, however, this cunning fools no one. The truth is that the nations of Latin America are way behind, even with respect to the Third World. Others have taken the initiative.

These are the plain and obvious facts that give us a better fix on the situation of our continent vis-à-vis the "outside" world. They should help us to figure out ways to enhance our own true interests and achieve a greater measure of real independence. It is in this context that we must see the relationship of our continent with the rest of the world, and particularly the relationship between the two Americas.

There is an urgent need for our nations to act in concert. One need only look at the United Nations to see the importance of international blocs. We must act in unison vis-à-vis the United States and vis-à-vis the rest of the world. No matter how many meetings and get-togethers we hold, we will not have any positive influence or negotiating power if we are divided. With the possible exception of Brazil, no nation in Latin America can afford to deceive itself on this point. The absence of real power of this sort is not a romantic assertion. It is a reality for which our nations pay dearly in real life.

11

New Dimensions

The Recurring Cycle

An examination of the situation in general terms helps us better to fix the parameters of current events in Latin America. It is obvious that the problems of today cannot be dissociated from past history, social structures, and the dominant ideas of Latin America. They are the historical constants that give us the reason behind many events.

Each nation does have its own personality, and there are marked differences between one Latin American country and another. Yet today they tend more to reveal certain general characteristics shared by all. Their economic and social processes are similar, as one can gather from reading some of the informational reports put out by international organizations. And once again we are seeing a recurrence, in somewhat different form, of the old cycle of democracy, anarchy, and dictatorship.

And so certain questions, hinted at already, surround the present-day life of our nations. Will they commit the same old mistakes under different names? Or will they have the maturity and self-awareness to recognize and overcome the causes that have prompted these mistakes in the past and now threaten to frustrate their future progress? In other words, will they prove capable of conceiving a viable historical project that will suit their real nature and legitimate needs and resolve their current problems, or will they continue to fluctuate from one extreme to the other as unstably as they have in the past?

These are not light questions, because right now in Latin America most of the democratic governments have toppled. Rarely have we witnessed the simultaneous establishment of so many dictatorships governing so many of our people.

There are new dimensions to the problems that confront the democratic system in Latin America today. For most of our past history the alternatives were rather simple: dictatorship on the one hand versus freedom and parliament on the other. There are considerable differences in that recurring cycle today. Once upon a time the conflicts were restricted to a thin upper crust of society; the common people were little more than a chorus, and usually they were not even heard. Today the collapse of some regimes upsets the whole social body. The incoming rulers must confront societies that are much more complex, economies whose problems are far more difficult to handle, social organizations and political parties with greater extension, and even revolutionary forces that use violence and terror as their weapons. Some currents question the very foundations of the system and propose other means to scale the heights of power. In their eyes no basic consensus exists; democratic government is not an ideal to be reached but an obstacle to be removed at the start.

Here it is worth noting what happened with the Socialist party in Chile. It was dominated by people calling for a revolutionary approach and a break with democracy. In 1965 its convention upheld those theses. In 1967 it ratified the following conclusions:

Our strategy rejects the electoral approach as a means for achieving our objective: the takeover of power. Revolutionary violence is inevitable and legitimate. It is necessary because of the armed, repressive character of classist states. . . .

It constitutes the only way to the takeover of political and economic power and its subsequent defense and reinforcement. Only by destroying the bureaucratic and military apparatus of the bourgeois state can we consolidate the socialist revolution. . . .

Peaceful and legal forms of struggle (through elections, fight for rights, ideological debate, etc.) do not in themselves lead to power. The Socialist party regards them as limited tools for action bound up with the political past. That leads us to armed struggle.

Such was the position of a party that had representatives in parliament, that would have a man from its ranks elected president in 1970, and that would be the axis of a government in which it not only maintained but intensified these opinions.

This blatantly frontal assault on the democratic system was not the only one. Other no less daring assaults were launched by activist minorities and various social sectors. They voiced their disdain for what they called "formal democracy." To them freedom was a delusion, elections a masquerade, and legality a bourgeois farce that ought not be respected. Those who proposed to move forward within that structure were labelled "reformists," a term of contempt for people who were traitors to the revolution because they did not opt for massive, total change at once.

If experience can teach us anything, it should make us reflect on the actual results of those formulations.

"Populism" has had equally catastrophic results in many of our countries. It confuses democracy with a great banquet marked by indiscriminate distribution of the goodies. The fact is that developing nations are those which call most urgently for sacrifice in order to create the goods they lack. Some governments have succumbed to a permanent state of agitation. It cannot affect the causes of the negative factors that weigh down upon the people. It leads to the weakening of authority. Instead of leading, those in power attempt to maintain themselves by appealing to passion; they lack substance and consistency.

The results of such a course are clear enough: runaway inflation, anarchy, and a generalized inability to work and lead. In all these phenomena, it should be pointed out, we can see the consequences of social dualism. A marginalized mass does not take cognizance of its responsibilities and is easy prey to any adventure or extreme.

From another standpoint we can see that a new form of "imitativeness" has appeared. The older Herodianism of the privileged classes now becomes an ideological imitativeness. Any foreign recipe is adopted without the least reflection. One moment it is Maoism. Another it is some philosophy, along the lines of Marcuse, that preaches violence. While these currents have had some fleeting notoriety in European intellectual circles, they have not taken hold among government or party leaders. In Europe some circles read these ideas with curiosity. Here some have tried to apply them. And all this goes hand-in-hand with a complete lack of realism, so complete in fact that more than a half-dozen avowedly revolutionary and populist governments have toppled amid the complete indifference of the very masses they sought to arouse. If they had had real roots in their nations, that could not have happened.

Herein lies the source of a certain kind of sociopolitical illusion in which we have indulged. For some reason we have thought that a nation can shape or reshape itself by magic, without having to solve its basic problems and to invest the necessary talent and energy required. We have frequently thought that we could correct everything by trading in one government for another, though they were at times different only in name. We have even gone so far as to think that all we had to do for success was to dictate new laws or to resort to the infallible expedient of applying exotic systems or promulgating a new Constitution.

All this is reflected in a fact over which one does not know whether to laugh or to cry. In the course of a century and a half more than 190 constitutions have been drawn up in Latin America, and there are probably a few new ones on the drawing board by now.

The more revolutions, the more constitutions. Each regime has thought that it could remedy the existing ills and write its names into the history books by simply drawing up a new constitution. Usually these have been copies of the latest model fabricated elsewhere, or else mosaic combinations of various models. Up to 1973, Chile was an exception to this trend. The country with the greatest political continuity, it contributed only two constitutions in 140 years. Uruguay can be mentioned as another example during the present century.

Those who fear reform and democracy anxiously follow these developments. They are masters at detecting their errors and winning power back from those who so docilely open the way for them.

These and other causes offer at least a partial explanation for the antidemocratic and antihistorical regression of our peoples. It has even happened to nations that were exemplary exceptions to this trend in the past: e.g., Chile and Uruguay.

Concrete Examples

The case of Chile deserves a special analysis of its own. Despite its small population and widely dispersed territory, Chile has had special resonance in the world. This was not due solely to carefully planned and directed propaganda. This would have had no success if people had not known that it had one of the oldest representative democracies in modern history. Chile indeed had earned a name and a reputation that even the Chileans themselves were incapable of appreciating fully.

In 1970 the theory was propounded that our democracy was formal and misleading, that it had to be changed entirely. There were countless declarations by the leaders of the ruling faction and their coalition parties. The legal approach was inadequate, they maintained. Violence and armed conflict was the only way. These concepts were given increasing stress and implementation as time went on. Various political factions took part in this view. Some, such as the Revolutionary Left Movement (MIR), carried it to extremes. In other factions it was difficult to tell where the basic view ended and sheer terrorist violence began. Other factions went to various other extremes.

Their basic mistake lay in the fact that they did not realize that our democracy was not so formal or abstract at all. Through a long period of development, and at an accelerated pace in more recent years, it was showing all signs of being a very real democracy indeed.

For more than 140 years a fully functioning parliament had existed in Chile. The chief executive, the congress, and municipal officials were elected in recent decades by all men and women over eighteen years of age, and the ballot was secret. There was clearly freedom of the press, radio, and TV. The Communist party itself owned newspapers, periodicals, radio stations, and publishing houses. So did the Socialist party, the Christian Democrats, and the political right.

Social legislation had become broad and widespread. Labor unions took in all segments of the working class, and it had real influence on the life of the nation. So did professional organizations, cooperative movements, and neighborhood communities. Elementary, high school, and college education was free. The student population had reached 98 percent. Illiteracy was being reduced to minimal levels. The universities enjoyed complete autonomy. A state health system covered all wage-earners and much of the middle class. Our progressive tax system had become a real tool for distributing income.

Agrarian reform was moving ahead surely and efficiently without hindering agriculture or the livestock industry; between 1965 and 1970 those fields of endeavor showed an annual growth higher than it had been in decades. The recovery of two basic resources, saltpeter and copper, began in 1965 when the state acquired more than 50 percent of foreign capital. Other basic areas already belonged to the state: electricity, petroleum, steel, coal, and a major portion of the means of transportation. The growth of production was steady even if not spectacular. Every day economic and social investment was on the increase. All this was well under way before the year 1970.

Yet this progress was judged in superficial, thoughtless, dogmatic terms. Against a democracy that had reached this stage of development people pronounced revolutionary shibboleths that did not correspond with reality. Without considering the real possibilities or the resources at hand, various sectors were threatened and our precious political, social, and economic capital was squandered. In less than three years the situation turned into chaos. In this laboratory, you might say, we can see where people are led by the uncontrolled abuse of freedom, by mutual fears and hatred, by an immature emphasis on ideology, and by the breakdown of the whole foundation for living together in society. In the end the country was plunged into a blind alley. Today we still suffer the consequences of those mistakes. Many now lament the ruin of all the things they were unwilling to continue and protect.

In Chile we have learned some lessons in fact rather than mere theory. Those who play with the destiny of a nation and advocate revolution, violence, and complete change immediately sacrifice freedom on the altar of their utopia. They thus support those who sacrifice freedom in the name of "order" and "security."

Another example worth mentioning here is Argentina, a clear case of what might be called political underdevelopment. It is a racially homogeneous country of

European composition. It had the highest real per capita income in Latin America. Its cultural, educational, and health indices were excellent. It had rich and extensive farmlands and its industrial development was sound. Destined to be a prime example of a state in good shape, it had everything except political sense.

I am leaving aside here the first decades of its life as an independent nation and the interminable quarrels between centrists and federalists. For about the past fifty years, however, it has gone from crisis to crisis, from one dictatorship to the next. For the most part this has all happened amid the indifference of the people. They have been impressed only by that curious and contradictory phenomenon known as Peronism, whose leader did such incredible things. For almost twenty years he dominated the political life of the nation from exile. Then he returned, again became president, and designated his wife to succeed him, though there was no sound precedent for such a decision.

Argentina's soil is so rich and its industry so active that it could be expected to move right to the top. All it had to do was avoid colossal political mistakes and provide a certain measure of peace and security. Yet it has been shaken periodically by contradictions and violence. Its life has been one of permanent, ongoing crisis; and the vast majority of the people have not yet found stable, organized expression.

We do well to remember how different things went for Argentina in the middle of the last century when it was governed by such fine leaders as Mitre and Sarmiento and by politicians of high intellectual caliber such as Alberdi. Then it showed a creative impulse that aroused general admiration.

So we could say that the collapse of democracy in Argentina was precipitated by political disintegration, the lack of authority, and violence.

Looking at these two examples among many possible others, we must recognize that the activity of enemies and military coups were not the main cause for the collapse of these democratic governments. It was due mainly to the errors and mistakes of their rulers or to the absence of sound common sense and conviction in its leaders at every level: in the executive and legislative branch, in the political parties, in the labor unions, and in the mass media. If people are unwilling to recognize this fact and correct their errors accordingly, then the future of these countries is not very promising.

To say it once again, this continuing evasion of one's own share of responsibility is at the root of many disasters. Blame is always laid at someone else's doorstep. It is the fault of the imperialists, or the coup leaders, or the enemy of the moment.

·Now such enemies do exist. There is no doubt about that. The point is that they could have been resisted and beaten hardily if we had not committed so many irreparable mistakes. The political catastrophes that have befallen our people suggest that there is some underlying ill that affects every person and group. We must realize that the germ of real revitalization can be found in each of us. Otherwise it will be difficult to generate a democracy that is more solidly rooted in truth and solid responsibility.

The Cuban Response

Our analysis would be incomplete if we did not include the case of Cuba, which is singular in more than one respect. It achieved its independence almost a century later than the rest of Latin America, and this was accomplished with the decisive intervention of the United States in the Spanish American War (1898). This event marked its birth as a republic. It also represented a degree of U.S. interference unknown by Latin American countries, perhaps with the exception of those in Central America and the Caribbean. The Platt Amendment epitomizes the situation, for it gave a foreign country a constitutional veto power.

Cuba's economy—agriculture, mining, and industry —was entirely dominated by U.S. interests. Its proximity to the United States turned it into a great tourist center. A vast organization of all possible vices was placed at the disposal of the tourist who wanted to "get to know" Latin America. All this profoundly warped the life of the nation.

Its rulers were almost always tyrants, surrounded by unimaginable corruption and backed by foreign interests. Thus the fall of the dictatorship in 1958 and the advent of a new regime was greeted with almost unanimous exultation.

This is not the place to examine the results of a government in existence for almost twenty years. My purpose is to see what sort of society is offered by this communist enclave in the Americas. I propose to examine it objectively, considering the political model it represents. Now there is a solid basis for doing this. We can consider the new Constitution, which was approved practically unanimously by the Cuban people.

Life teaches us that it is very difficult to find criteria on which all will agree in a family, among friends, or in any human institution. It remains a mystery, then, that in some regimes millions of people or an entire country express uniform opinions.

It is also worth noting the timing of this ratification. The new Constitution took effect on February 24, 1976, the eve of a Communist Party Congress in Moscow. At that meeting in Moscow there surfaced the ideological differences that are now to be found in Eurocommunism and other nations within the Soviet orbit. The French and Italian Communist parties were already talking about democracy and pluralism. They were speaking out against the dictatorship of the proletariat as a basic thesis. And people knew of the criticisms being made by Soviet dissidents, the cream of the U.S.S.R.'s intelligentsia.

At such a juncture in history we can learn a great deal by seeing how the form and institutional structure of a communist state is conceived when that state is not geographically close to the U.S.S.R. For in such a case there is no validity to arguments based on strategic security, the kind used by some to justify the U.S.S.R.'s intervention in Hungary and Czechoslovakia. The answer in this case is astonishingly clear. We can have no doubts as to where this conception of the person and the state leads and as to how total and seamless it is. Here are some passages from the Cuban Constitution:

Article Five. The Communist Party of Cuba—the organized Marxist-Leninist vanguard of the laboring class—is the superior guiding force of society and the state, organizing and guiding the common effort toward the lofty goals of constructing socialism and moving toward a communist society.

Article Six. Under the direction of the Party, the Union of Communist Youth, the organization of avant-garde young people, works to prepare its members to be future communist militants and helps to educate the future generations in the ideals of communism. . . .

In its educational policy it adheres to the following principles:

a. Its educational and cultural policy is grounded in the scientific conception of the world laid down and elaborated by Marxist-Leninism;

b. Education is a function of the state. Hence the teaching centers are state-owned;

c. It seeks to foster the communist formation of future generations and to prepare young children, teenagers, and adults for social life;

d. Artistic creation is free so long as its content is not contrary to the revolution. The forms of artistic expression are free.

The education of children and young people in the communist spirit is the duty of society as a whole.

Freedom of speech and the press is accorded citizens in conformity with the ends of communist society. . . .

The material conditions for their exercise are given by the fact that the press, radio, TV, and other mass media are owned by the state or society. In no case can they be an object of private ownership. This ensures that they will exclusively serve the working people and the interests of society. . . .

The law shall regulate the exercise of these freedoms.

The Socialist state, which bases its activity and educates its people on the scientific materialistic conception of the universe, recognizes and guarantees freedom of conscience, the right of each individual to profess whatever religious belief and to practice whatever cult . . . within the bounds of law.

The law shall regulate the activities of religious institutions.

It is illegal and punishable to oppose faith or religious belief to the revolution, to education, to the carrying out of one's duty to work, to defending the homeland with arms, to reverencing its symbols, or with whatever else is established by the Constitution.

Obviously this Constitution contains a series of principles that are to be found in other constitutions. But an examination of the provisions cited above enables us to characterize the regime it sets up with a fair amount of objectivity. One is forced to say that rarely does one find clearer indications of a monolithic, nonpluralistic society. It consecrates the absolute and monopolistic permanence of a single party and a single doctrine. Indeed the latter is turned into a dogma.

As is the case in other Constitutions, this one specifies that the law will regulate the exercise of certain functions. But we must remember that in this case the law emanates from organisms composed of members from only one party. There can be no dissent from its viewpoint. The basic picture, then, is clear beyond any reasonable doubt.

In that society there can be only one line of political thinking. Adolescents are to be educated only in the one offical doctrine of Marxist-Leninism; and their guides must be associated with the one existing party. All the information and communications media are the property of the state. One might claim that they are socially owned, but this is a fiction because society is ruled by a single party and a single ideology. The same holds true for the alleged religious freedom. There is no doubt who calls the tune when and if religion stands opposed to the revolution. What worth does a religious entity have if it cannot impart any teaching of its own? It is illegal to challenge the official brand of education, and this education is based on a philosophy that denies, both in theory and practice, any truth other than the legally permitted one.

The Constitution also recognizes Cuba's "right and international duty to help those who are attacked and those who are fighting for their liberation." This clearly suggests that it has the right to intervene whenever, wherever, and in whatever way it deems necessary. Cuba's activity in Africa is already an open fact.

An interesting intellectual exercise would be to imagine what would happen if a Constitution with similar articles but of different inspiration were promulgated in another country: e.g., by the Democratic Action party in Venezuela, by the Liberal party in Colombia, by the Christian Democrats in Italy, or by the Social Democrats in West Germany. Undoubtedly there would be a hue and cry around the world, lamenting the death of democracy in those nations. All the "libertarians" on the left and the right would raise their voices in condemnation.

The Cuban case, as I indicated earlier, takes on relevance in the light of the historical circumstances in which its Constitution was promulgated. Far from having merely local significance, it is a clear example for the whole world. Thanks to it, we can judge the terms of the alternative that concerns us.

Organized Violence

I have dealt with these concrete examples, however briefly, because they shed a great deal of light on the magnitude of the situation confronting millions of human beings in Latin America. But there is another factor that is one of the determining influences on what is going on now and what may happen in the future. It is the phenomenon of violence and of what is called "subversion." It clearly is affecting the whole world, but we are particularly interested in its manifestations here in Latin America.

Violence, of course, is not a completely new fact in human society. Some now justify their actions by claiming that nothing similar has ever happened in history before and that a normal government regime just cannot handle it. That is simply not true, and we do well to remember some history.

Barbara Tuchman has written about the wave of violence that swept over Europe and the United States in the period just before the start of World War I. Victims of assassination included: President Carnot of France in 1894; Prime Minister Cánovas of Spain in 1897; Empress Isabella of Austria in 1898; King Humberto of Italy in 1900; President McKinley of the United States in 1901; and Prime Minister Canalejas of Spain in 1912. None of these victims could be called a tyrant: "Their deaths were the gestures of desperate or deluded men to call attention to the Anarchist idea. . . . They came from the warrens of the poor, where hunger and dirt were king."[1]

Those who committed these acts and other similar ones were enemies of private property, as Proudhon pointed out. They saw it as the root of all ills. This school of action was opposed to that of Marx and his followers, which maintained that the revolution would come from the industrial proletariat once it was organized and trained for the job.

Bakunin, who favored violence, had a different view. He believed "that revolution could explode in one of the more economically backward countries—Italy, Spain, or Russia—where the workers, though untrained, unorganized, and illiterate, with no understanding of their own wants, would be ready to rise because they had nothing to lose."[2]

A wave of violence reached its culmination in Chicago in August 1886. It caused the death of many policemen and demonstrators. The chief figures involved were hanged, including August Spier, the publisher of a periodical whose summons to vengeance would today be dramatized by explosives.

The Anarchist wave spread throughout Europe. Bombs went off in cafés, killing peaceable citizens. Two were thrown into the famous Teatro Liceo in Barcelona in 1893, killing many in the audience. Another was thrown into the French Chamber of Deputies in the same year. Bombs were planted in railway stations, police headquarters, and restaurants. They went off in Italy, particularly in Milan; in Spain, especially in Cataluña and Andalucía; in Switzerland; and in Germany. No country on the continent was safe from the threat. One English visitor to Paris described the atmosphere, and Barbara Tuchman sums it all up:

The city, wrote an English visitor, was "absolutely paralyzed" with fear. The upper classes "lived again as if in the days of the Commune. They dared not go to the theaters, to restaurants, to the fashionable shops in the rue de la Paix or to ride in the Bois where anarchists were suspected behind every tree." People exchanged terrible rumors: The anarchists had mined the churches, poured prussic acid in the city's reservoirs, were hiding beneath the seats of horsecabs ready to spring out upon passengers and rob them. Troops were assembled in the suburbs ready to march, tourists took flight, the hotels were empty, busses ran without passengers, theaters and museums were barricaded.[3]

The European press demanded collective measures to combat anarchism. In the United States President Theodore Roosevelt had this to say about it: "Anarchism is a crime against the whole human race and all mankind should band against the anarchist." Congress should "exclude absolutely all persons who are known to be believers in anarchistic principles or members of anarchistic societies."[4]

Anarchism had well known theorists of its own: Bakunin, Prince Kropotkin, Malatesta, and Reclus.

Others had considerable intellectual influence on the direction of the labor movement. And the chief exponent of violence as a revolutionary method was Georges Sorel.

Yet their influence waned and their disciples ceased to be a threat. By the start of this century terrorism still survived only in Spain and Russia. The fact is that the preaching of violence and the execution of deeds designed to upset things did not mobilize the masses. They failed, even though some fanatics committed spectacular assassinations with cold-blooded resolution.

Without renouncing their own nature, the democracies withstood these assaults and were not toppled. But the chief cause for the failure of these assaults lay in anarchism's own intrinsic aversion to organization. That is why it was replaced by communism, which took over worldwide direction of the revolutionary movement after 1917.

The reappearance, or better, the recrudescence of this sort of violence today bears some of the hallmarks of anarchism. Though some of the techniques are new, it is likely to suffer the same fate. But we must not be too quick to equate the new with the old, even though they share certain traits. Today the phenomenon has spread to the whole world. Urban and rural guerrilla warfare seeks to destroy the existing structures of society and replace them with others. But now iron-clad organization and rule by dictatorship have replaced the utopian view of earlier anarchism. There is also more consistency and greater organization to the use of tactics and available resources.

This activity has had an undeniable impact on Latin America. By a curious paradox it has been fully successful in its fight against democratic governments, not to install its own proponents in power but to bring about dictatorial governments that put an end to them.

Violence will not lead to any authentic solution now any more than it has in the past. It has never had deep roots among the people because their age-old wisdom tells them that it is a blind alley and a course leading to disaster. Hatred cannot bring about peace, much less freedom and justice.

Some claim that this coercive approach is justified because an "institutionalized violence" exists as well. Such violence certainly does exist. But as we shall see further on, one does not justify the other. We cannot use violence to put an end to violence. Jorge Millas has offered some profound comments on this matter:

Contrary to what Marcuse would have us believe, hate seems to be an indispensable element of violence in the eyes of many revolutionaries. That is not surprising. As good technicians of this diabolical instrument, they think about its effectiveness first and foremost. Hate also suits the aim of negating its victims and masking their martydom. Thus every vestige of compassion and every inconvenient feeling of guilt is curbed while the whole standard of ethical values is changed. . . .

Let us hear the words of someone who knew more than anything about these matters and who was elevated to sainthood by many through this ambiguous ethics: "Hate is an element in our combat. . . . Implacable hatred of our enemy pushes us above and beyond the material limitations of humans and transforms us into a select, effective, cold killing machine." Is that an unpublished text of Mussolini's son jubilantly describing the bombardment of hapless Ethiopian blacks? No, it is a well known comment of Che Guevara. There is a difference, of course. The fascist displays inhuman esthetic enjoyment over the martyrdom of other human beings . . . while the guerrilla leader proposes "committed" human hatred and a utilitarian indifference to his enemy's death. But the ethical result is one and the same: the suffering of some human beings no longer counts for other human beings in circumstances which the latter have the right to define and choose.

Whether the aim is the morbid delight of a soul corrupted by power or the attainment of political ends by a hate-driven soul, we arrive at the same terrible result: in the name of values that human beings themselves have created, other concrete human beings are turned into something that can be transcended. This being the case, it is easy enough to see how we can fashion a politics of violence, a lyrical poetry of violence, and even a metaphysics of violence. It is as if the victims did not exist at all, or existed but completely lacked importance, or were important only as abstract factors in abstract historical equations.[5]

This emphasis in favor of violence is not an isolated one; it is a basic principle that is constantly upheld. Thus there exists an ideology of violence. "It is not simply force in general, but a way of using it. Force is to be employed without any concern for the victim and without any suprapersonal norms governing the responsibility of the sacrificing priest."[6]

This ideology and line of action is upheld only by minority groups in Latin America. It has no real roots among the people. But its importance is much greater because these few can threaten many. They can inspire insecurity and terror in societies that are ready, at the first sign of danger, to throw overboard a legally governed state for the sake of their own protection.

The Counter-Response

This new system of revolutionary warfare has evoked a counter-response from other sectors. Against such an attack, they do not see democracy as an effective response; or else they see this as their chance to replace democracy with a system that will defend their interests or fulfill their yearnings for power.

To ensure the success of this antirevolutionary action, a whole theoretical and practical methodology has been worked out. This strategy for antisubversive combat is bound up with what is called the "doctrine of national security." Here there is no need to trace its historical origins or to consider its initiators and interpreters. There are numerous books, studies, and documents that deal with the theme, though only in exceptional cases have they reached the general public.[7]

One of the expositors of this new strategy has this to say about the basic situation:

Since the end of World War II a new kind of warfare has been created.... Today's warfare is the clash of a series of systems—political, economic, psychological, and military—which tend to overthrow existing governments and replace them with others....

We must realize at the start that in this modern warfare we are not fighting against an armed band that appears in a given territory but against a dangerous and well armed clandestine organization whose chief aim is to impose its will on the population. Victory will come only when we manage to destroy that organization.

In the period when our enemy is still making preparations and has not yet initiated open hostilities, this enemy usually finds protection under the standard of a legally established political party.[8]

In order to destroy the enemy, which simply must be done according to the advocates of this view, strict control over the masses becomes a necessity. Society must be organized as a pyramid, and intelligence-gathering services must be developed and implemented. It is necessary to discover who the enemy is, and for this a large string of informants is needed: "We must create numerous training centers where militants willing to cooperate can receive the necessary instruction. Once trained and molded, these agents will be distributed wherever there is a great deal of human activity: e.g., factories, offices, schools, and public places. But our best agent will be provided by the enemy itself, if we know how to do things right."[9]

Every method, including torture and murder, becomes legitimate in this view so long as it does help to destroy the enemy's organization. Once we find ourselves in a war, everything is permitted. The dissenter now becomes an opponent, a traitor. Not only the actual enemy but also all those who refuse to take part in the fight are pursued and attacked: "Particularly dangerous are those who propose a return to legal ways or who defend 'human rights,' because they pose difficulties to the police and intelligence services. Dissent is also unacceptable because that will embroil us in polemics with the people, and such polemics only benefit our enemies."[10]

This conception of community life and government organization considers ends and means in terms of a declared war. The notion of "national security" becomes all-embracing. Everything else is redefined in terms of it, including the values on which the society is based. All means, including the Armed Forces, are to be used to eliminate subversion and all political expression that does not emanate from the regime. The governing regime is the sole center of power.

This is the doctrine officially held and implemented by various government rulers on our continent. In reality we are confronted with a total kind of warfare, they maintain. Those who run the forces of government should have total control over the whole activity of the country. Everything is part of the total strategy, the chief aim of which is national security and the destruction of the enemy.

Here once again we run into the curious twist of Latin American imitativeness. These theories were elaborated by people who cannot put them into practice in their own nations. Here in Latin America some regimes are taking over these very theories and implementing them.

Neither in the United States nor in any nation of Europe is this theory determining the organization of the government or the role of the Armed Forces. The latter continue to be professional cadres of the highest caliber and position, but they are carefully confined within the limits of the juridical structure. Their role is to guarantee internal and external security, but not to become involved in political activities that vitiate their purpose and dissipate their effectiveness.

There was the famous warning given by President Eisenhower, all the more relevant because he himself had been a military man. Indeed he had been in command of the Allied Forces that triumphed in one of the largest wars ever fought. He said that an undue growth of the influence of the military-industrial complex would become a potential danger. It could lead to disaster, jeopardizing the freedom and democratic procedures of the people of the United States.

So in the United States a man from the ranks of the military does not hesitate to issue such a warning. What is the situation here in Latin America? Dictatorial regimes link up with those sectors that have the most economic and social power. They implement policies that do not so much block further change as cause retrogression, thereby jeopardizing fundamental changes. Besides, these mistaken policies affect essential institutions that support these regimes.

None of the great nations under democratic rule fail to show respect for the Armed Forces and their proper role. That is why the latter have a high level of efficiency that continues to grow. But these nations refuse to let the military become a political power, much less subjugate the life of the nation to the demands of a domestic "war" against all subversives and dissenters. Yet that is precisely the notion that has been imported here and implemented in concrete practice.

The frontiers of this war are ideological rather than geographical, as was pointed out above. The central aim is to cross this invisible barrier and pinpoint the enemy physically. That is why the intelligence apparatus acquires such a fatal priority. Its agents must discover the "enemy" so no one and nothing can be allowed to hinder their mission. Laws and rights are subtle obstacles in which the enemy takes refuge. Every organization outside the official ones is suspect, and hence must be subjected to surveillance and control. The tribunals of justice are annulled by some emergency system of juridical control. To protect the rights of the accused would be to aid and abet the enemy.

Since the Armed Forces constitute the main, if not the only, support of the government, their members are subject to even more rigorous control than the citizenry at large. Flaws and disagreements in that group would be more dangerous than in any other. Under such circumstances both the government and the Armed Forces become virtual prisoners of the mutual vigilance on which they depend. "Conscientization" of those forces also becomes a necessity because they possess important information and they must evaluate its content to write up reports.

The intelligence-gathering organisms, the organisms charged with vigilance and security, take on a life of their own and professional deformation inevitably occurs. This problem is compounded by the fact that a certain type of human being is more suited to this task and that the organisms must constantly try to justify their existence by discovering new threats to the government they serve. Their chiefs can stress certain dangers, distort any incident, stir or influence those in power, and thus justify the elimination of a given individual or organization. Mistakes do not matter because security takes precedence over the lives of individuals, even as it does in a nation at war.

Thus the two extremes of violence end up looking more and more alike. Both share the same apocalyptic vision: putting an end to the enemy. Everything is permitted because the end result will be a paradise where happiness reigns among human beings.

Envisioning such a world, these groups feed on mutual hatred and terror. They vitiate the notion of security and turn society into a battleground between irreconcilable forces. But domestic warfare to eradicate ideas, even going so far as the elimination of people, cannot be a viable, rational formula for any nation. National security is certainly an important function of the state. No nation and no government can dispense with that responsibility, whatever its orientation may be. But it is something very different when national security becomes the axis of the whole political construct. Then what we get is a regimented society in which self-appointed elites or castes define the objectives and life-style of every individual as well as the nation as a whole.

Understood correctly, democracy and national security are not antagonistic. Rather, a strong democracy is the best guarantee that the Armed Forces, as permanent entities, will be efficient and well supported. Everyone, including themselves, will have an interest in defending the overall institutional system.

Security is essential if a national community is to exist and achieve its aims. But it is perverse to convert this condition into an objective, particularly into the supreme and ultimate objective to which everything else must submit.

Security is an essential condition, not only for living in society but also for making progress in a world that is now fraught with snares and complexity. But it is quite wrong to start from the opposite direction, to suppress individual guarantees and the exercise of rights so that people may live in a seeming tranquility.

In more primitive groups, when human societies were beginning to organize, security was intimately bound up with the force and power needed to ensure survival. To go back to that point of departure, however, would be to deny the whole process of history. That process has been nothing else but the struggle of human beings against any power or authority that seeks to absorb them or to disregard their inalienable rights as humans.

12

The Present Political Task

Repression: No Solution

The ideas of the famous German strategist Karl von Clausewitz underlie both the doctrine of revolutionary warfare and the doctrine of counterinsurgency warfare. Trotsky and Lenin, the latter in particular, adopted these ideas in their own line of action. Lenin used them to make the postulates of Marxism truly operational, and Mao Tse-tung also used them in developing his notion of revolutionary warfare.

Mao noted that in China war was the principal form of struggle and the army the chief form of organization: "All Communists must realize that power is born from the gun. Our basic principle is that the Party commands the gun. We will never allow the gun to command the Party." Here Communists prove to be the most orthodox followers of the Prussian general, for von Clausewitz maintained that "the only possible course is the subordination of the military point of view to the political point of view."[1]

The opposite extreme has its own version of the same basic viewpoint. Entertaining the same conception of war, it implements it at home in the name of national security. The difference lies in the fact that it subordinates politics to the military point of view and allows the latter to control the former. This is what is happening in various Latin American countries today. The people of those nations are forced to face a permanent state of domestic warfare.

The situation is not always presented in such naked terms. Despite the various shadings and distinctions, however, it is the basic fact of life in a large portion of Latin America. Indeed it is so much a fact that democracy has disappeared from most of our republics. It has been imprisoned between two irreconcilable factions and the aggravating effects of terrorism, counterinsurgency, and violence of all sorts. Once again we are faced with the infernal cycle that dominated our continent at the start of the last century. The clash of extremist forces gives rise to instability, hatred, and vengeance.

The concept of security, properly conceived and understood, is not meant to shackle human beings. It is meant to guarantee them the exercise and enjoyment of their rights, to prevent others from violating them.

The whole work of civilization has aimed at creating the juridical norms that would allow for rational coexistence in society. Roman law and Christian teaching contributed greatly to this effort. Though often violated or ignored, those truths have been proclaimed for centuries. If we ignore them now, there will be no limit to sheer force and we can readily imagine where the human race will end up. Indeed we have seen enough already in the recent history of Latin America.

The task of politics is to achieve a consensus, affirm a sense of solidarity, and try to involve all the members of the community in the quest for the common good. Some might say that this goal is not always achieved, or that those who practice politics undermine the effort. That is true enough. Yet it is also true that laws are not always obeyed either. Who would want to abandon them as the guiding norms of social life for that reason? Further progress in the right direction depends on the goals that are set and the means that are employed to reach them.

As was pointed out many years ago, politics is a failure if it can triumph only through the use of force. It must create a consensus and a legitimacy that will make coercion and violence unnecessary. The aim of war, on the other hand, is the destruction of the enemy. Friends versus foe is the only relationship it allows.[2] Arriagada puts it this way: "In politics nothing is more dangerous than risky generalizations. If one fails to recognize the disparate interests existing in a society, if one fails to note the interplay of conflicting points of view at every level, then one is simply ruling out the possibility of legitimacy and consensus. One has started down the road to a government based on terrorism and dictatorship."[3]

Attempts have been made to fashion a society on the basis of divisiveness and irreconcilable factionalism. Attempts have been made to resolve the inevitable conflicts to be found in society by eradicating all the various forms of ideological expression. But these attempts have always ended in total failure.

The lesson of history in this case is clear and unmistakable. India and Spain offer recent examples. For forty years or more efforts were made in Spain to silence every current of political thought except the official one. Despite the economic development that took place during that period, we can now clearly see the end result of that effort. The simplistic way of looking at problems and the reliance on an omnipotent authority may seem to be successful in the short run; but in the long run peace cannot be established by the use of force alone.

A New Juncture in History

Our peoples are at a new stage in their history. It is no less difficult than the phase that confronted them when they had won political independence. At that time they had to face up to the changes required for economic development, social integration, technological progress, and continued existence in a worldwide economic and political order posing ever new challenges. Today they find themselves challenged by those who want only revolution on the one hand and those who want to crush revolution at any price on the other hand.

If either of these extremes triumphs, there will be no future for our people; nor will there be any peace or justice. The fatal dilemma of violence versus counter-insurgency is a somewhat different version of an older process of historical frustration. Our nations will be the victims of this process unless the majority of the people impose their control over the two forms of violence, be it institutionalized or not, and thus find a rational approach to liberation.

The majority of which I speak here does really exist. Despite surface appearances to the contrary, the common people possess a strong feel for reality, an authentically democratic spirit, and a love of freedom that remains undiminished by mistakes and failures. These traits continue to survive and deepen even in an atmosphere of imposed silence. The majority of the people know that democracy, with all its limitations and failings, guarantees them some minimum of dignity and respect. They know that it offers them the prospect of exercising their rights, learning how to use them, and progressing in real self-expression.

Unfortunately most of our Latin American nations have confronted a worsening situation in recent years. Pressure from extremists has become more intense and widespread, and the techniques of subversion and repression have grown more refined. The ideological assault on democracy from one extreme or the other has also intensified. The truth is that never has human freedom been more in jeopardy, and never has it been so downtrodden in many areas.

The indubitable fact remains: the vast majority of our people reject violence and dictatorship, and they refuse to be the tool of one or another extreme. They wish to live in freedom, not in insecurity or anarchy, for they have an innate sense of solidarity.

This majority is large and imposing at every level of society. It is particularly strong among the laboring class, peasants, the middle classes and, despite certain estimates to the contrary, young people. Up to now these sectors have refused to give their support to subversion and violence. This is an objective fact that can readily be verified. The subversion and violence has been provoked by minority groups, usually of bourgeois origin. The majority of our people have shown that they do not believe in the methods or the objectives that these minorities propose in order to effect social and political change. The common sense of the majority leads them to mistrust wild adventures, for they realize that they themselves will ultimately have to pay a high price without achieving any real positive result.

So true is this that many segments of the ultra-left and the ultra-right are at one in rejecting what they call the electoral approach. Time and again both have failed to win the votes of the people. In this case the figures do not lie. Nor can one maintain that national majorities are supporting the dictatorships now enthroned in Latin America. To keep themselves in power these dictatorships must continue to repress and suppress all the rights of the citizenry that stand in their way.

But we must not make any mistake here. This precious reserve of moral and human force can be dissipated if democratic government does not reflect the legitimate needs and hopes of the people in its proposals and its activities. A vast segment of our people is being crushed under an intolerable burden of injustice, inequality, and misery. Those people want to know right now what concrete steps will lead them out of their present situation. Too slow to act, seemingly incapable of implementing the changes which would correct this inhuman situation, democracy is causing them to lose heart; it is leading them toward skepticism and even despair.

We come back to what I said earlier. Many democracies in Latin America and around the world are becoming the victims, not only of their enemies but also of their own weaknesses and mistakes. We cannot just talk about democracy. Those who believe in it must be able to offer a concrete, up-to-date historical proposal, a modern project that will break the stranglehold of opposing forces and allow our people to make their way out of the abyss in which they now find themselves.

A modern democracy must also engage in a continuing process of improvement designed to uphold and exalt human rights. Without justice there can be no freedom. By the same token freedom—that is, the full exercise of human rights—must serve as the foundation of justice.

Democracy cannot be bland, much less weak. To be legitimate, the authorities must be chosen by the people and must operate within the law. They must also guarantee peace and security in order to establish the basic minimum of social tranquillity that will ensure progress for our peoples.

Our experience of democracy in Latin America provides us with a clear lesson, though unfortunately the periods of flourishing democracy have been all too few. When democratic governments have been in operation, they have produced clear-cut progress. When violence and dictatorship have prevailed, they have led to insoluble conflicts and paralyzing retrogression. In cases such as that of Chile, where democracy was constantly operative for more than a century, this system of government clearly brought material and human development to the nation and its people. Such was the case until the framework of consensus was broken by the factors and forces noted above. Then it became impossible for democracy to endure.

The least bit of reflection forces us to conclude that those who preach total revolution, and of course those who advocate the sinister exercise of violence, are not capable of liberating our peoples at any time. Moreover, dictatorial regimes may bring about order for a time but basically they offer no solution either. They only produce an accumulated store of tension that portends a gloomy future for our nations.

To bemoan the process which has dominated the past is not to provide a solution for the present. That process has hurt all, and all share some measure of responsibility for it. What we must do now is to find some way out of the dilemma in which we find ourselves. The only real way out is to revitalize the foundations of democracy, the principles of humanism in which it finds its inspiration, and to restructure its organisms of action in accordance with the demands of our world in the future.

PART III

SHORING UP THE FOUNDATIONS OF DEMOCRACY

13

Preconditions

Overcoming Fear and Contempt

In Latin America there is an urgent need to bolster democracy in those countries where it still exists and to restore it in those countries where it has already disappeared. Today this means that we must propose a viable "historical project." Such a project would revitalize the foundations of democracy and offer a satisfactory solution to the problems that so deeply affect our nations.

Now if the need to restore democracy is pointed out to those who presently live under "authoritarian" regimes, they are almost unanimous in agreeing with that proposition. But they will immediately add that right now they are afraid to go back to the disorder and anarchy that has been manifest in some democratic governments. Others maintain that communism or terrorism will flourish without the intervention of a "strong arm." Rather than let that happen, they are willing to pay any price. They are even willing to give up all their rights as citizens: the right to express themselves, the right to elect officials or be elected themselves, the right to know the when and why and wherefore of the laws and institutions that are imposed on them, and the right to decide who will formulate or amend such proposals.

Factors other than rational arguments underlie these debates. Some are caught up in self-satisfied egotism; others fear the risks of freedom; still others have an innate distrust of the common people, questioning their ability to think and to participate in an open community. Here again these groups display what has been called "political underdevelopment." At the first sign of danger they are tempted to take refuge in some sort of dictatorship.

At the end of World War II Western Europe offered a dreary spectacle: materially destroyed countries, razed cities, countless dead, millions of prisoners to be exchanged, deep-rooted hates in every nation, famine, and unemployment. In such a situation some people in Latin America would have immediately opted for the establishment of dictatorial regimes. They would have regarded the maintenance of democracy as an aberration. The Europeans, however, not only maintained democratic government but also restored it where it had ceased to exist. So successful was its functioning that in a few short years those nations reached heights of prosperity they had never known before.

Some years later De Gaulle was summoned back to power. He had to face an acute political crisis, which was further aggravated by the Algerian War. He could have taken the easy way out, closing parliament and relying on the Armed Forces to exercise unlimited authority. Though he had to repatriate almost a million French people who were extremely bitter toward him personally, and though he faced more than one attempt on his life, De Gaulle did not stop the functioning of democratic institutions. A part of the army and well known generals stationed in Africa rebelled against the legitimate authorities. Night after night his opponents set off bombs throughout Paris. But De Gaulle stayed within the bounds of the Constitution. He found a way to create new juridical norms and institutions that enabled France to come out of its crisis without destroying democracy. In less than two years he consulted the nation in two plebiscites, affirmed the status of legitimate authority, and maintained respect for freedom even when it went to excess. Thus the Fifth Republic was born and the crisis of decolonialization was resolved.

In France, then, the people were able to confront and solve a delicate political situation. At the start, to be sure, De Gaulle had to rely on the support of the Armed Forces. But he never failed to rely on the people and their consent. He certainly did not take advantage of the critical situation to establish a dictatorial government.

In like manner we cannot underestimate the trials through which democracy in the United States has passed in recent years: a humiliating defeat in the Vietnam war; dissent and confrontation in the universities; the assassination of one president and the resignation of another; violent racial conflicts and the assassination of the most important black leader. Yet all these crises were surmounted.

In similar circumstances the immediate reaction of many rulers in our nations would have been very different. Their spokespeople maintain that the democratic experiences of the United States and Europe cannot be readily transposed to Latin American countries because of their different structures, traditions, and cultural levels. Without saying so outright, they intimate that our peoples are so inferior that they must be ruled by interdict. Why? Because they simply do not know how to use freedom correctly. They suggest that our nations cannot achieve real economic growth without iron-clad discipline, and that only dictatorial regimes can guarantee such discipline. In this respect they are in agreement with Marxist-Leninism and fascism, though they may not realize it. For these, too, require the implementation of rigid authoritarian systems and iron-clad discipline.

Many rulers in Latin America, Asia, and Africa, who invoke differing and even opposed ideologies, are at one in insisting that only one form of government is possible in their countries. They maintain that they must assume full and total power, suppressing every form of opposition. This basic attitude is echoed among some people in the highly developed nations. Their overt or covert feeling is that democracy is a luxury in poor, backward nations.

Such views could not be more depressing. They imply that democracy should be discarded both as a basic principle and as a system. They also imply a denigratory judgment on our people, suggesting that they are so immature and backward that they must live under the tutelage of others.

The truth is very different. It is not correct to say that democracy is a luxury for certain countries. Democracy is vitally required for the social, cultural, and human development of peoples, as well as for their economic growth. Its flaws and defeats do not justify its replacement by a closed, repressive society. This judgment is based on concrete experience and its convincing lessons, as I have tried to show in previous chapters.

The exercise of democracy is not the privilege of only certain nations. Every democratic nation has had to learn how to live out democracy concretely, and in many nations its history is of very recent vintage. Some nations of Europe have been unified for little more than a century. With few exceptions they have experienced upheavals, revolutions, and dictatorships—the Nazi regime and fascism, to mention only two.

Finally, we must not forget that the democratic persuasion has deep roots in Latin America itself. Its nations were brought up in the tradition and culture of the West and Christianity. Those who freed and founded our republics were motivated by the same convictions and philosophy that gave rise to the democracies of Europe and North America. So despite mistakes and vacillation, our peoples have always yearned for a regime based on law and rights. Even when they are reduced to silence, the hope of breathing the air of freedom remains imbedded in their breasts.

Prefiguration of a Democratic System

There is no doubt that it is not easy to restore full democracy once a democratic government ceases to exist. The transition from one state of affairs to another always seems difficult, especially because of the mounting tensions that are not resolved by the de facto government. This is not a matter of theory but of empirical fact.

One of the major obstacles to be overcome is the inertia of those who fear the possible alternative. They refuse to discuss democracy as a technical ideal. Instead they demand that its workings be spelled out in advance down to the last detail. They want to know what its new forms and institutions will be and how they will function. In short, they want a complete and perfectly detailed picture from the very start, an asceptic model that will not entail any risks for themselves. They must have all sorts of guarantees to move out of the state of security and tranquillity in which they assume they are now living. Such demands are typically presented when people are more interested in posing obstacles than offering solutions. It is a mark of hypocrisy or of unconscious feelings. Every proposal concerning a democratic project is examined with the utmost caution and care, and objections will always be found to make sure that they do not have to alter the silence and the vacuum in which they feel they can remain quite comfortably.

Here we might do well to reflect on Revel's report of what happened in Spain in 1975. The Spaniards were wondering about the post-Franco period and speculating on the transition to democracy. A high official of the moribund dictatorship offered this elemental observation of the whole issue: "All our discussions on the nature of democracy are simply a way of stalling its return. A child of ten can understand what democracy is. There can be no doubt as to what its incontestable features are: free elections, universal suffrage, the right of meeting and forming associations, freedom of opinion and expression, and so forth. Their presence or absence indicates the presence or absence of democracy." Revel then goes on to complete the remarks of the official with his own observations: "I would add that when people get entangled in discussions about the essence of democracy, it is evident that they really want to reject it, whether they be leftists or rightists. . . . The evident signs of democracy are clear and unmistakable. One need only suppress one or another feature to see that they all are essential constituents of democracy."

In other words, those who see only the defects of democracy, which are real defects inherent in human nature, are blind to the complications that result when democracy itself is eliminated. Some people in Latin America do demand perfection before democracy is to be restored. They are like people who refuse to treat a festering sore that grows more lethal every day. As time goes on, it becomes more difficult to resolve problems in a rational and peaceable way. Such is what happens when dictatorial regimes remain in power.

The ultimate consequences of a regime based on force or dictatorship are not the only thing worth recalling. We might also consider the consequences of the old colonialist regimes in Africa and Asia. Until recent times they were grounded on the alleged inability of the native populations to govern themselves even if they were liberated. Today we can see that such subjection could not possibly endure. While those colonial regimes lasted, intolerable socio-economic situations accumulated and cultural regression took place. The blame seemed to rest squarely with the government administration. Here again we see how abnormal it is for peoples or nations to be subjugated and oppressed. Sooner or later this sub-human condition must come to an end because it is contrary to all logic.

Looking at the other side of the coin, we are surprised to note that these same people, who are so thorough and implacable in their critical scrutiny of democracy, are curiously calm and "understanding" when it comes to dictatorships. On one occasion a pro-democracy convention was being held in Caracas, Venezuela. Delegates from all over the continent were in attendance. A group of individuals held counter-demonstrations to prevent the convention from proceeding with its agenda. When silence was restored and my turn came to take the rostrum, I pointed out the paradoxical aspect of the Venezuelan demonstration. Under the dictatorship of Pérez Jiménez these same demonstrators displayed no reaction whatsoever; now when there was freedom, they were suddenly brave and aggressive in their criticism.

Here we have one of the great paradoxes in contemporary life. Some people will tolerate no obstacles when democracy holds sway, abusing it to the utmost. Yet these same people will often surrender abjectly to those who not only set limits on their rights but suppress them completely. They want everything right away from a democratic government but they are totally submissive to any regime based on force; and the latter is often the result of irrational and aggressive demands made on democracy by such people. They will give a totalitarian regime all the time it needs or demands, excusing its mistakes and keeping silent about its abuses. And since such regimes have no definite time limit, they can keep inaugurating new plans without anyone computing the cost of their failures. Yet democracy is called to account every single day.

That in itself is not bad, of course, because it forces a democratic government to keep purifying itself. What is inacceptable is the laxity which those same people judge those who seek not to correct democracy but to suppress it altogether.

As we have already noted, it is clear that Latin American democracies have had grave defects, and these defects have sometimes precipitated their downfall. However, the only way to rule out the correction of these mistakes is to prevent the re-establishment of democratic government. The sensible course is not to suppress such governments but to give them a chance to correct their mistakes. No kind of totalitarianism allows for such correction. Still less is it permitted by dictatorships that lack supporting doctrines and seek to establish themselves in power indefinitely instead of looking for a quick return to democracy.

Upholding the Necessary Presence of Humanism

The only sound objective, then, is to shore up democracy where it exists and to restore it where it has disappeared. But of course this proposal will not come true merely by wishing it to be so. We cannot defend democracy simply by trying to maintain a basic conception of what it entails. We must also constantly revitalize and actualize its underlying principles and its structures so that they correspond to the new situations of human life, different communities, and diverse states.

Brzezinski is undoubtedly right when he points out that we are witnessing the birth of a "technetronic era"[1] and goes on to spell out the main features of our new postindustrial society. Clearly the basic outlines of our older industrial society are being altered. And while the process is mainly affecting the more advanced nations at present, it is also having its influence on the lifestyle of all other nations as well.

Given this situation, we must inevitably reform and revitalize the forms in which a democratic society finds expression. For society has been profoundly altered by the new factors and forces conditioning human life on both the individual and the collective level.

Whatever these changes may be, however, democracy cannot dissociate itself from its source of inspiration in humanism. For besides giving it consistency and projection, humanism ensures that it will be more than simply a new technocratic form of living together in society. The medium and the instruments may well change, as Brzezinski points out. But the human being ever remains the center of the process, no matter what the circumstances may be.

As I noted earlier, this humanistic vision is not the exclusive patrimony of one current of thought alone. Still I believe that Christian humanism does have a decisive contribution to make to the historico-cultural reality that is Latin America. It may not be the only possible contribution, but it is an irreplaceable one. And here I am definitely not talking about the religious arena; I am talking about the temporal realm of history and politics.

We know that the peoples of Latin America have been brought up in the teachings and traditions of Christianity. This heritage is engraved on every aspect of their life and culture, on their customs and their juridical institutions. A network of schools, universities, cloisters, and churches stretches from Mexico to the tip of Cape Horn, embodying one of the most impressive human undertakings. To appreciate it fully one need only gaze in admiration at the buildings and works of art that are to be found in countless cities and sites throughout the continent. The skill and genius of native artisans incorporated this Christian inspiration into their work. We find it on doors and gateways, on the facades of monuments, in their rich architectural work, and on their dazzling altars and baroque choirs. Indeed we find it in all their varied artistic work, be it literature, painting, or sculpture. This creative impulse engraved in every aspect of their lives bears witness to a culture that did not destroy the earlier cultures but rather revitalized their forms of expression and then passed them on.

The existence of this tradition is an integral part of our peoples, present during the colonial, independence, and republic periods. We cannot hope to construct anything solid if we propose to ignore it or erase it. To be sure, the tradition has suffered many crises that obscured its lineaments. The confused intermingling of throne and altar and the involvement of the clergy with conservative parties and the landholding classes are facts. Moreover, we must not forget that in the nineteenth century the church engaged in a futile struggle against liberal democracy because the latter advocated the separation of church and state and the laicization of public institutions. Mutual bitterness and fanatic sectarianism were evident on both sides. In the eighteenth century, and even more in the nineteenth century, both the church and the temporal embodiments of Christianity reflected a form of worship and of socio-political action that alienated them from the burgeoning middle classes and the people in general. Though some practices were solidly rooted in the life and being of our societies, the spirit of the gospel could hardly be glimpsed underneath so much plaster and masonry.

But whatever the facts of history may be, it is obvious that the Christian current of thought must be an essential element in the task of fashioning a new form of democratic society in Latin America. That is why the change that took place within Christianity around the middle of this present century is of such importance for the present and the future. It has broken with a whole series of positions adopted over previous centuries and sought to return to its pristine spirit. This change must be considered important and dramatic insofar as Latin America is concerned, for our region contains the largest number of Catholics in the world. More and more this revitalized teaching is being picked up here, and the church is moving away from its ties with power, money, and the established order.

So we find that a current of thought and a tradition with deep roots in the history of our people is striking out on new and promising paths. This opens up a moral and human perspective that we cannot possibly overlook or ignore. Insofar as it is projected into the political arena, however, it cannot take the form of neoclericalism. The human values entailed in its principles will call for a new form of social and economic organization, suitable structures, new techniques, dialogue, alliances, and so forth. In the political arena they are the responsibility of human beings who act on their own initiative and risk without involving religion or the church. They cannot presume to represent the church, much less to embody a particular movement that is the one and only embodiment of human values.

In other words, humanism is not a historical project peculiar to Christians alone. Insofar as it is in line with their thinking, they have the duty to support it. But it is an undertaking for all those who share the values and convictions based on humanism, however much they may differ in their other beliefs and ideas. All those whose basic philosophy is some authentic form of humanism are called upon to find the formulas that will translate its message into a workable system of democracy. They must offer an alternative that peoples and nations can understand and accept as their own.

At this juncture in history the responsibility of such humanists could not be greater. They are not strangers or newcomers in Latin America. They are an integral part of a culture that has deep roots in our nations and has done much to shape them. The absence or weakness of humanist elements could open up a fatal gap through which the forces of dehumanization and totalitarianism might enter. But if they are to be present in a meaningful way, the forces of humanism must revitalize their sources of inspiration and display a creative imagination that measures up to the pressing demands and expectations of the day.

Our people are beginning to learn the lessons of history. They can see now where extremism and its dialectics of hate and violence lead. They are in a position to appreciate fully the conceptual validity of humanism. This is not enough, however, since it only creates more demands. Principles do not act or operate in and of themselves. However reasonable they may be in theory, they prove to be tiresome if they are not translated into realistic and effective action.

This is the great temporal and historical undertaking that must be shouldered by the advocates of humanism. It is their particular task and they can rely only on themselves. They must rely on their own moral energy, their own creativity, and their own ability to think, act, and convince.

Repudiating the Myth of Simplistic Solutions

Today we live in what is obviously a conflict-ridden world. There are new and different conceptions of what national and international society are supposed to be. There are varying interests at work: political, social, economic, regional, and local. In such a situation the first temptation we must avoid is the myth that there is some easy or simple solution. Simplistic solutions are attractive but misleading; they usually deal only with some features of the conflicts we are now facing.

Time and again some magic formula is presented as the solution to our problems: e.g., an emphasis on security and order, or direct democracy, or extra-parliamentary methods, or a classless society. Even highly advanced societies may be enticed by such fabled solutions; but simplistic solutions are dangerous. As Paul Ricoeur points out:

The society of the future will not be simpler than ours today. There will be even more cities and computers. The problems of communication will be even more complex, both on the material level of speech and on the administrative and political level. . . .

We must not minimize the growing potential for violence at the borderline between organized society and a potential "alternative" society. . . .

By "violence" here I do not simply mean what is usually called "subversion." Even more important is the store of intolerance that organized society tends to accumulate: e.g., a lack of understanding of young people, hatred of dissidents, and so forth. . . . Once again we are led into the vicious circle of dissidence and repression.[2]

The growth of the middle classes, for example, was a motive force behind change at one stage of societal development. Today that is generally not the case. This also applies to certain more qualified segments of the industrial proletariat as well. For they are inclined to defend their own advantages against those on the margins of society, against rural peasants and the rest of the lower proletariat.

These examples suggest some of the complications in the problems that must be tackled, and difficult problems have never had simple solutions. Opting for simplistic solutions is one way of evading the issues.

A sample case might make this point clearer. In the face of growing problems one simplistic approach maintains that representative democracy is at the end of its tether and should be replaced with direct democracy. Here is what Ricoeur has to say about that option:

This dreamy notion of direct democracy is also fraught with violence. There is a strong temptation to short-circuit existing juridical procedures and go directly to popular tribunals. There is also a strong temptation to drop the delegation of power and to focus on direct, brutal reclamation of one's rights. To opt for such a course is to forget that political democracy was a slow, laborious achievement and that it is very fragile. It is based on subtle procedures of discourse and on complicated conventions for arbitrating conflicts. One author has pointed out that democracy is a way of proceeding, and that is certainly true. When we forget that point, we succumb to terrible illusions. . . .

By the same token the response of institutional society is as much to be feared. Today the shadow of the police state is lengthening over the old democracies. It is nourished by the aggressively defensive reactions of the middle class, and perhaps of a portion of the working class as well.[3]

Hegel described this basic situation in his *Phenomenology of Spirit.* In analyzing the French terror of 1793, he talked about the "rage for destruction" that takes control over freedom when there are no institutions.

We live in a society where there is a great diversity of opinion and a wide variety of problems to be solved. In many instances there is no prior experience to guide us. In such a situation many people lose confidence in reason as the basis for some accord that will make community life possible:

To the dissidents, existing institutions seem to be an indivisible bloc of power and repression. The authorities are "the establishment," whether we are talking about the banks, the churches, big business, the universities, or politics. So envisioned, society is bound to be associated with a strategy of confrontation and polarization and to wear the face of repression underneath its liberal mask.[4]

The polar counterpart of this view is the temptation to seek order and security at any price:

The individual is concerned to hold on to something that seems to offer solidity and consistency in the midst of the general confusion. . . . Faced with the more or less aggressive nomadism of dissidents, people favoring order picture themselves as settled human beings or as castaways on an island fraught with dangers.[5]

In short, conflict lies at the very base of society and the exercise of power and authority. Increased communication and participation in no way diminishes it; indeed it may intensify it, since more people and groups are involved and interested in issues every day.

The myth of simplistic solutions inevitably generates one-sided views of the matter. For example, some rulers have felt that their great objective was to educate; others have felt that their task was to create suitable physical infrastructures; still others have focused on economic development, and then decided that it must go hand in hand with social progress.

The truth is becoming plainer every day. The fact is that we cannot rule or guide a nation without some overall conception of society, one that takes due account of the interaction and interdependence of the most varied factors: human, ecological, technological, cultural, social, and economic. And all of them are intimately bound up with phenomena that extend beyond given frontiers and limit our sovereignty.

Reaction to all this complexity may give rise to new forms of oversimplification. When a problem is difficult or ambiguous, when it seems beyond government control or threatens certain sectors, then people seek out elemental solutions that disregard the existing conflict or try to eliminate it. They think that repression will silence the clash of different interests, however legitimate they may be. Authoritarianism is attractive because fewer people do any talking; there are no risks, no debates, no differing points of view.

This translates into a pragmatism that has an obsession against political parties, parliaments, and any other form of societal organization. There is danger in their talk, so it is much better if they keep quiet. Thus conflict does not really disappear; it is simply silenced. But it remains alive under the surface of life, silently looking for ways to break out and becoming dangerously explosive.

For many of our peoples the observation of Daniel Cosio Villegas on social change is quite true:

Social changes do not take place daily in a normal, fluid way. Instead they occur every once in awhile, say every twenty or thirty years. But then the change is thorough, total, and radical. It violently tears down laws, institutions, habits, and customs, usually reaching the point of civil war. In short, social change becomes revolution, and at times it reaches the level of a geological cataclysm.[6]

Oversimplification can also be found in those who find it difficult to appreciate and value "procedure." Their thoughts are taken up with direct methods and a direct democracy; but this utopian notion has never stood the test of actual survival. Authority both represents and serves the community; it is the embodiment of organized solidarity. Insofar as it is direct, it leads to tyranny. Why? Because it thereby bypasses the community as an organically expressed entity, and only this can both delegate authority and keep control over it. Every dictatorial and totalitarian regime would like to see an inorganic community confronting an unchecked and uncontrolled authority.

A new vision of Latin America should not cause us to be disheartened over the multiplicity and complexity of the different interests we find. Negotiation is difficult, and the quest for consensus is often exhausting. Lack of maturity and underlying political or ideological factors often make the quest for a solution even more difficult. This is particularly true when people lose sight of concrete, specific objectives and conflict is looked upon as a way of intensifying antagonisms rather than resolving them. The matter becomes all the more complicated when different groups are able to express their opinions about the proposed solutions to the problems confronting them.

How pleasant it is for some people when the law does not require previous discussion, when there is no recourse to parliament, when the interested parties need not be heard, and when the issues are not discussed and analyzed by the information media. All that is required in such a case is a decree framed by anonymous advisers and promulgated by the authorities. If that decree proves to be ill advised, then it is corrected with another decree; but no one is held accountable for the mistake committed or the damage caused.

How easy it is when the press and the other communications media cannot express disagreement, when they can only laud the authorities or express cautious reservations that sound more like praise.

That is what happens in all authoritarian and totalitarian regimes. The only echo we hear then is the product of the herd mentality and the social inertia of people who are weary of thinking for themselves and wish only to be relieved of the burden.

The stance of humanism is the direct opposite of this simplistic primitivism, which is a sheer negation of what the human condition and contemporary society should be.

14

Basic Ingredients

A Strong Democracy

The existing conflicts are rendered more acute in our nations because of inadequate structures and sharp inequalities. It is not enough to take note of these conflicts, however; we must also try to resolve them without having recourse to violence or stripping people of all their rights, including their right to life.

The problem is not only difficult but also fraught with uncertainties. Every effort of human beings to gain dominion over nature or advance the cause of justice and freedom has entailed risks. No essential progress has ever been achieved easily. The effort to keep moving forward must be undertaken at every moment and by each succeeding generation.

The only alternative is an inhuman society. Whatever form it may take, it leads to bondage and the destruction of the values for which human beings have fought since they stepped on the stage of history. We must recognize the difficulty of the task if we are to avoid the dangers of simplistic solutions. The product of ignorance, they only hold up progress or cause retrogression.

By the same token, however, a "historical project" based on respect for human beings and their freedom does not signify a democracy that is helpless in the face of complex problems or a government pictured as a neutral arbiter in the interplay of paralyzing democratic currents. Conflict cannot be evaded or turned into a tactic. Instead it must be fully faced in the ongoing quest for solutions that are solidly grounded in an adequate vision of humanity.

If a democratic society is to exist, one basic condition is the presence of some minimum consensus. That is what Maritain called "the creed of freedom." It must operate within the framework of laws and institutions that give it definition and set limits. Only then can communal life go on without falling into savage claims for the assertion of one's own rights.

A free society arises from a delicate balance between respect and renunciation vis-à-vis one's neighbor. There must be limits. If individuals demand everything they conceive as their own rights, then life in common becomes impossible.

Democracy, then, cannot be left defenseless. There must be certain guiding principles. Consensus and reason do not rule out firm leadership and guidance and the unhesitating defense of those values that allow for the "creed of freedom."

The role of the government, which symbolizes the unity of the nation, must be established clearly. The very complexity of the problems demands that its authority and functions be spelled out precisely. For millennia human beings have lived in agrarian and pastoral societies; now they confront demands and pressures that were scarcely imagined a few years ago.

One of the features of the new situation is the emergence of power centers that propose to go beyond the state and even control it. Some are foreign centers of power: Consider the influence of the great powers and multinational corporations. Others are domestic centers: e.g., financial organisms, communications media, partisan political groups, and labor unions. If the government is weak or defenseless in the face of these pressures, then it will become the prisoner of new currents of feudalism that seek to give priority to their special interest over those of society as a whole. That will lead inevitably to the old cycle of revolt and anarchy.

There will always be a clash of conflicting partisan interests that can bring more or less pressure to bear. The basic *raison d'être* of authority is to take account of all that within the broader framework of the common good. But if the dynamics of power lead governments to absorb more and more areas of activity, then it will begin to suffer from congestion. This will seriously diminish the autonomy of individual persons and intermediary groups who form the social fabric of the nation. The system will inevitably become a threat to freedom and individual rights.

By virtue of the problems they confront today, human societies are slipping into governmental centralism and bureaucracy. In such a situation it is difficult for isolated individuals and intermediary organisms to preserve even a minimum of independence. Paradoxical as it may seem, omnipotent centralized governments always end up serving the interests of a single party, or of the groups and the technocrats who serve as administrators. They do not serve the common welfare, the ordinary human being.

Dictatorial regimes consider it necessary to eliminate every form of organization that might oppose them. They create a social no man's land that enhances their own maneuvering. If that is combined with total control over the economy and communication and the fusion of the executive, legislative, and administrative functions, then democracy becomes a meaningless word.

In the present circumstances it is obvious that societies need strong and effective governments that can act. But that is hardly the same thing as the unlimited exercise of authority over defenseless and helpless social groups. The government must be the apex of an integrated social structure, a structure made up of other organisms that have enough autonomy and vitality to exercise their proper functions. Thus the governing authority should divest itself of tasks that should be taken up by other social and regional groups who know the problems at first hand and must deal with them directly. The role of the government should be to give orientation and direction to the various sectors of the national community, to superintend the interests of the common good, to stand above private interests and narrow pressure groups.

Within such a framework many different talents and initiatives will be given free play. The government will not waste its energy in subordinate conflicts, and it will be able to lead the nation forcefully and effectively toward the national objectives. Such a policy requires the establishment of institutions that will enable rulers to carry out their objectives authoritatively on the basis of a national consensus and a shared solidarity. That is the only way in which democracy can stand strong and firm against assaults from outside forces.

Authority and Freedom

Certain criticisms are frequently lodged against democracies. It is said that they are weak, that they cannot maintain respect for the law in the face of violence, and that they seek to fashion unity in the face of different partisan groups and pressures that never stop trying to step out of bounds.

These accusations are important because there is often some truth in them. Moreover, lack of adequate authority permits abuses and offenses that often have their greatest impact on the average people who want to live in peace. They are willing to make great sacrifices for the security of their children and the guarantee of daily work. People do not want to be oppressed or threatened by violence. As Camus points out, these are traits of human nature. The lowly and the humble enjoy brotherhood and simple happiness, and we should be willing to defend these yearnings.[1]

An alliance between the ruling authority and the people is a recurring phenomenon in history. Toward the end of the Middle Ages there was such an alliance between the monarchy on the one hand and craftsmen on the other to combat oppressive feudal conditions. The latter saw this as a step toward their own liberation.

Some sectors of society stand in most need of seeing society transformed and its defects corrected. It is they who are in most need of a government capable of carrying this process through. If the government fails to do this, then there may be anarchy; or else other power centers and interest groups will dominate the picture, operating against the interests of the most needy. The more serious and urgent problems are, the more firm and effective the authority of the state must be.

Some democratic parties and governments feel reluctant to pronounce the word "authority" and to exercise it. They forget that authority is the "formal" element, i.e., the element that gives specific form to a society. When authority disappears, the way is open to abuse and violence. I would suggest that this abdication is the principal cause for the downfall of many democracies. When government is weak almost to the point of complete paralysis, then everyone wants to issue orders except those who have been entrusted with the task.

Social justice is the first victim of misgovernment, or all the human appetites are unleased at once. As Lacordaire pointed out, when it comes to a contest between the strong and the weak freedom kills while the law redeems. When laws and institutions do not function, then the common welfare is attacked by partisan groups of every sort. The absence of authority tempts individuals and groups to abuse freedom in favor of their own special interests. Maritain has this to say:

In the sacral society of the Middle Ages the heretic was the breaker of religious unity. In a lay society of free men the heretic is the breaker of the "common democratic beliefs and practices"; the one who takes a stand against freedom, or against the basic equality of men, or the dignity and rights of the human person, or the moral power of the law. . . .

People who remember the lessons of history know that a democratic society should not be an unarmed society, which the enemies of liberty may calmly lead to the slaughterhouse in the name of liberty. Precisely because it is a commonwealth of free men, it must defend itself with particular energy against those who, out of principle, refuse to accept, and who even work to destroy, the foundations of common life in such a regime, the foundations of which are freedom and the practical secular faith expressed in the democratic character.[2]

There are individuals who appeal to revolution to paralyze democracies, to reject every economic program, and to wage a persistent battle for unrestrained freedoms. They know that such efforts can unhinge the system and thereby pave the way for the triumph of their revolution. But we must remember that the ultimate victory in such a case may go to either one of two possible extremes.

A democracy without authority cannot survive. Indeed the absence of authority may destroy society itself. In such circumstances people tend to look for someone who can fill the void, for the void frightens them even more than injustice. That often explains why some manage to come to power, replacing those who did not know how to exercise authority within the law.

Today it is worth noting that communism often presents itself more as a political solution than as an economic solution. Those in authority will ensure order, coordinate action between the party, the Armed Forces, and the government bureaucracy, and rule out dissidence and violence. In some countries the communists start by destroying the existing consensus in order to appear as the faction that can guarantee "security."

In an article on authority Engels pointed out that the principle of subordination would have to be retained in industry even after the victorious socialist revolution.

Roy Medvedev, who continues to regard himself as a Communist, feels that Engels was completely right in opposing the antiauthority factions. He points out that modern industry cannot operate without firm management, whether that is exercised by a capitalist, a functionary, or someone directly chosen by the workers. Whatever its origin and structure, some degree of authority is required in connection with the material conditions that foster industrial growth and market distribution.[3]

Thus every social system requires some operative authority to avoid the excesses of particular groups and all extremists. Lack of an effective authority will destroy any social system.

One of the great problems facing democracy is to find the proper balance between authority and freedom. That balance cannot be static, hence it must be redefined periodically. This problem will continue to plague human beings and society because it is part of the very fabric of their lives.

The concept of the state compels us to clarify the notion of authority, by which I mean the proper exercise and limits of the directive function assumed by those who govern. The natural tendency of authority is to increase its power and its range of action. The more complex problems are, the more this tendency is intensified. Hence a democratic project must define its moral and legal foundation, its sphere of action, its powers, and the proper boundary line between functioning authority and the rights of the community.

Democratic Structures

I think it is correct to say that today we find ourselves facing two structural tendencies. One has to do with the growth and extension of the public sector. It means that authority is intervening more and more in political, social, and economic life; individual freedom and personal initiative are being reduced correspondingly. The other tendency is the growing demand for participation in the decisions that affect the public sector. In Latin America, for example, our people have become much more conscious of the importance of their tasks. They possess a wide range of information that enables them to form judgments about the problems facing them.

The latter tendency forces us to reconsider the function of political structures in a democratic framework so that the exercise of authority and the influence of countervailing organisms may be effectively integrated. Whatever form these entities may take, every democracy must take due account of certain basic principles.

It must be clear, first of all, that authority in a democracy is distinguished by its source. It is delegated to those who govern the land by the people themselves. Their sovereignty is not surrendered, it is delegated; and this delegation takes place in periodic elections that entail universal suffrage, free choice, and a secret ballot. In a democratic regime authority cannot be concentrated solely in one body, much less one person, that exercises all political functions: executive, legislative, judicial, and supervisory. When such concentration takes place, democratic authority ceases to exist. Countervailing powers are of the essence of democracy; they must be maintained.

Parliament is an essential structure in democracy. There people express and debate their views about the general problems affecting the community. There laws are passed, and a watch is kept on the acts of public authorities. That is why parliament should directly represent the people.

Corporative parliaments cannot adequately carry out this mission. The functional groups that make up such a parliament have different reasons for being and particular interests of their own. Various intermediate groups (e.g., labor unions, professional organizations, and cultural, economic, regional, and local bodies) make up the social fabric that permits individual human beings to participate legitimately in certain spheres of activity and to be integrated into the life of the nation through appropriate channels. But decision-making on the political level is something else again. It derives from an overall view of the nation's whole life, not from a consideration of special interests, however legitimate they may be.

There is no doubt that democratic parliaments in Latin America are not properly organized to deal with the new realities they face. Their organizational structure and their work procedures must be amended if they are to fulfill their mission. Today public opinion is greatly influenced by debates that take place outside parliament: e.g., on radio and TV. There are other levels of discussion and diffusion in specialized organisms. All that does not change the essential function of parliament, but it does alter the way it must work if it is to carry out its commitment successfully.

Parliament must formulate laws, maintain a check on the vast and complex apparatus of government, and carry out rather specialized tasks. This means that its members must have the status and the technical advice needed to study the legislative proposals of the executive branch, to draft appropriate laws, and to make sure that the government is effectively controlled without paralyzing administration.

To be sure, there is no insuperable difficulty in finding the technical juridical measures needed to make sure that parliament can handle these new functions. What is more difficult to change in this respect is the mentality of those who make up that body. They must see the need for new procedures and new approaches to its task in a society where other organisms are stepping into the picture more and more and debating the issues at hand.

Moreover, another point must be noted here. Whatever the form of government may be, planning organisms are assuming more importance every day. They elaborate projects and programs that are both middle range and long range. Time, continuity, and consistency are required if those programs are to be fully worked out and implemented. Parliaments should take part in the general discussion and decision-making process with regard to these programs. But they should not go into the details involved in their implementation. Laws adopted on such matters should follow these guidelines. More and more parliament should be the center where basic options are made and their implementation is reviewed and checked. But it should not interfere in the operational and regulatory details of planning and implementation to the point where management of the modern state becomes completely impossible. The existence of parliaments and the participation of the citizenry in national life should rule out authoritarian absolutism; but their role should not shackle the executive branch so that it cannot operate effectively.

The executive branch must be the supreme instance, and hence it must be able to count on the legal instruments it needs to effectively direct the course of the nation. Where socio-economic policy is concerned, this direction takes on a more pointed sense when it is bound up with a concrete plan that seeks to carry out an overall historical project. For such a project is a broad-ranging and coherent vision, not only of economic development but also of the whole life of the community; it seeks to reconcile quantitative and qualitative production growth with the civil, cultural, and social progress of the people.

Organized justice implies that there must be autonomy in the origin and setup of judicial authority as well as in the procedures that administer it. In general we can say that in our countries today the exercise of rights in the courtroom is slow and burdensome. In practice that translates into inequality and even the negation of rights. It is not enough to have tribunals that are honest and independent in carrying out their functions. Simplifying the whole court process and injecting speed and flexibility is of equal importance. If the law cannot be applied promptly, and if there is no equal access to the courts, then the judicial process will lose prestige and the civic conscience will suffer deterioriation.

The formation of a moral conscience and the inculcation of respect for the law can be effective only if certain things are done. The courts must judge and punish crimes against property and persons. They must also punish infractions of laws and regulations governing the obligations of the citizenry and their social conduct. Honest payment of income tax would be an example.

Of equal importance today for the proper functioning of a democratic system is the existence of a supervisory public administration that will maintain control over civil service and the acts of the executive and legislative branches. Acting as an autonomous body, it would determine whether their actions are in accord with the legal regimen in force.

Proper balance in a democratic setup will rest upon these bases. Such has always been the case, and it is even more necessary today. On it depends the further consolidation of democracy. To its absence is due the decline or disappearance of democratic government. If people insist on clinging to democratic forms that cannot measure up to the conditions of the time, then democracy itself cannot help but being ineffective or doomed.

Political Parties

No matter what conception of the state and society we may have, and no matter what sort of institutions may embody that conception, we must consider the problem of political parties. Even in many states that deny political democracy we find that political parties have not disappeared. We cannot imagine a communist state without a Communist party, and the same holds true for other dictatorships of a more nationalist cast. In such nations political parties have been a central factor in the preservation of doctrine, a motor force behind the government, and a factor controlling all the vital centers of the nation including the Armed Forces.

Political parties are completely suppressed only in very primitive dictatorships that have no underlying philosophy. Yet even these look to certain groups or currents for support, desperately trying to find some underlying ideological inspiration. If that is so in such instances, then it is obvious that we cannot imagine a democracy in which political parties are not present.

In democratic regimes political parties are the channels through which human beings express their sympathies, involve themselves in specific issues, and deal with the problems that affect the whole community. Political parties are to democratic societies what the nervous system is to the human body. Each organ of the body has its own function, but the nervous system transmits reactions that affect the whole organism. In a democracy political parties are the two-way channel of communication, transmitting information from the bottom to the top and directives from the top to the bottom. In short, political parties are the "real motive force behind political life in modern states," even as they were in the past under somewhat different historical conditions.

Political parties should be instruments for sounding out, coordinating, universalizing, and defending the interests and aspirations of the whole community. They should serve as the link between grassroots citizen participation on the one hand and the final decision-making process on the other. And when a national community is working on a historical project that embodies its vision of the future, then there should be politically organized people to promote it out of a sense of conviction, a set of rigorous ethical norms, and a deep passion for a cause. In short, there should be some activists and militants.

By their very nature as public administrators in concrete areas, technocratic administrators and civil servants cannot serve as this link between the government and the people. Neither can specific functional groups or special interests insofar as we are talking about overall guidelines that affect the whole community, for their relations are partial and "self-interested," in the legitimate sense of the term.

From the days of Athenian democracy to our own, the link between communities and their governments has been the same. It has been made by political groups who represent the ideas held by people about the organization of their lives, the community, and the state as well as the function and role of social, economic, technical, and cultural forces. In the course of time they have moved in the most varied directions, but they have always represented the opinions of large societal conglomerates. That is why the existence of political parties is now more important than ever before.

The classic distinction between a presidential government and a parliamentary government is today less important than the distinction between a one-party system and a multiparty system. As one study and action group has put it: "If the freedom of the citizenry seemed important in Montesquieu's day so that 'power might restrain power,' then freedom will not exist today except in nations where 'party restrains party.' "

There can be no doubt about that fact. If France or the United States were suddenly to adopt the one-party system, then democracy would cease to exist in those countries even if they retained all the legal codes and institutional apparatus. And if the U.S.S.R. or some other Communist nation were to allow the existence of parties who enjoyed freedom of expression, then dictatorship would disappear even if they did not change an iota of their present laws and their constitution.

In some countries where there is only one party we find parliaments known as the People's Assembly. That does not affect the substance of the regime at all because they are monolithic systems in which all organisms are subservient to a single idea and have only a single form of expression.

In communist states the single party performs a key role; it determines the ideological orientation and controls life on both the individual and collective level. The role of parties is quite different but equally decisive in democratic states, whether one party obtains a majority or a coalition government rules. The latter are not directly elected by the people. They are the result of agreements reached between parties who will play a decisive role in them. This is particularly true of the party leaders involved, since it is they who will discuss and debate the bases of any such pact.[4]

Jean Ladrière, the philosopher, has gone deeply into an analysis of political parties. He has this to say:

In principle, by virtue of the theory implied in universal suffrage, there is no intermediary between the citizenry and their representatives. . . .

It is considered that the assembly of representatives directly reflects the will of the citizenry and effectively embodies the "general will" of the nation. But that "will" is not homogeneous, and the relationship of the citizenry with the power center is not immediate. It comes about through the mediation of parties. . . .

The confidence that the citizens place in their representatives is not indeterminate. It is conditioned by a specific overall conception of public life and a particular vision of politics. If the system is to function, this political vision must find expression somehow; and so there must be some organization that will put it forward. . . .

Thus political parties have a specific and indispensable role to play in the whole power structure. They must ensure mediation between the citizenry and government power by proposing political projects. That means not only specific measures to be adopted but also an overall conception of the state's mission as a whole.[5]

The elaboration of a political project is therefore an essential task of any party. It must work up such a plan, propose it to the public in basic propositions, promote and organize those citizens who agree with the plan, and work out a line of action that will enable the party to win power and implement the program.

Once it has attained power, however, there is the problem of defining the role of the party vis-à-vis the government. Here Ladrière spells out certain indispensable guidelines:

We must not confuse the program of the party with the program of the ruling government. A party program is oriented mainly to public opinion. It may refer to certain specific points, but it does not cease to have the air of broad generality. To be sure, it is conceived in terms of the overall project and program of the party; but it also takes account of public opinion and their expected reaction to it.

A government must be precise. It must take account of real-life problems in all their complexity. Now the fact is that government problems are becoming increasingly complex and that a wide range of information is needed to work out the desired objectives. For this reason it is becoming increasingly difficult, if not impossible, for a political party to formulate a program that is directly applicable on the governmental level. Hence the role of political parties is not so much to fix a precise program of action. It is rather to provide a certain political orientation that will find concrete embodiment in the shape of the ruling government. It will be up to the government itself to determine its specific program. Of course the government and its officials will take due account of public opinion, but its relationship to public opinion is not the same as that of political parties. The latter are much closer to public opinion than the former. Governing officials have a particular role to play by virtue of their place in the political system. They are supposed to give impetus to collective will, which is ultimately responsible for social change.

Even when the governing ruler is closely tied to one or more political parties, that ruler has a real sphere of personal initiative, a proper field of action. The ruler can and ought to impress a specific orientation on the life of society as a whole.[6]

Many of the conflicts that arise between parties and elected officials stem from the failure to recognize these two distinct functions. The former, who have the role of giving direction to public opinion, sometimes propose to alter concrete governmental programs without possessing the competence or the elements required for a sound judgment. By the same token those in government who seek to implement certain programs often do not give sufficient weight to public opinion and its reaction. Political parties often sense this reaction because they are in closer touch with the real feelings of the public at large.

If that is the mission of political parties, it is obvious that they play a very important role in the life of a country. Thus their organization and their leadership are not simply intramural matters; they are bound up with the whole structure of democracy. Party leaders channel party activity, integrate its inner tendencies, and offer the people a choice of possible candidates who were chosen by active party members. The weakening of political parties through a failure to modernize their organization and their line of action foreshadows a crisis in the democratic system because no other political organism can replace them.

From a different vantage point we can say that the excessive or unlimited proliferation of political parties is also a clear sign of a decaying system. If the number of parties keeps growing, it will be impossible for them to orient and channel public opinion as they are supposed to do. As splinter-groups multiply, they lose all sense of their real function and try to survive at any cost. We arrive at absurd situations where the life of a government often depends on some small splinter-group that desires to wield great influence out of all proportion to its representational status.

This defect must be eliminated or minimized by legal mechanisms that will require political parties to have some minimum voting strength before being allowed to exist. The intent here certainly is not to rule out new movements representing shifts in public opinion. If a new movement does have solid content and interprets a solid segment of the community, then it should be able to obtain the minimum voting strength required to make it legal.

Looking at the other side of the coin, we can see why many political parties in Latin America have gone into a period of decline. They have lost sight of any overall vision and they have proved incapable of integrating the major currents of political opinion. Lacking principles and projects for inspiration, they have given up both their intellectual and their ethical mainsprings. Their active party members have lost their motivation and their spirit of service to the cause. They have fallen into narrow partisanship and a concentration on personalities. More interested in intramural quarrels and power plays, they forget the aspirations of the larger community and ignore the opinion of outside sympathizers among the masses. This is fatal because the latter once felt represented by them; it was the support of these sympathetic masses which gave the party its true dimensions. Now the parties cease to be instruments in the service of the whole country and democracy.

To fill the vacuum created by a dearth of ideas and an absence of general guidelines, the parties resort to maneuvering and all sorts of compromise in order to attain power or maintain their modicum of influence. This inevitably leads to personal quarrels, factional divisions, and struggles for control of the party. This sad spectacle of pettiness and myopia rapidly leads a party into decadence or extinction. If that happens on a sufficiently wide scale, there will be no way to maintain the democratic system in a country, for one of its essential components will have gone up in smoke. It will mean that the citizenry has lost the faith and drive that gives reality to democracy, that it is ready to succumb to one sort of dictatorship or another.

Yet the fact remains that the corrective for many of these defects lies in freedom itself. Public opinion moves away from those who do not interpret it adequately. The vigor of a democracy lies in the fact that the citizenry move closer to other partisan movements that fulfill this function.

That expedient is not sufficient, however. Once we recognize the important function of political parties, we must create the juridical mechanisms to regulate them properly. Their existence must be recognized in the constitution. Their actions must be subject to a set of juridical statutes that will spell out the choosing of party leaders, their proper role, their rights, and their responsibilities.

It is equally necessary that party financing be public, not only in elections but also in their normal growth and operation; that will guarantee their independence. The law should also provide that they will have access to the communications media.

Inner party structure should allow for the systematic expression of views from the grassroots up. In this way the leaders will truly represent the grassroots level, preventing others from using nineteenth-century tactics to splinter the party and obtain personal advantages. All too often the reverse has been the case, and those least qualified have come to predominate. Their narrow sectarian view has led them to ignore the general will of the people.

The measures noted above, and others too, are indispensable. But they cannot substitute for another important consideration. The fact is that political parties must be organs that give expression to ideas, programs, and a conception of community destiny; they must also be capable of offering effective and feasible solutions. No law or set of regulations will save them if they lack such a vision, if they do not have the moral strength that will make them worthy of the public's confidence.

15

Essential Factors

The Programming of Development

Modern governments are creating organisms to research and develop long-range and middle-range programs of development. The structure and name of these organisms may vary greatly from one nation to the next, of course. But today more than ever before it is impossible to carry out any political policy with one's eyes focused only on the immediate present. That will inevitably lead to serious mistakes in the future. So today every nation interested in planning must consider certain institutional aspects of such basic factors as the programming of objectives, ecological problems, and the contribution of new technologies.

This fact cannot be overlooked, and it is recognized in various camps. As Brzezinski has said, there is general agreement that planning is desirable, that it is the only way to tackle the various ecological threats that face the world. And given the continuing progress of computers and communications systems, there is good reason to feel that modern technology makes such planning feasible. For example, the multifaceted scanning and analysis of satellites promises more effective planning with respect to the earth's resources.[1]

Economic and social plans should be conceived in broad terms; they should be macro-level plans. They should not descend to the micro-level and the intangible variety of individual and community life, for there the unforeseen and unpredictable initiative of human beings is at work.

As I indicated earlier, the whole planning process varies in accordance with the doctrine that inspires it and the technical model that is utilized in it. In a democracy, however, planning cannot be the result of centralized decisions by technobureaucrats. It is certainly true that technological tools, those of the information sciences for example, have come a long way. They enable us quickly to size up the past and probable future behavior of every production unit or social unit. But no matter how perfected these tools may be, they are no substitute for the creative contribution of human beings to the multifaceted areas of life.

The plan or program should certainly organize and reflect the fundamental options of the community. Discussion of it should allow for the participation of the principal categories and centers of both public and private activity in the nation. This means that we must be able to overcome the difficulties and complicated dialectics existing between the public sector and various community groups, particularly those social organizations that are truly representative. But as one report points out:

We must not underestimate the difficulties or the opposition that labor unions or business groups habitually tend to pose to any policy that is proposed or approved. It is necessary to move these groups toward a new stance beyond their traditional emphasis on their own demands and rights. They cannot limit their vision to such matters as salaries, for example. They must also see the importance of qualitative factors relating to both working conditions and living conditions. The focus must not be on industry alone but on industry in relation to the whole socio-economic and cultural context.[2]

Political representatives must know how to get across these points so that laborers, business executives, and professionals will appreciatc the objectives of the plan and offer their collaboration. To the extent that this is done, there will be greater trust on all sides and positive participation in the implementation phase.

I have already suggested what is needed if this trust is to be won. In the whole programming process there must be adequate coordination of all the sectors involved with economic and social policy; only then can they operate with each other harmoniously at each stage of formulating and carrying out the established priorities. The creation of such institutional bodies as economic councils or social councils accords with these objectives, for the various sectors involved in socio-economic development are properly represented in them. Those sectors include: the government, which acts as promoter, coordinator, and arbitrator; business executives; workers; and social entities of both a public and private character.

In our countries there are perennial problems. They include the proper distribution of income, employment opportunities, and inflation. Such problems can be resolved only if all the sectors involved have a real understanding of the policies to be applied. And such understanding will result only after proposals and objectives have been discussed openly and then agreed upon by all.

One primary objective must be to give new content to the process of development by placing primary stress on the rational utilization and distribution of income: i.e., on the collective forms of consumption and savings. The rate of population growth in Latin American nations takes on considerable importance in this connection. Though of course it varies from country to country, the present rate indicates that the population of Latin America will double by the end of this century. That is only about twenty years away.

This challenge must be faced, but it does not justify a

compulsive solution. Such basic factors as food supply and occupational opportunities, which are already critical today, must be taken into account. So must the whole matter of protecting the basic resources of our nations. The solutions to these issues cannot come simply from initiatives taken in the private sector. Groups in the private sector obviously are looking out for their own interests, which do not always coincide with those of the community. In a free society we must provide an integrated program that offers a basic and permanent solution to these and other fundamental problems.

Insofar as consumption is concerned, we find that the more developed countries must now correct past excesses by altering the artificial scale of values that has influenced consumer taste. Underdeveloped societies possess even less resources. In their case it is essential that individualism not be equated with an erroneous conception of freedom when it comes to choosing forms of distribution and the utilization of income. It is not right that certain "Herodian" minorities should confuse democratic freedom with the privilege of choosing an artificial and sumptuous way of life that does not correspond with the real potential of their country, that distorts and sacrifices objectives which are indispensable for the rest of the community.

The full realization of a democratic society does not lie in the maintenance of an absolute freedom to consume. It lies in giving priority to the production and equitable distribution of basic necessities, so that every member can achieve some minimum of dignity and a reasonable way of living. In other words, the exigencies of development in such countries as ours require us to adopt policies that will establish certain priorities. Those priorities should enable us to cover the basic consumption demands of the vast majority of our people.

Under normal circumstances the market may act as the regulator of supply, demand, prices, and production volume. But in developing nations the government and the community can and should establish the basic context in which these factors operate. This is particularly true in countries where vast numbers of human beings lack even the bare necessities.

This point does not apply solely to the ordinary process of consumption. It also applies to the decisions made with regard to the source and volume of savings and their allocation to economic and social investment. If a nation lacks housing for a large portion of the population, for example, then the satisfaction of this need should be established as a priority. People must be discouraged from investing material and financial resources in construction projects that go beyond certain pre-established limits.

Whatever measures are adopted, it is obvious that savings are basic to the investments that will determine the magnitude of future progress. They are a crucial item in the elaboration of any program, representing the community's willingness to make sacrifices now in order to improve the living standard of the populace later on. There is no way to escape this sacrifice if our peoples really want to make progress, to overcome poverty, and thus to become less dependent.

In short, our societies must operate on the basis of rational knowledge and prior reckoning. Investments, production, and the distribution of goods and services must be planned out both qualitatively and quantitatively. That is the only way to enlist the solidarity of the vast majority of the people. All of this must be given consideration in elaborating, discussing, and approving the overall plan.

Once the process of dialogue and approval of the program has taken place, however, the plan must be carried out. At this latter stage the executive branch, the center of authority, must be able to count on the instruments and the force required for its execution. No one should be able to block implementation. Specific legislation should ensure this; it should also establish procedures for review and revision in accordance with the changing demands of a constantly evolving world.

The means at our disposal today enable us to use models, to weigh the suitability of various options, and to point up priorities. Both the government and the community can make proposals, and all can offer their opinion. But once the majority has legitimately made its choice, it should be implemented resolutely, logically, and consistently. The adopted plan or program involves a commitment to long-term tasks that will not show immediate results. That is why debate cannot keep going on indefinitely once the will of the parties has been established.

It should be stressed that democracy does not imply instability, endless discussion, and the proposal of legislation that would go against the middle-range and long-range goals already approved by parliament. The right of minorities to express their opinions must be respected, but we cannot allow them to paralyze government action or to block the execution of plans already approved by the majority.

The democratic process of participating in the decision-making process entails many difficulties. It takes time, and various forms of opposition will undoubtedly crop up. But all that is to be expected within the framework of a free society.

Some people feel that it is more proper for programs to be worked up by technical organisms and planning bodies, so that the difficult stage of decision-making is rendered much more simple. It is a tempting thought, especially when people fear controversy, when there is not enough communication with the general public, and when populist organizations cannot find out the objectives to be pursued and the price that must be paid for them.

Here again some would compare democratic government unfavorably with dictatorial and totalitarian regimes. The latter seem to expedite matters better because there are no intermediate levels in the decision-making process, because orders come down from the centralized organs at the top and no one is allowed to express dissent or suggest anything different.

Time and again, however, these seeming advantages have been shown to be illusory. Underneath the surface of strength, effectiveness, and unity we find great fragility and numerous mistakes and contradictions. We cannot build anything solid if we ignore or mistrust human beings. Truly human progress must be grounded on confidence in human beings. Otherwise our efforts will eventually reach some crisis point and start going backward rather than forward.

There has been much progress in Latin America with regard to ideas concerning development and its programming. We now have many qualified experts who are capable of working up models and elaborating programs. They constitute an indispensable corps for any democratic project, and they were not available to us a few short years ago.

Our nations must make use of the institutional and technical efforts that have already been carried out in connection with programs for economic development. They must broaden these programs to take in the social aspect and then implement them without succumbing to the distortions of political opportunism. All this will be even more necessary if we try to bring our nations together to form a Latin American Common Market and thus try to successfully challenge the other international blocs who have combined to defend their economies. A basic precondition for the development of such a Common Market is the long-range planning of our production capabilities. That in turn will entail organized planning of the rest of the products produced in the member nations.

Our task here, then, might be summed up in the following terms. We must make feasible the programming of economic and social development. We must create the channels that will allow all segments of society to participate in the decision-making process and know about the results. And we must establish the institutional mechanisms required to effectively implement those decisions. This in turn calls for juridical reform so that we can regulate the process of discussion and approval of the program and provide the authorities with the tools they need to implement it without negative interference.

The Development of Knowledge

A second factor is just as important as programming. We must make progress in the realms of science and technology and develop a knowledge industry.

No one in Latin America would object to this general statement. In practice, however, our nations are far from having worked out any policy that deals with this problem adequately. This tardiness accounts for our regression vis-à-vis the progress that has been made in the industrialized nations.

Of course there is discussion of this topic. Centers are being organized to incorporate the new bits of knowledge. Congresses and seminars are being held. Yet there is still no clear awareness of the consequences of technological advances and how they might be utilized for further development.

People display totemic admiration for the new scientific discoveries and desire to acquire them for our nations. They even would like to see such discoveries generated in our countries. But there is no organized system to transfer these discoveries, catalogue them, pinpoint the most necessary ones, and evaluate the suitability of their incorporation here in Latin America. That must be done, however, because they often come from highly developed countries whose overall situation is very different from that of our nations.

Some technological advances could be easily absorbed

in our nations, and they would generate new jobs and occupations. Some are indispensable even though they do not create new jobs. Some should not be imported because they can be replaced here with an abundant supply of manual labor that needs employment. And some cannot be assimilated to our milieu or represent a threat to the quality of life. We must be able to evaluate these technological advances, to use them profitably, and to reject those not suitable for our societies.

Theo Lefèvre has been in charge of the scientific policy of Belgium for many years. He has this to say: "It is of the utmost importance that we continue adapting scientific developments and the objectives of scientific policy to various societal models. Nations and different groups of nations display clear-cut differences in economic structure, people's motivations, value systems, and overall civilization. A realistic scientific policy must take all these things into account."[3]

This brings us to an even more general conclusion: Choosing a technology and making optimum use of it implies some notion of what is expected from it. This vision is elaborated insofar as we program the development of a society with respect to its human aspects. This overall vision and the corresponding research calls for organic collaboration between the universities and scientific circles in both the public and private sectors. Even the most highly developed nations are now reconsidering the bases on which their scientific technology has been built. They now realize that previous neglect of human and moral elements has caused clear and serious damage to the quality of life in various communities. Renewed interest in ecology and the protection of the environment is one reflection of this new concern.

Like other nations in the Third World, the nations of Latin America must consider these factors so as not to repeat mistakes that others are now trying to correct. Moreover, the transference of technologies, perhaps more than any other issue, raises the whole matter of our growing dependence on, and subordination to, enterprises that are growing increasingly powerful because they control and dispense these sources of technological progress. Of course we can point to seemingly important advances when we make use of inventions that others create and sell, or whose operation is taught by them. Even on this level, however, we are often way behind. We acquire some new apparatus that is already outdated without even knowing whether it can be usefully adapted to local conditions.

Until a short time ago technological changes were spaced well apart. New discoveries could gradually be adapted to local conditions. When science and technology were distinct activities, the application of new knowledge proceeded slowly. The current refinement of technology has resulted from the fact that these two somewhat different modes of thinking have come together. Their integration has produced a dizzying rate of accelerated change and unforeseen situations. Now there is no real correlation between the scientific concepts that are changing the physical world and the concepts that govern the political and social organization of society.

One of the many consequences of this rapid evolution is the fact that some societies find it increasingly difficult to keep pace with other societies. Equitable relations between the two have become almost impossible. We confront a world divided into greatly contrasting zones. Concentrated in one zone is a rapid pace of industrial and technological advance. This translates into the production of goods in which a large store of knowledge is incorporated. The value of the incorporated knowledge grows increasingly vis-à-vis the value of the raw materials used. Indeed the value of the latter continues to decrease correspondingly.

The general rule is that the price of more advanced products is showing a real increase. When raw materials were converted into industrial products a few decades ago, they came back to their point of origin with a value six or seven times greater than they originally had. Today in some instances that value has increased a hundredfold or even a thousandfold. This represents a sharp and quick alteration, both quantitatively and qualitatively, in international trade relations. As Lefèvre puts it: "In relation to the United States and Europe, the economic situation in the poor countries . . . is simply regressing. This divergent evolution is a source of bitterness and discontent. It is unacceptable when more and more resources are at hand, when we have the knowledge data that would enable us to put science and technology in the service of development."[4]

There are many causes behind this phenomenon. One is the fact that greater scientific dominion over nature and better knowledge of its laws makes it possible for us to use new raw materials. This allows for much greater flexibility in replacing the traditional raw materials.

But there is something else. This greater control over knowledge is itself becoming a substantial part of the relative changes. Computer systems offer a clear example. Their physical size is becoming smaller and smaller, and of less and less importance relative to the cost involved in acquiring mastery of their operation. It is estimated that the sales value of the operation process, which would include the training of personnel, will grow at an annual rate double that of the sales of equipment and hardware. Salvador Lluch points out the consequences of this fact: "While knowledge is growing in value as a factor, the physical embodiment of it is decreasing in value. . . . This holds true also for the raw materials that have traditionally been the determining ingredients in the physical hardware. . . . The cumulative effect of these tendencies suggests that stopgap measures such as preferential treatment or accords will not suffice to maintain prices."[5]

We must realize, therefore, that we have no alternative but to get involved in this whole realm of knowledge and information. If we do not, then we are condemned in advance to a position of inferiority. Neither can the problem be solved by trying to equalize the balance of trade through setting limits on the new modern equipment. Less advanced nations get all the production machinery and know-how from abroad. To reduce these acquisitions would be equivalent to depriving our nations of the basic work tools that they need for their development.

The obvious alternative would be to manufacture this equipment, or a large portion of it, in the needy nations themselves. That of course presupposes two things: We must know how to do it, and we must be able actually to do it. The design and construction of complicated industrial machinery implies that there is a scientific and technical infrastructure with a market able to sustain it. Most if not all of the nations of Latin America are not in a position to handle this individually. As individual nations they lack the minimum dimensions required to justify and support such a scientific and technological establishment.

Two consequences flow from this. First of all, they could not even begin to consider certain kinds of scientific activity. Second, if they chose to specialize in some highly technical process, their products would probably not be competitive because of their high unit cost in such restricted markets. In reality they would be subsidizing the more advanced nations because the latter can benefit from knowledge data that cannot be implemented in our countries.

Another point is worth noting here. An almost irreversible logic is at work in such a situation. Insofar as higher human capacities lack stimulation and support, they tend to be absorbed by the more powerful centers. For these can provide qualified people with the tools they need for their research, and they can also implement their findings.

Taken as a whole, however, Latin America is capable

of creating and sustaining such a production structure. It is also capable of generating a demand that could support major centers of scientific research and technological application.

There is no doubt that our nations, taken in isolation, do not possess the economic and human resources required to carry out research projects that could compete in the world market. Once again we see that they must get together. They must pool programs, resources, and markets. They must avoid duplication in matters of importance, such as those noted above. If they do not do this, they will not be able to carry through a project that could bring incalculable benefits to our continent and its scientific development. We must not only manage to transfer foreign inventions here; we must also participate in the process of creating them.

However the basic political objectives of our individual nations may differ, this item is a centerpiece in any model of development. It represents one of the best, if not the best, precondition for the qualitative and humane development of our societies, for it entails a general expansion of education and of top-notch joint centers in the scientific and technological sector.

Such centers are not just indispensable for sound, independent progress. They should also be places where Latin Americans who are highly qualified in science and technology can meet and work together. A project of this scope should also radiate great benefits and hopes to the people at large and upcoming generations. They should stimulate them to ever greater improvement and give those involved the satisfaction of seeing their work having an impact on the quality of life shared by their people.

In today's world no factor offers greater positive prospects for the future. The mere existence of such joint centers should raise the level of the cultural milieu in which our nations operate.

16

Primary Objectives

Respecting Human Rights

A historical project must be reflected not only in concepts and structures but also, and even more importantly, in the objectives it pursues. The ends are just as important as the means used to attain them, and the two interact mutually.

A democratic state cannot perdure without the essential institutional elements. It is not enough for these elements to exist, however. They must also be geared to accomplish certain goals. The government must be capable of achieving those goals, thus resolving the basic problems that a given society faces at a given point in space and time.

Insofar as Latin America is concerned, the goals are fairly obvious and can be readily appreciated by all. The first of these should be full respect for human rights as they are enunciated in the Universal Declaration of Human Rights promulgated by the United Nations. Some people think that these rights are being respected when one or another of the Declaration's articles is being observed: when no one is subjected to cruel or inhuman torture, or when there is no arbitrary interference in the private lives of individuals (Articles 5 and 12 of the U.N. Declaration).

This is a restricted view of the U.N. Declaration. Its

thirty articles make up a basic code dealing with the essential rights of human beings: i.e., the right to life, liberty, security, work, and health; the right to equality before the law; the right to get a hearing before independent and impartial tribunals in public sessions, so that no one is condemned on the basis of laws that did not exist when the alleged act or omission was perpetrated. The U.N. Declaration also asserts that all human beings have the right to circulate freely, to leave any country including their native land, and to be protected from arbitrary loss of their nationality. Human beings have the right to establish a family, to possess individual or collective property, and to enjoy freedom of thought, conscience, and religion. They should be able to participate in authentic elections. The U.N. Declaration also talks about the establishment of a national and international social order in which all these rights and freedoms are fully real and respected.

The situation in Latin America today seems almost incredible in this connection. Once upon a time those rights would hardly have been disputed in most if not all of our nations. Today they are little more than an ardent hope for millions of our people. If these sensible and simple yearnings were respected by all the nations who subscribed to the U.N. Declaration, humanity would make enormous and revolutionary progress. The real situation is far different, however. The mere attempt to defend or implement the Declaration provokes international disturbances and dramatic conflicts within nations. Some people are upset when human rights are invoked because they think it is a matter for each government to decide. Some governments violate human rights with impunity, then hypocritically accuse other nations of doing the very same thing. Still others feel that their own offenses are justified by the fact that others are doing the same.

Those who love democracy, those who think that all human beings possess certain inalienable rights, must defend and fight for the U.N. Declaration. To do so is to defend the cause of humanity as a whole. When one of its articles is violated, then all citizens are threatened with danger. Some may feel secure and indifferent because the violation does not reach their doorstep today. But tomorrow it is they who may be crying for help. The violators may shift their direction or focus, or they may be replaced by some opposite extreme that is only too glad to follow their example.

The task of humanism is to clarify, perfect, and defend the intellectual and ethical principles that underlie a democratic society in which human rights are not only respected but actively enhanced. But if human rights are to be defended in Latin America, and elsewhere in the world, then democracy must find the mechanisms required for the task. It must correct the injustices that have led to "social dualism" in our countries. As of today, unfortunately, the democratic framework supports only certain sectors of the population; for other sectors it is totally meaningless.

The exercise of freedom and the community as a whole are harmed when essential human rights are violated. The same holds true when we maintain a situation that causes social divisiveness and perpetuates injustice. It is not just that the existence of freedom is morally and materially ruled out. What is ruled out is the bare minimum of equality, solidarity, and respect for human life and people's rights.

The growing emphasis on the issue of human rights today is beginning to change the situation somewhat. A concern to defend those rights has surfaced from within the bosom of democracy itself. A moral banner has been raised, one which goes beyond the issues of economics, politics, and military security; and its impact has been widely felt and noted. Against this backdrop the nations of Latin America should work up and project a cultural, social, and economic model in which those rights can be truly implemented.

Achieving National Integration

The defense of human rights, then, means more than preventing flagrant abuses; it means establishing the conditions that will allow for their full exercise. We must hasten the process of social integration in every Latin American nation. We must ensure the existence of a community where the necessary consensus and national solidarity are present.

In our nations, where sharp social contrasts are evident, such solidarity can result only from a conscious decision to put an end to glaring inequalities. Each nation must be able to establish a truly integrated social system, and this calls for the responsible organization of the nation's inhabitants. They must have entities that truly and legitimately represent them. Otherwise they cannot get a hearing, they cannot participate in the national dialogue, they cannot fight for their rights, and hence they cannot feel any share of personal responsibility in the task of constructing society.

Poverty, lack of education, and marginality are the root causes of instability. For families that live in such conditions, any chance of change represents a hope whether it is truly feasible or not. It is even more enticing if it offers them some chance to take vengeance on those who are oppressing them. The only logical way to rule out extremism is to get rid of the underlying causes. So long as the underlying conditions remain, democracy cannot be fully operative.

It is a false illusion to assume that inequalities can be eliminated by the good will of certain groups or by appeals to generosity and benevolence. Even when good will does really exist, it is not enough. We cannot construct a social order by demeaning some human beings into being the mere recipients of alms and making them dependent on their benefactors. Human egotism is insatiable in any case, and it is a mistake to try to base one's hopes for a just system on human generosity.

The lessons of human history, and of our own nations, are clear on this point. Paternalistic governments and dictatorships of whatever sort immediately try to eliminate existing social organizations. Even if they choose to retain them for tactical purposes, they will deprive them of substantive power and their representative function. In the end they only aggravate the existing inequities.

The right of association is a key factor in the quest for justice. It should be granted to every stratum of society: laborers, peasants, intellectuals, the middle classes, and businesspeople. Each group will then have the opportunity to define and perfect its function within the overall project that the national community has drawn up. Decentralization of power is meaningless if there is no real organization of the social bases, if the latter are not in a position to assume their fair share of responsibility for the tasks that will promote participation and national integration. It will be impossible to defend human rights if individuals find themselves isolated over against an all-powerful government.

Organized labor is a key element in this process of participation. Its opinions must find a hearing in the business world, in regional and national institutions, and in general discussions. That is the only way that individual workers will feel that they are being given a hearing, that they are truly a part of the national process. It is also the only way that the government can speak with moral authority and ask people to accept the discipline required for carrying out its policies.

In this way the people will not just manage to defend their own aspirations. They will also learn to comprehend the problems of the nation, come to respect limitations, gain access to the higher levels of decision-making, and acquire a broader view of their own rights, responsibilities, and obligations.

Unlike the people who constitute it, a nation does not have a soul. Its reason for being in the task of carrying out a national "project" resides in the consciousness of its members. It depends ultimately on their understanding, their social commitment, and their willingness to fashion an integrated country while respecting its characteristic culture and traditions.

In short, then, one central goal should dominate authentically democratic regimes in Latin America and their efforts to carry out a historical project. They must seek to integrate all into the life of the nation. They must put an end to social injustice, extreme poverty, and the overall misery that oppresses and marginalizes hundreds of millions. No society can endure today if it is based on the old encomienda system, if it suddenly pushes millions of people into urban conglomerates where they find no form of mutual interrelationship. The process of disintegration can be seen in the cities themselves, where we find two different worlds, two different lifestyles, and two different sets of customs and opportunities. There cannot be peace in such circumstances. That is why governments based on force appear periodically to maintain the surface appearance of unity and to avoid the danger of revolutionary explosions.

As I noted earlier, in more advanced societies the advocacy of violence is reduced to small, marginal groups. In our nations it is a latent danger in large sectors of the population because of blatant injustices. Some groups seek to alleviate the situation by implementing reforms from above. Ignoring the people, they propose to "help" them in one way or another as the enlightened despots of the eighteenth century sought to do.

Only authentic social integration can really change the situation, however. Society must be organized in such a way that all the components of the community are involved in it. They must feel responsible and at one with it. They should not feel that they are the passive receivers of benefits granted them by others. That is the way to put an end to the existing social dualism. That is the way to bring about authentic transformation in society, correcting the defects of the existing order and creating a truly communitarian society.

Overcoming Poverty

To talk about overcoming poverty today is to talk about economic and social development. Whatever term we may use, however, the fact remains that poverty can be overcome only if each national community enjoys a daily increasing volume of goods and services. In a stagnant economy an effort at distribution alone will simply turn into demagogic populism and an inflationary force.

The indigence of Latin America could not be more alarming and we simply must face up to it, even though there are no dogmatic or exclusivist formulas for solving it. Each national model will have to accommodate its procedures to the peculiar tenor of the country, its present level of development, its human and natural resources. Yet certain basic aspects and conditions are general enough to require serious consideration from any viewpoint.

For example, the development sought and needed by the people of Latin America cannot come from the mere application of classical capitalism. The existing inequalities will not be wiped out by an "overflow" system, whereby the upper classes are stimulated to get rich and the overflow eventually trickles down to the lower classes.

In this connection the behavior of some in Latin America is indeed curious. They set up the most rigid dictatorships, reject the most elementary freedom as dangerous, and hurl anathemas at freedom of expression on every level. Yet these same people are inflexible proponents of freedom and liberal capitalism in the economic sector. They would accept and promote laissez-faire to a degree that is no longer accepted in the countries where that doctrine originated.

In those nations where the free enterprise and the free market system prevail, we find a strong organization of labor free to operate. This is true, for example, in West Germany, France, and the United States. In our nations, by contrast, governments refuse to recognize the labor movement, or annul its prerogatives, or simply destroy it. By the same token rightist groups in the developed nations have a disconcerting point of view. They think that our people are not capable of living freely in a democracy; yet in the area of the economy, where we are especially weak, they stump for complete freedom.

There is no solid proof that the laissez-faire economic model leads to real economic development in our nations. On the contrary there is every indication that it does not produce social development; that it intensifies and increases inequalities, that it promotes social dualism by leading to a further concentration of economic power, and that it leads to a kind of accumulation that was operative in Europe at the start of the industrial age more than a century ago. Remember that at that time there was no kind of labor organization, no social legislation, and a great deal of illiteracy. In many cases, moreover, the country in question possessed a large colonial empire that it did not hesitate to exploit.

Some economic policies now being implemented in Latin America by authoritarian regimes are little more than attempts to revive that old model from the past. They have little to do with a "social economy of the market," which they claim to imitate. Experience and application vary from country to country, but in general these policies are based on the total subjugation of the laborers and uncontrolled freedom in an unrestricted market.

The need to accumulate capital—i.e., to save—is certainly a compelling one. The affluent countries know that their future depends on it, and the socialist countries impose great sacrifices on their people in order to obtain high rates of savings and investment. The real problem, of course, is to find out who is accumulating or saving money, how, and why. Mexico and Brazil, for example, have had phenomenal success in certain sectors. But in Brazil we find that the social and regional imbalances continue to be awesome, and that dependence is even greater now in some cases. Yet Brazil possesses unequalled resources; and in many other domains, in the conduct of foreign policy for example, it has demonstrated more flexibility and breadth than any other similar regime.

The truth remains that one may choose one or another formula to obtain authentic socio-economic growth and wipe out poverty. But the job will be feasible only if one can persuade the people and mobilize them in a positive way. But they will have to know why they are working, for whom they are working, and to what extent the labors and the ultimate benefits will be shared. Our countries must realize that greater development and decreasing dependence can be the result only of a domestic effort in which all their people participate.

Capital investment, credit, and technical assistance from outside are no less than indispensable. Even the most powerful governments resort to these expedients. But we cannot rely on these as the basic solution. That lies in choosing satisfactory socio-economic policies and having the support of the people. Foreign aid, however necessary it may be, ever remains chancy and costly.

A truly self-conscious democratic society must realize that creative effort is indispensable. It must find its own road to greater and better development. This is not easy to do when nations are caught somewhere between complete underdevelopment and a real takeoff point, as our nations are. For then they face greater demands without the people being fully conscious of the time and the sacrifices required to meet them; and the people lack such knowledge because they have been pushed to the sidelines in the decision-making process.

Indiscriminate imitation of methods that are alien to their own reality is often futile. Often they live on prestige investments without noticing that the overall poverty is increasing rather than decreasing. President Julius Nyerere of Tanzania spoke about building a nation in the following terms:

Building a nation is not simply a matter of building paved roads, tall edifices, luxury hotels, and so forth. Truly building a nation ... means building the character of its people, ... building a mental attitude which will enable us to live together in unity.... It is the dignity and well-being of our people that stands at the beginning and the end of all our efforts....We have decided that all shall be equal in dignity in this country; that all have an equal right to be respected, to have the opportunity for a good education, and to satisfy the basic needs of their lives; and that all citizens shall have an equal opportunity to serve their country in accordance with their abilities.[1]

A socio-economic model for Latin America should seek to overcome poverty and misery, to integrate all the people in the country into the national community, and to create occupations for the millions of men and women who are unemployed or underemployed. If it does seek to do this, then it must give a human connotation to development and set the dignity and well-being of the people as its beginning and end.

These objectives will require the adoption of well defined policies concerning the goals and orientation of public expenditures as well as the stimuli and the brakes to be applied to the various areas of the private sector. It will be equally important to determine the forms of capital accumulation, the tax structure, and ways in which income is to be distributed. Distribution might be direct or indirect (e.g., through social investments). And of course much can be done through fairer stipulations for land holding and land ownership.

The measures effected by the government of Chile between 1965 and 1970 show concretely how the state can redistribute income and effect real changes in the living conditions of the people. One detailed study has analyzed the impact of government activity on the dire poverty of the nation in 1969.[2] Using complete figures for the distribution of income and family expenses in the nation, it analyzed more than 140 public-expenditure programs, the total tax system, state subsidies, and the social security system in order to find out who benefited from the public programs and who helped to finance them.

The results of that analysis show how the poorest in the nation were helped by the net effect of expenditures, taxes, subsidies, and social welfare. The poorest economic group received benefits equivalent to one third of their liquid income. Toward 1970, 30 percent of the neediest families in Chile improved their real income by about 52 percent because the government provided health services, education, economic housing, food, support for small producers, areas of agricultural reform, and so forth.

In short the state provided important subsidies to those who were poor and neediest. Because of their limited ability to pay, they would not have had access to many services otherwise. Middle-level groups also benefited from government involvement, increasing their income by 7 percent. Only the higher-income groups contributed more to the state than they received back in public services, paying mainly by way of increased taxes.

I cite this detailed study because it shows how much was being done by the government in Chile in those years. At that time Chile was more effective in reducing economic inequalities than any other nation in Latin America that has information on this matter. Chile and its government directed 43 percent of its fiscal expenditures toward the low-income groups.

Growth does not mean having the latest automated plant if thousands of people in the vicinity are without food, work, or housing. To build such plants under the circumstances is to create exotic islands in the middle of a dark and bitter sea. Growth does not mean simply investing in the whole production apparatus either. It must go hand in hand with qualitative, humane social development. The latter cannot be regarded as a consequence of the former, to be postponed until the first and primary stage is completed.

In short, social investment has equal priority. We must invest in health, education and housing. Education itself is a chief factor in any kind of development, offering the most concrete possibility for real equality of opportunity. Nothing is more important for a nation than its commitment to make full use of its human capital. If access to the higher levels of education is restricted to a narrow stratum of young people, then the nation is losing enormous potential reserves of intelligence and creativity. No injustice is more odious than inequality of educational opportunity. From a human standpoint it impoverishes a nation and closes off the horizon to many potentially capable people.

The most unacceptable discrimination of all is that which uses money as the basis for selection. To be sure, university education cannot be for all, as some of its would-be destroyers maintain. But it should be for all those who have demonstrated higher capabilities, whatever their background and resources may be.

No investment has more productive and positive consequences for the life of a community than one which goes to the education of its people. Empirical proof of this assertion can be found in our own countries and in other regions around the world.

In short, we must draw up models based on the fundamental lines indicated above. With the help of these models and the information sciences we should be able to glimpse where we want to go in general terms. We should be able to foresee the decisions we want to adopt, the priorities we want to establish, and the limitations facing us.

Our first priority should be to rescue the vast masses of the people from the intolerable poverty and misery in which they find themselves. Everything suggests that this is indeed possible. No region of the world still in the process of development seems to be more favorably situated for a real economic takeoff. Consider the economic level already attained in Latin America, the enormous store of available natural resources, the relation of the human population to the physical landscape and the available space, our shared traditions and cultures, the educational advances already made, and countless other assets that might make other underdeveloped regions envious.

The task of overcoming poverty is indeed feasible. To fail to carry it through would be to maintain a state of inequality and injustice. That would inevitably provoke an ongoing clash between extremes, leading to a pattern of irrational behavior that is already evident in many Latin American nations. A society is fatally jeopardized and morally corrupt if it is willing to allow one-third of its population to live in dire need. For it cannot evade the consequences of an undercurrent of egotism, hatred, and vengeful thoughts.

The decision to overcome poverty is an act of justice. It is also the precondition for further progress and development. It will raise millions of people to a new level of existence, turning them into a market for our economic expansion and a source of labor and active endeavor. It will also lead to a freedom firmly rooted in the heart of each individual.

Reaching a Basic Consensus

Many of the points discussed here confirm the notion that we are faced with a growing process of "socialization."[3] No human society seems exempt from this process. It is extremely important because there is a growing interdependence between human beings and an accelerating thrust toward one world. As Vatican II noted in *Gaudium et Spes* (no. 25):

Man's social nature makes it evident that the progress of the human person and the advance of society itself hinge on each other. . . . Among those social ties which man needs for his development some, like the family and political community, relate with greater immediacy to his innermost nature. Others originate rather from his free decision. In our era, for various reasons, reciprocal ties and mutual dependencies increase day by day and give rise to a variety of associations and organizations, both public and private. This development, which is called socialization, while certainly not without its dangers, brings with it many advantages with respect to consolidating and increasing the qualities of the human person, and safeguarding his rights.

The dominance of this social dimension and its concerns is now a worldwide trend. The upward thrust of labor, population increase, and an accelerated process of urbanization are creating closer ties between human beings. This in turn is requiring greater government involvement in both economic and social activities within nations. The facts just mentioned and others typify the process of socialization that can be noted in the contemporary world, and hence in Latin America.

"Socialization" finds expression at every level of community life and in the organizational forms adopted in the processes of production and distribution. The tendency towards greater work participation is clear and unmistakable. It lies in the very nature of present-day society and in the implications of the new technological era. Progress along these lines, however, should not and cannot imply the destruction of private enterprise out of dogmatism or immaturity. In free societies private enterprise has proven to be an effective instrument of economic development. The effort to give greater influence and participation to labor should not entail the undermining or elimination of private enterprise. The whole world can now see the results of collectivized economic planning with its centralized decision-making and its ruling bureaucracies. Those results are not exactly alluring.

In our nations it would be particularly damaging to prescind from the dynamic impulse of creativity and renovation that is characteristic of a free society. That applies both to private enterprise and to self-governing cooperatives and community organizations. "Socialization" does not mean shifting from the individualism of bourgeois liberalism to the collectivism of completely centralized states.

Respect for human persons and community values complement each other in the functioning of a truly human economy. Lebret spells out what this might mean:

A supremely human economy is one that takes care of authentic needs: e.g., the need for life's basics, the need for dignity, the need for functional facilities, and the need for spiritual progress. The great need of humans is the need to be more, starting from where they are and from their inner and outer potential.... This need is always relative to a given individual and to the environment in which he must fulfill himself.

There is great danger in doing what all too many do, that is, in judging what is more truly human solely in terms of quantitative criteria and consumption possibilities. Such criteria prompt us to judge what is more human in terms of greater possibilities for individual satisfaction and comfort, and to base our evaluation on the spiritual values peculiar to one particular kind of civilization.[4]

That is why I think the term "socialization" is more appropriate here. It suggests a better balance between the individual and the surrounding community; without the community the individual cannot attain complete fulfillment. But "socialization" is very different in meaning from the terms "socialism" or "Socialist." Actually the term "socialism" has so many different connotations today that it hardly defines anything in itself. And of course some local interpreters would automatically give it a pejorative connotation.

For the average individual socialism is a philosophy reacting against capitalistic individualism. It places collective interest above particular or individual interest. In that sense the term has universal significance.

However, the main currents that go by the name of socialism today find their inspiration in Marxism. Some of them reject Lenin's later interpretation. Other currents of socialism claim to adhere to democratic or humanistic philosophies, and they actually do. Thus socialist movements now range from communism on the one hand to various reformist currents and schemes for state socialism. We cannot overlook the various brands of national socialism.

We must be careful, however, not to confuse Social Democrats or the British Laborites with the socialism of the various People's Democratic Republics or with the programs and actions of socialist factions in Latin America and the rest of the Third World. The latter espouse violence and revolutionary upheaval, and it is hard to see any party relationship between them and the socialist currents of Western Europe and such places as India.

The British Laborite Anthony Crosland, who was foreign affairs minister of Great Britain, has pointed out that the Socialist Party of Germany (S.P.D.) gave up public ownership as a major goal in 1955; Brandt and Schmidt have sustained this thesis. He says the same thing of Austria, Switzerland, and even France. In recent years even the Italian and French Communists have come out with similar views. Insofar as Great Britain is concerned, Crosland notes that public ownership is only one of several instruments available to the government in its fight against monopolies, underinvestment, and defective planning designed to utilize national resources for the benefit of the whole community.[5]

It seems quite clear that there is little relationship between these brands of socialism and the socialism of one-party regimes. The former fear any threat to freedom. The latter want total public ownership by the state, so that the economy ends up having only one employer instead of many. From the standpoint of freedom the latter alternative hardly seems like progress. When political power and economic power merge completely, the margin of freedom is narrowed considerably and may even disappear completely.

In a human economy with a mixed structure the government assumes functions relating to the common good of the nation and the ownership of its basic elements. But it also maintains a private sector where there is plenty of room for the free initiative of individuals and community entities at every level. This guarantees the independence of people and their ability to participate in the overall process.

Thus the term "socialism" takes in a variety of positions. Some entail profound conceptual differences; others differ in their practical applications. Some socialist parties in Europe have maintained their fidelity to democracy and their unreserved respect for electoral decisions. In West Germany the Christian Democrats and the Social Democrats continue to vie with one another. This is useful because it generates criticism, ensures alternating control of the government, and invigorates democracy. Moreover, both maintain a consensus about certain essentials, so that one party can replace the other in power without jeopardizing the life of the system.

Of decisive benefit to Latin America would be socialist currents or movements equally concerned with the defense of freedom. They could dialogue with the forces of Christian humanism and help to establish a basic consensus that would shore up the existence of a democratic regime. Our societies need broader accords and agreements. Our people must learn to live with mutual respect and to implement the essential objectives they share. This means that various political movements must be able to agree on certain principles, even though partisan differences may separate them.

Such agreement might be based on a shared belief in the invaluable benefits of freedom, on a shared acceptance of a pluralistic society, on a rejection of all political and social monolithism, and on a shared conviction that democracy is a value in itself rather than merely a tactical resource for winning power. Agreements of this sort do not mean that individuals have to renounce their own convictions. In a democratic society, encounter and dialogue are possible between people who are clear about their views and differ with one another. Above all the quarrelling and name-calling, it is possible to find the bases for an understanding that will allow for the participation of widely differing segments of the population.

An agreement or understanding of this nature would have deep roots in the character and life of our peoples. For this reason it would be supported by a large majority of the citizenry. Only by reaching such an agreement and giving it expression will we be able to establish a new form of democracy that will resolve the crucial dilemmas and open up a realistic, creative perspective.

The accord proposed here cannot be achieved simply by agreements made between leaders or at the superstructural level. Such agreements are indispensable, of course, but they will not suffice in themselves. All too often such high-level accords come down to allocating spheres of influence or power quotas; they lack the transcendent dimension required to ensure the permanence of democracy. The Argentinians often refer to such pacts as an "abusive coalition" (*contubernio*), and public opinion often refers to them as "political" combinations in a pejorative sense.

A movement capable of implementing a new historical project and revitalizing democracy calls for a new attitude and new strength. Besides allowing for ideological and political pluralism it must be able to unite the masses of our people in a common political movement. Our peoples, who have matured through these years of testing, are waiting expectantly for such a movement. They see the need for it more or less clearly. Until it finds concrete expression in Latin America, no democratic regime will be stable from a political standpoint.

17

A Creative Task

The Role of Human Conduct

Institutional structures, social consensus, the specific structure of a democracy and its objectives will not suffice to ensure that its essential commitment is carried out. If it is truly to be "a rational organization of freedoms based on law," it must be cemented by a factor that is indispensable and basic, i.e., the conduct of human beings.

When that basis is lacking, it is all too easy to fall prey to the structuralist fallacy. One keeps trying to make sure that the facade looks good while the supporting beams are rotting away. No law can perdure, however perfect it may be, without some animating spirit.

A democracy based on humanism is itself an effort of intelligence, a constant appeal to reason, prudence, justice, mutual respect, and courageous fortitude. As Pascal put it: "We must make sure that what is just is also strong. When it turns out that the just is not strong, we find that what is strong becomes what is just." That is why the deeper thrust of the humanist message lies in the inner reform of human beings and its reflection in their personal and societal life. We must not imagine that we can organize a society by rejecting ethical principles and norms. To do so is to build upon sand.

Ideals cannot fail to take due account of human conduct. But we cannot turn evils into first principles and refuse the task of correcting them simply because we recognize the natural failings of human beings. For example, we all realize that profit and the desire for gain motivate human beings more powerfully than does generosity. A society, however, cannot ground its laws and institutions on the principle that the former should serve as the basic pillars of society. There will always be a wide gap between ideals and actual practice, but progress lies not in reducing human aspirations but in trying to improve actual practice.

It is just as unreasonable to assume that human beings are angels. Golda Meir makes this point in summing up the experiences of a lifetime:

My dream of a just world united under socialism has gone by the board. National interests have prevailed over international interests. Swedish Socialists have shown themselves to be first and foremost Swedish, English Socialists have shown themselves to be first and foremost English, and Israeli Socialists have shown themselves to be first and foremost Israeli. . . .

I am not cynical at all. I have simply dropped my illusions. Forty years ago, for example, I thought that a Socialist was always a good person incapable of telling lies. Now I think that a Socialist is a human being like everybody else. Socialists can be just as dishonest as everybody else. That is disheartening of course, but it is no reason to lose confidence in human beings.

That judgment does not apply to Socialists alone, of course. It could be applied to people of any ideological or political persuasion. It could be applied just as well to those who call themselves Christians, for they do not always act in accordance with their professed beliefs. They, too, are quite capable of lying and hatred.

It is a mistake to give way to cynicism or disillusionment on that basis. The correct conclusion is that we must take human beings as they are, with all their virtues and all their failings. Christianity recognizes the weaknesses inherent in human nature, but its whole inner thrust is to make sure that human virtues prevail.

Humanism offers us an invaluable principle when it distinguishes between human beings and their errors. We must fight against error, but a human being is always worthy of redemption. To deny that assumption is to open the door to hatred and to rule out peaceful coexistence in society.

Totalitarian regimes and dictatorships divide up the whole world into good and evil people. They arrive at the most illogical conclusions, maintaining that those in power possess the whole truth while dissenters are completely wrong. This oversimplification goes against nature; hence it is ultimately deceitful and malevolent. In recognizing the true condition of human beings as ever fallen and ever redeemable, democracy has solidly Christian roots even though its advocates may not always share our Christian beliefs.

There will always be people who accept the idea of democracy but are disillusioned with it in practice. A keen observer offers this judicious comment:

Who can be surprised by that? Wasn't Plato disillusioned by Athenian democracy? Didn't Mussolini and Hitler in their heyday proclaim the failure of European democracies ... as Lenin had done earlier? It would be really surprising if democracy, given its nature, did not encounter difficulties in those whose spirit has been cast down or affected by the lust for power .... Democracy is essentially an imperfect regime, which accepts human defects and tries to make their social consequences less painful. It adopts an experimental approach to life that is not always reasonable. It makes all participants in the difficult enterprise of generating law and it contains mechanisms for self-correction. In that sense democracy is always "failing," because it ever remains an ongoing experiment. Some rectification is always possible for the democratic way of life.

For that very reason it is the most realistic and humane of political systems. It is as tense, as uncertain, as inventive as life itself. But it possesses one characteristic that lies at the heart of its abiding prestige: It is the only form of societal life that reduces to a minimum the subjection of the individual to an alien power—the terrible condition surrounding life in society.

Only those who comprehend this condition as a challenge to reason and the human yearning for fulfillment can appreciate what democracies mean to human beings, however difficult they may be to realize as an ideal.[1]

Without a doubt democracy is being constantly created by the intelligence, which can operate only in freedom. Like everything genuinely human, it is as uncertain and inventive as life itself.

In primitive societies rule was based on force. As time went on, there emerged social systems calling for ever larger doses of rationality. Eventually people arrived at the conception of democracy. Eliminating democracy, therefore, would be taking a step backward.

Reason alone does not suffice, however. People who have lived for awhile learn to appreciate the virtues of the soul more and more. Goodness, loyalty, moral courage, and modesty do not glitter as much as intelligence does; but their absence can trigger unrestrained urges for power and lead to all sorts of excess. In a famous poem Claudel described this dramatic process, depicting how the *animus* (the intelligence) can be moved by pride to abandon the *anima* (the soul). This is an ever present danger, and it may well be the cause behind the crisis now facing modern societies. These may display great reserves of inventiveness and intelligence, but they may also be losing their souls.

The Need for Prophetic Minorities

The formulation and implementation of a democratic project requires human beings who are imbued with a faith that can mobilize the people. Communism, for example, is a faith. Who would deny that? Its parties are

composed of militant minorities who are totally dedicated to the cause. That is why they have managed to
exert great influence in some democratic countries, taking over key positions in the whole process of giving
direction to social and cultural change.

Other minorities are equally dedicated to their cause.
By comparison the advocates of democracy often seem
to be lifeless, perhaps because democracy embodies a
rational way of life. In any case the masses of plain
people now feel forsaken and helpless because those who
should be leading them often seem divided, vacillating,
and far from the scene.

Nothing is needed more today than the presence of
prophetic minorities who are capable of expressing the
themes of humanism, giving them direction, and thus
shoring up belief in freedom. Maritain had this to say
about prophetic minorities:

It is not enough to define a democratic society by its legal
structure. Another element also plays a basic part, namely the
dynamic leaven or energy which fosters political *movement*,
and which cannot be inscribed in any constitution or embodied
in any institution, since it is both personal and contingent in
nature, and rooted in free initiative. I should like to call that
existential factor a prophetic factor. . . .

And those servants or prophets of the people are not—not
necessarily—elected representatives of the people. Their mission starts in their own hearts and consciousness. In this sense
they are self-appointed prophets. They are needed in the normal functioning of a democratic society. . . .

The people are to be awakened—that means that the people
are asleep. People as a rule prefer to sleep. Awakenings are
always bitter. Insofar as their daily interests are involved,
what people like is business as usual: everyday misery and
humiliation as usual. . . . It is a fact that, for good or evil, the
great historical changes in political societies have been
brought about by a few.[2]

These minorities are even more indispensable in
times of great change such as the present. People need

their words and their witness. They particularly need the latter because those who are suffering in silence need more than fine words.

Of course minorities are a basic phenomenon in human history, and there does exist a danger that such minorities may first become rulers and then despots themselves. Aflame with their ideals and dedicated to political and social struggle, they may come to feel that they are predestined to save the people. They may appoint themselves as the leaders of the people because they think they know more and can do more. They may assume the right to speak for the people even though the people have not appointed them as their spokespeople. They may even go against the express will of the people when the people refuse to go along with them. Maritain describes what tack they take next:

There is only one way to make good the risk that such a minority is taking, namely, *the out and out use of violence*, in order to succeed at any cost and by any means. . . .

The deep trend toward emancipation . . . requires *breaking of the law* as a perpetual and necessary condition of progress, and blossoms forth into the messianic myth of *the Revolution*.[3]

And so the minority group comes to spurn the people whom it had pledged to redeem, denying the ability of the people to judge for themselves. It would take us too far afield to enumerate all the revolutions that have ended up in terrorism being imposed by those who thought they were the full possessors of truth. Such minorities are not in the service of human beings; they are fanatics willing to enslave people.

What distinguishes minorities inspired by humanism is their resolution to serve, to convince, to seek peace, to win over the intelligence of human beings, and ultimately to submit to the verdict of the people. In the last analysis it is the people who should decide their own destiny. This is the cornerstone of the humanist attitude and its subsequent actions.

Hope Grounded in a Real Option

It is commonly said in Latin America today that this is the time for clear and definite action; that we need people of great firmness who will not vacillate, who will not think too much or try to make a lot of distinctions. Those who think too much are suspect right now.

This is not the first time that we have heard the cry of "death to intelligence." Unamuno challenged that same cry some years ago. Some people feel resentment toward those who try to reason things out. We have reached such a state of upset that some people are proposing radical theses to deal with the matter. Their theses can be expressed very simply in everyday terms. They suggest that we should kill not only those who kill but also those who might kill. We must eliminate such people right away, and it does not matter if some innocent person suffers by mistake; for the important thing is to ensure the "tranquillity" of millions of people.

Such a primitive line of thinking can only generate more and more conflicts that will prove to be insoluble. Those who entertain it usually do not know where to stop. Soon they look with suspicion on all those who talk about justice and peace, who defend human rights, or who simply disagree with their actions. This picture might seem like a caricature. Unfortunately it is an everyday occurrence in many countries of the world, and also here in Latin America. People deliberately propagate the notion that every government that operates within the law and respects the will of the people is weak.

The advocates of the humanist message must not be intimidated by such criticisms or give in to such aberrations. They should realize that they will always be assaulted by two different fronts. Some will accuse them of being allies of subversion when they defend human rights; others will accuse them of being reactionary because they reject violence and vengeance perpetrated by groups outside the law.

To carry out their commitment, the advocates of humanism will need deep-rooted convictions, a strong faith, moral courage, and perseverance. Only then will they be able to look beyond success or failure. In the long run the battle will be won in the minds and hearts of all the people, if the people find a response to their questions in our words and our personal witness.

The people, I have suggested, seem to possess some secret instinct for detecting what is true and what is false. They may make mistakes about particular matters or particular people, but they rarely err when it comes to basic options. Sound common sense enables them to distinguish between the real work of justice and inconsistent promises. The common people are closer to the fonts of life, work, and sorrow. That is why there is such a thing as popular wisdom, which rarely errs in its fundamental judgments.

However, the common people cannot do much unless there are people who rely on their worth and are sincerely on their side. Silenced people, who get only limited or adulterated information, need others who will speak the truth. This task requires time and a great sense of reality. One pays dearly for hasty improvisation in organizing the people, and usually it is the people themselves who pay most dearly. Lack of maturity and sound judgment has led to many catastrophes. As Lebret points out in the work cited earlier, even the objective of a human economy can be reached only by halting, imperfect steps. It will take time. A whole series of operations must be coordinated and controlled, and they will often take years or decades.

Yet some, as I noted in a previous chapter, demand that democratic government accomplish everything here and now. Often its own supporters are the most impatient and dissatisfied. The dissatisfaction itself is legitimate, to be sure, so long as it does not turn into an illusionary approach that blocks real progress.

A "historical project" grounded on humanism can be profoundly transforming, but it must be efficacious. If it is thought out, explained and supported by prophetic minorities who truly stand by the people, then it will surely evoke a response. Besides being the only rational approach, it is also the only positive approach. If it is spelled out in all its dimensions, it should manage to awaken the faith of the people, to mobilize their energy, and to point out the path that truly leads to their liberation. It is an intellectual, cultural, and human enterprise of a civilizing nature that goes far beyond what is commonly understood as "politics." But it should also foster and support *Political* action, and I capitalize the word here to give it its full, authentic dimensions.

We all have seen the end results of demagogic lack of realism, light-headedness, irresponsible action, continuing injustice, and violence. We all have seen freedom disappear because of its abuse by some and because of the fear, blindness, or ambition of others. We all have seen what happens when our people are subjected to governments that deny their most fundamental rights.

A "historical project" for Latin America, as I have described it in these pages, should lead us to a real democracy inspired by the authentic values of humanism. It should put an end to the ongoing instability that has characterized the life of our nations.

The execution of this "project" will depend on the will power and moral commitment of those who support it. It will also depend on a clear notion of what the bases for a solid democratic consensus are. Let me spell out our essential obligations with respect to forming such a consensus:

—We must create an awareness that freedom is not giving free rein to our passions and appetites, that the exercise of freedom is the most distinctive embodiment of the human condition, and hence entails a high level of responsibility.

—We must realize that a free society cannot function without some firm and stable authority that guarantees peace, security, and the common welfare of the nation above and beyond the special interests of the individual or a group. This authority is delegated by the people to act, but sovereignty resides in the people. To be legitimate, therefore, delegation must come in free elections held periodically which are based on universal suffrage and the secret ballot.

—We must organize society under a pluralistic, communitarian system that is based on justice, toleration, and unreserved respect for human rights.

—Our central objective must be to overcome poverty and put an end to social dualism by integrating the national community. Up to now it has been splintered by the existence of two different worlds.

—We must alter the present structure of the various branches of public authority, of the whole government administration, of political parties, and of various social organizations. They must be accommodated to the new realities we face, so that they can defend and promote the interests and aspirations of the community as well as further advances in the process of "socialization." Democratic institutions must be effective, and they must correspond with the new world conditions created by science and technology.

—We must promote political, economic, social, cultural, and human development in accordance with the distinctive nature of our milieu, our people, and their enormous resources. This development must be both quantitative and qualitative. Its central focus should be human beings, the family, and the perfecting of community life. Prestige, power, concentration of wealth, and unrestrained consumption cannot be goals of a truly human economy.

—We must realize that such an undertaking calls for

continuing effort and sacrifice as well as high levels of intelligence, knowledge, and labor. We must appreciate the fact that we are living in a difficult and increasingly complex world, that we must reject simple-minded views and the magic of simplistic, cure-all solutions.

—We must open the way to greater participation by all in basic decisions. In this way the people will feel a part of the common effort. Through their own organizations their voice will be heard and they will learn the how and why and wherefore behind the actions of those who are directing their destiny.

—We must categorically reject all forms of hatred and violence, and we must not allow the guarantees offered by democracy to be used to undermine it, immobilize it, or destroy it.

—We must realize that our nations will have a very limited destiny if they stand alone and isolated. Only a truly integrated Latin American community of nations can create the human and economic conditions required to establish it as a broad and satisfactory market. Lacking that, our nations will not be able to ensure their development, their real independence, or the defense of their legitimate interests. Nor will it be possible for them to undertake the venture of scientific creation and its technological applications so that they may have a voice in the larger world community.

—We must understand that the integration of regional units should culminate in a world community. This is a basic precondition for promoting justice between nations, defending the basic resources available to humanity, confronting problems that go beyond national frontiers, and ensuring adequate social, economic, and human development for all the peoples of the world.

The points just mentioned above can provide the fundamental basis for consensus and progress. It should not be described as a task for rightists or leftists, for the extremes are not where we will find reasonable human beings today. In our deeply confusing world they do not seem to stand for a clear, reasonable position or a solid political approach. As Maritain put it, rightists and leftists have become "emotional complexes aggravated by their mythical ideal. Political intelligence can do little more than utilize them in the service of passion. To choose not to be on the right or the left means to choose to preserve reason."[4]

Some think that an undertaking of this magnitude is not only difficult but impossible to accomplish. They think it is utopian when in fact it is the assumption that the forward march of our peoples can be stopped that is unrealistic.

There is every reason to believe that we can build a better society on this vast continent, a society where human beings can live out their lives in peace and dignity. Our nations are still young. They can look to the future with joy and optimism, unfettered by the bonds of violence and hatred.

The world has a right to expect this much from Latin America, and we should measure up to that expectation.

Notes

Chapter 1

1. See Donella Meadows, Dennis L. Meadows, J. Randers, and W. Behrens, *The Limits to Growth* (New York: Universe Books, 1972).

2. H. Cole et al., *Thinking About the Future: A Critique of the Limits to Growth* (Chatto and Windus: Sussex University Press, 1973).

3. Mihajlo Mesarovic and Eduard Pestel, *Mankind at the Turning Point* (New York: Dutton, 1974).

4. Fundación Bariloche, *Modelo mundial latinoamericano.*

5. See Christopher Friedmann, *The World Models and Their Sub-Systems.*

6. See Roger Garaudy, *Parole d'homme* (Paris: Editions Robert Laffont, 1975).

Chapter 2

1. For a treatment of these points see Michel Crozier, Samuel P. Huntington, and Joji Watamuki, *The Crisis of Democracy* (New York: NYU Press paperback, 1975).

2. Aid from the United States is about 0.2 percent of its national product; that of the U.S.S.R. is about 0.1 percent.

3. Arnold Toynbee, *The World and the West* (New York: Oxford University Press, 1953), p. 11.

4. Henry Kissinger, *A World Restored: Metternich, Castlereagh and the Problems of Peace 1812–22* (Boston: Houghton Mifflin, 1957).

5. Robert S. McNamara, *The Essence of Security: Reflections in Office* (New York: Harper & Row, 1968), pp. 29–30.

6. V. Giscard d'Estaing, *Démocratie française* (Paris: Fayard, 1976); Eng. trans. *French Democracy* (New York: Doubleday, 1977).

7. Roger Garaudy, *Parole d'homme.*

8. Willy Brandt on "Democracy, Freedom and Socialism," in *Revista Nueva Sociedad*, no. 23, 1976 (San José, Costa Rica).

9. Arnold Toynbee, *The World and the West*, pp. 13–14.

Chapter 3

1. Jacques Maritain, *Le crépuscule de la civilisation*. For an English translation see *The Twilight of Civilization* (New York: Sheed & Ward, 1943). For a good brief overview of Maritain's thought on man, humanism, and democracy see Parts Three and Four of the anthology, *A Maritain Reader*, edited by Donald and Idella Gallagher (New York: Doubleday Image Book, 1966).

2. J. Maritain, *Le crépuscule de la civilisation*.

3. Ibid.

4. Alexander Solzhenitsyn, *Nobel Lecture*, bilingual text (New York: Farrar, Straus & Giroux, 1972), p. 22.

5. J. Maritain, *Le crépuscule de la civilisation*.

6. Ibid.

7. Ibid.

8. Georges Pompidou, *Le noeud gordien* (Paris: Editorial Plon, 1974).

Chapter 4

1. J. Maritain, *Le crépuscule de la civilisation;* see note 1 of Chap. 3 in this volume.

2. Ibid.

3. J. Maritain, *Man and the State* (Chicago: University of Chicago Press, 1951, paperback edition), p. 60.

4. Roger Garaudy, *Parole d'homme*.

5. Aurelio Peccei, personal communication to the Club of Rome, 1973, cited in Meadows, Meadows, Randers, and Behrens, *The Limits to Growth* (New York: Universe Books, 1972), pp. 151–52.

Chapter 5

1. Arnold J. Toynbee, *Civilization on Trial* (New York: Oxford University Press, 1948), p. 55.

2. Jacques Maritain, *Humanisme intégral: Problèmes temporels et spirituels d'une nouvelle chrétienté* (Paris: Aubier, 1938); new Eng. trans., *Integral Humanism: Temporal and Spiritual Problems of a New Christendom* (New York: Scribner's, 1968).

3. Ibid.

4. Jacques Maritain, *Lettre sur l'indépendance* (Paris: Desclée, 1935).

Chapter 6

1. The word "liberal" has many different meanings. It involves a semantic problem. Liberals may be those who love freedom. In the United States it often means those who are advanced in their ideas. Or

it may refer to certain political parties that appeared in the nineteenth century. It may also refer to an economic and political doctrine that holds that individual freedom is the supreme value in society and that laissez-faire should be the guiding principle in economics. Here we are using it mainly in the laissez-faire sense.

2. All the Maritain citations in this chapter are from his *Lettre sur l'indépendance*.

3. Louis Joseph Lebret, "Manifesto for a Solidary Civilization," Span. edition (Santiago, Chile: Pacífico, 1975); in French see *Pour une civilisation solidaire* (Paris: Ouvrières, 1963).

4. See, for example, Albert Speer's *Inside the Third Reich* and William Schirer's *The Rise and Fall of the Third Reich*. There are also various books on Stalinism and on the fall of the Portuguese regime.

5. Jacques Maritain, *Lettre sur l'indépendance*.

6. See Alexander Solzhenitsyn, *The Calf and the Oak*, Eng. trans. (New York: Association Press, 1975).

7. Roy A. Medvedev. For an English translation see *On Socialist Democracy* (New York: Knopf, 1975).

Chapter 7

1. Darcy Ribeiro, *El dilema de América Latina* (Mexico, D.F.: Siglo Veintiuno, 1971).

2. Gabriela Mistral, Prologue to my book, *La política y el espíritu* (Santiago, Chile: Pacífico, 1946).

3. Gabriela Mistral, personal letter to me, June 1939.

Chapter 8

1. In subsequent chapters I shall cite comments by Carlos Dávila and Carlos Rangel, among others.

Chapter 9

1. Augusto Orrego Luco, "La cuestión social en Chile," reproduced in Nos. 121–22 of the *Anales* of the University of Chile, 1961.

2. Helio Jaguaribe, *Crisis y alternativas de América Latina: Reforma o revolución* (Buenos Aires: Paidos, 1972).

3. Juan Carlos Mariátegui, *Siete ensayos de interpretación de la realidad peruana* (Lima: Biblioteca "Amauta," 1928), Eng. trans.: *Seven Interpretive Essays on Peruvian Reality* (Austin: University of Texas Press, 1971).

4. See José Pareja Paz, *El Maestro Belaúnde* (Lima: Universitaria, 1968).

5. José Vasconcelos, *Nacionalismo en América Latina*.

6. Two examples are the novel by Alberto Blest Gana entitled *Los transplantados* (Santiago, Chile: Zig-Zag, 1966), and the work by Joaquín Edwards Bello entitled *Criollos en París* (Santiago, Chile: Zig-Zag, 1965).

7. Gabriela Mistral, Prologue to my book entitled *La política y el espíritu.*

8. Carlos Rangel, *Del buen salvaje al buen revolucionario* (Caracas: Monte Avila, 1976).

9. See José Pareja Paz Roldán, *El Maestro Belaúnde.*

10. Carlos Medinacelli, cited by Mariano Baptista Gumucio in *Historia contemporánea de Bolivia* (La Paz: Gisbert, 1976).

11. *Time* magazine, February 21, 1977, p. 33.

Chapter 10

1. Víctor Raúl Haya de la Torre, *El anti-imperialismo y el Apra* (Lima, 1928).

2. F. H. Cardoso and E. Faletto, *Dependencia y desarrollo en América Latina* (Santiago, Chile: ILPES, 1967).

3. Aldo E. Solari, Rolando Franco, and Joel Kurt Kowitz, *Teoría, acción social y desarrollo en América Latina.*

4. Cardoso and Faletto, *Dependencia y desarrollo.*

5. Ibid.

6. Daniel Cosio Villegas, *Rusia, Estados Unidos y América Latina* (Mexico, D.F.: Hermes, 1966).

7. Linowitz Report.

8. Foro Latino-Americano, Mexico, D.F., May 1977.

9. Ibid.

Chapter 11

1. Barbara Tuchman, *The Proud Tower: A Portrait of the World Before the War* (New York: Macmillan, 1966), pp. 63–64.

2. Ibid., p. 65.

3. Ibid., p. 88.

4. Ibid., pp. 107–8.

5. Jorge Millas, "Las máscaras filosóficas de la violencia," in *Dilemas* (Santiago, Chile), no. 11 (1975).

6. Ibid.

7. Extensive bibliographies can be found in the United States, France, Brazil, and now Chile.

8. Roger Trinquier, "La guerra moderna," cited in Genaro Arriagada et al., *Seguridad nacional y política* (Santiago, Chile: Pacífico, 1976); Trinquier's work originally done in French.

9. Trinquier, ibid.

10. Ibid.

Chapter 12

1. Genaro Arriagada, *Seguridad nacional y política.*

2. See Gerhard Ritter, *The Sword and the Scepter: The Problem of Militarism in Germany,* Eng. trans., 4 vols. (University of Miami Press, 1969–1973).

3. Genaro Arriagada, *Seguridad nacional y política.*

Chapter 13

1. Zbigniew K. Brzezinski, *Between Two Ages: America's Role in the Technetronic Era* (New York: Viking Press, 1970).
2. Paul Ricoeur, *El conflicto, ¿signo de contradicción y de unidad?* Spanish version.
3. Ibid.
4. Ibid.
5. Ibid.
6. Daniel Cosio Villegas, *Los problemas de América* (Mexico: D.F.: Hermes, 1966).

Chapter 14

1. See Albert Camus, *L'homme révolté* (Paris: Gallimard, 1951); Eng. trans., *The Rebel* (New York: Knopf, 1954).
2. Jacques Maritain, *Man and the State* (Chicago: University of Chicago Press, 1951), paperback edition, pp. 114–15.
3. For an English translation see Roy Medvedev, *On Socialist Democracy* (New York: Knopf, 1975).
4. See Jean Ladrière, *El poder* (Santiago, Chile: Pacífico, 1975); French original.
5. Ibid.
6. Ibid.

Chapter 15

1. Zbigniew Brzezinski, *Between Two Ages: America's Role in the Technetronic Era.*
2. Final document of a study-action group composed of delegates from the Christian Democratic Party. Their meeting was held in Rome.
3. Theo Lefèvre, *La science d'aujourd'hui pour la société de demain* (Brussels: Editions Vie Ouvrière, 1971). He served as the minister of scientific policy and was also rector of Louvain.
4. Ibid.
5. Salvador Lluch, *La integración y el desafío del conocimiento,* privately published.

Chapter 16

1. See Julius K. Nyerere, *Freedom and Unity: A Selection from Writings and Speeches, 1952–1965* (Oxford University Press, 1967). Also see idem, *Freedom and Socialism: A Selection from Writings and Speeches, 1965–1967* (Oxford University Press, 1968).
2. Alejandro Foxley, *El estado y la pobreza hoy* (Santiago, Chile), no. 3, June 15, 1977.

3. The term was used by Pope John XXIII.

4. Louis Joseph Lebret, *Manifiesto para una civilización solidaria.*

5. See Charles Anthony Crosland, *The Future of Socialism*, revised and abridged (New York: Schocken Books, 1964); also *Socialism Now* (British Book Centre, 1976).

Chapter 17

1. Jorge Millas, "La ilusión necesaria," *Ercilla*, No. 2151.

2. Jacques Maritain, *Man and the State* (University of Chicago Press, 1951), paperback edition, pp. 139, 142.

3. Ibid., pp. 143–44.

4. Jacques Maritain, *Le paysan de la Garonne* (Paris: Desclée, 1966); Eng. trans., *The Peasant of the Garonne* (London and Dublin: Chapman, 1968).

Other Orbis Books . . .

HEALTH AND DEVELOPMENT
presented by Kevin M. Cahill, M.D.

"A penetrating symposium by ten writers, four of them medical doctors, focusing on the need: two thirds of the human race malnourished, medical services reaching only ten percent of people in developing nations; the interrelatedness of social, economic and political factors in health problems and solutions." *Missionary Research Library*

ISBN 0-88344-178-0   *Cloth $6.95*

THE UNTAPPED RESOURCE
Medicine and Diplomacy
edited by Kevin M. Cahill, M.D.

"Presents eight diplomats, doctors, ministers and philanthropists who argue on the basis of experience that the mission of healing is higher, holier and more effective for every good purpose than a mission of force." *World Call*

ISBN 0-88344-522-0   *Cloth $4.95*

A NEW DEVELOPMENT STRATEGY
by Robert Alexander

"Alexander holds that the developing nations can take much of their destiny into their own hands by an import-substitution strategy that encourages domestic production of products for which a home market has already been created by imports. Points out the political and social changes required by this strategy. Cites Latin American examples." *Booknotes*

ISBN0-88344-328-7   *Cloth $6.95*

WHY IS THE THIRD WORLD POOR?
by Piero Gheddo

"An excellent handbook on the Christian understanding of the development process. Gheddo looks at both the internal and external causes of underdevelopment and how Christians can involve themselves in helping the third world." *Provident Book Finder*

ISBN 0-88344-757-6   *Paper $4.95*

POLITICS AND SOCIETY IN THE THIRD WORLD
by Jean-Yves Calvez

"This frank treatment of economic and cultural problems in developing nations suggests the need for constant multiple attacks on the many fronts that produce problems in the human situation." *The Christian Century*

ISBN 0-88344-389-9   *Cloth $6.95*

THE LAW AND THE POOR
by Frank Parker, S.J.

"This interesting and extraordinarily practical book shows how to make the laws work for the poor rather than against them." *Choice*

ISBN 0-88344-276-0   *Paper $4.95*

DEVELOPMENT: LESSONS FOR THE FUTURE
by Thomas Melady and Robert Suhartono

"This volume is written in clear and readable English, with a minimum of professional jargon. It should be of interest to both professionals and interested laymen." *Journal of Economic Literature*

ISBN 0-88344-079-2   *Cloth $6.95*

THE ASSAULT ON AUTHORITY
by William W. Meissner

"This is a sober study of authority from a socio-psychological perspective, with strong emphasis on problems of the religious community." *The Critic*

ISBN 0-88344-018-0   *Cloth $7.95*

PILGRIMAGE TO NOW/HERE
by Frederick Franck

"Every now and then a true gem of a book appears that fails to get caught up in the tide of promotion, reviews, and sales, and, despite its considerable merits, seems to disappear. Such a book is Dr. Frederick Franck's *Pilgrimage to Now/Here*. His *Zen of Seeing* has been a steady seller, and *The Book of Angelus Silesius* is moving well. What happened to *Pilgrimage*, which in many ways is a more important book? Since Orbis is known as a religious publishing house, many distributors and booksellers are reluctant to stock it. Yet this is a religious book in the most significant sense of that word—in what Frederick Franck would call the search for meaning—for it is an account of a modern pilgrimage by jet, bus, train, and on foot to visit holy places and meet Buddhist leaders and Zen masters in India, Ceylon, Hong Kong and Japan." *East West Journal*

ISBN 0-88344-387-2   *Illustrated Paper $3.95*

THE PATRIOT'S BIBLE
edited by John Eagleson and Philip Scharper

"Following the terms of the Declaration of Independence and the U.S. Constitution, this faithful paperback relates quotes from the Bible and from past and present Americans 'to advance the kingdom and further our unfinished revolution.'" *A.D.*

ISBN 0-88344-377-5   *Paper $3.95*

THE RADICAL BIBLE
adapted by John Eagleson and Philip Scharper

"I know no book of meditations I could recommend with more confidence to learned and unlearned alike." *St. Anthony Messenger*

ISBN 0-88344-425-9
ISBN 0-88344-426-7   *Cloth $3.95*
                    Pocketsize, paper $1.95

TANZANIA AND NYERERE
by William R. Duggan & John R. Civille

"Sympathetic survey of Tanzania's attempt to develop economically on an independent path." *A Journal of World Affairs, Tufts University*

ISBN 0-88344-475-5 CIP   *Cloth $10.95*

DOM HELDER CAMARA
by José de Broucker

"De Broucker, an internationally recognized journalist, develops a portrait, at once intimate, comprehensive and sympathetic, of the Archbishop of Olinda and Recife, Brazil, whose championship of political and economic justice for the hungry, unorganized masses of his country and all Latin America has aroused world attention." *America*

ISBN 0-88344-099-7   *Cloth $6.95*

THE DESERT IS FERTILE
by Dom Helder Camara

"Camara's brief essays and poems are arresting for their simplicity and depth of vision, and are encouraging because of the realistic yet quietly hopeful tone with which they argue for sustained action toward global justice." *Commonweal*

ISBN 0-88344-078-4   *Cloth $3.95*

AGAINST PRINCIPALITIES AND POWERS
Letters from a Brazilian Jail

by Carlos Alberto Libanio Christo

"This book is a collection of slightly edited letters from a Dominican seminarian in prison to his family and friends. No attempt has been made to render the letters more literary or palatable. They come through in all their starkness as an inspirational witness of a Christian intensely involved in the history of his people and their struggle for liberation from unjust human structures and systems." *National Catholic Reporter*

"A testimony of faith from a churchman in prison, related to liberation theology." *Publishers Weekly*

ISBN 0-88344-007-5 CIP
ISBN 0-88344-008-3   *Cloth $8.95*
                                Paper $4.95